$\mathcal{R}$obert Louis Stevenson

HIƧ BEƧT PACIFIC WRITINGƧ

*Selection, Introduction
and Commentaries
by Roger Robinson*

Foreword by Albert Wendt

BESS
PRESS

3565 Harding Ave, Honolulu, Hawai'i 96816
808/ 734 7159   www.besspress.com

Library of Congress Cataloging-in-Publication Data

Stevenson, Robert Louis.
   Robert Louis Stevenson : his
best Pacific writings ; selection,
introduction and commentaries
by Roger Robinson ; foreword
by Albert Wendt.
      p. cm.
   Includes illustrations.
   ISBN 1-57306-171-9
   I. Robinson, Roger.
II. Title.
PR5482.R62 2003   828-dc21

Introduction and commentaries
Copyright © 2003 Roger Derek Robinson.
Foreword Copyright © 2003 Albert Wendt.
This edition Copyright © 2003 Bess Press, Inc.

ISBN 1-57306-171-9

Published in North America by
Bess Press, Inc.
3565 Harding Ave, Honolulu, HI 96816, USA
Tel: (808) 734 7159. Fax: (808) 732 3627.
email: info@besspress.com   www.besspress.com

Cover design by Craig Humberstone.
Design and artwork by Streamline Creative Ltd
Auckland, New Zealand
Typeset in Adobe Garamond.
Printed in China through Colorcraft Ltd, Hong Kong.

To Tom, Jayne, Claire, William
& Jim, Nikki, Maria, Sophie

ACKNOWLEDGEMENTS

Of the almost innumerable biographies and studies of Robert Louis Stevenson, those I have turned to most often for different aspects of this book have been Isobel Strong and Lloyd Osbourne, *Memories of Vailima* (1903); H.J. Moors, *With Stevenson in Samoa* (1910); David Daiches, *Robert Louis Stevenson* (1947) and *Robert Louis Stevenson and His World* (1973); Margaret Mackay, *The Violent Friend* (1968); Jenni Calder, *RLS: A Life Study* (1980); Ian Bell, *Dreams of Exile* (1992); Frank McLynn, *Robert Louis Stevenson. A Biography* (1993); Hunter Davies, *The Teller of Tales* (1994); and Angelica Shirley Carpenter & Jean Shirley, *Robert Louis Stevenson: Finding Treasure Island* (1997).

Most of Stevenson's Pacific writings are now very hard to find – hence this selection. A notable exception is *A Footnote to History*, introduction by Malama Meleisea (Pasifika Press, Auckland, 1996). There are also excellent accessible editions of some of the fiction, notably Barry Menikoff (ed), *The Beach of Falesá* (Stanford University Press, 1987); Peter Hinchcliffe and Catherine Kerrigan (eds), *The Ebb-Tide* (Edinburgh University Press, 1995); and Roslyn Jolly (ed), *South Sea Tales* (World's Classics, OUP, 1996). Jenni Calder (ed), *Tales of the South Seas* (Cannongate Classics, 1987) includes *The Wrecker*, as well as other fiction and some non-fiction.

Several major libraries and collections have once again proved themselves the modern world's best repositories not only of rare books, but of courteous assistance: the Alexander Turnbull Library, National Library of New Zealand, Te Puna Mātauranga o Aotearoa, Wellington, New Zealand;

Beinecke Rare Books and Manuscript Library, Yale University; the British Library, London; Huntington Library, San Marino, California; the Library of Congress, Washington DC; the New York Public Library; Robert Louis Stevenson Museum, Vailima, Western Samoa; the Silverado Museum, St Helena, California; and Victoria University Library, Wellington, New Zealand.

Two research grants from the Faculty of Humanities and Social Sciences, Victoria University of Wellington, are warmly acknowledged. Naomi Barton provided research assistance that enabled the project to start at a time when I was committed elsewhere. Friend and colleague Paul Millar enabled me to develop some key ideas in a shared course at Victoria University. Jeremy Commons led me to Jack London's *Son of the Sun*. At least one point in my commentary reflects the privilege of supervising John O'Leary's PhD, 'The Colonising Pen'. The writings and conversation of Albert Wendt are a positive presence. Support from Doris Humphries Robinson was warmly appreciated.

My greatest personal debts, not for the first time, are to the friendship and skill of Tim Chamberlain and the encouragement and love of my wife, Kathrine Switzer, who was with me at Vailima, the starting line of the idea. For their cheerful tolerance of an eccentric absentee father and grandfather, the book is dedicated to my sons and their families – children of the Pacific.

Roger Robinson

CONTENTS

TUSITALA:

THE LEGEND, THE WRITER &

THE LITERATURE OF THE PACIFIC

Robert Louis Stevenson has been a presence in my life ever since I was born. From our family home in the Vaipe, Apia, you can always see Mount Vaea and its summit where Stevenson is buried. Stevenson's burial was one of the first facts we learned from our grandmother and parents. So, daily, when we got up and gazed up at Mount Vaea, we 'saw' Stevenson and the legend of Tusitala. (By the way, Stevenson himself misread the meaning of Tusitala – it isn't Teller of Tales, it is Writer of Tales.)

That legend, according to my grandmother and her generation, went something like this: "Tusitala was the most famous writer of his day, a Scotsman who, when he came here, was ill with consumption. He chose our small and insignificant country to write and die in. And when he died, our chiefs and warriors, because of our enormous love for him, carried him on their shoulders over the steep Road of Loving Hearts to the top of Mount Vaea, which he'd chosen as his burial place". Stevenson himself and Europe's romantic notions about the South Seas helped create and enlarge that legend.

Most of my generation had to memorise 'Requiem', at school – one of the first poems in English I memorised and can still recite today. Years later, when I was Principal of Samoa College, the Samoa College Old Pupils' Association and our school organised groups to climb Vaea and clear Stevenson's grave of weeds and vegetation that were threatening to smother it. Four times we climbed and worked. Tough in the sweltering heat, but well worth it when we rested by the grave and re-read/recited 'Requiem' and gazed out into the magnificent panoramic view of our islands and the enormous ocean and heavens. Stevenson was 'egotistical' enough to have chosen that view, forever, for himself!

There weren't many books at my Intermediate School in Samoa but I read *Treasure Island* and *Dr Jekyll and Mr Hyde* and found them compelling and addictive. (Since then I've seen many film and television versions of the two novels.) Alas, when I went to boarding school in New Plymouth, New Zealand, and became addicted to the school library, I couldn't get into much else of Stevenson's work. However, at the end of my prep school year, at the annual prizegiving, I was awarded *Kidnapped*.

Later at university, while I was researching the Samoan Independence movement, I found *A Footnote to History*. For me, that has remained Stevenson's most relevant work. It showed his astute and perceptive and enthusiastic support for our struggle against the foreign powers and colonialism. After all, Stevenson grew up in the Scottish anti-colonial struggle. And his views of colonialism were well ahead of his times.

Over time in my own writing, he has also become a presence. In my novella, *Flying Fox in a Freedom Tree*, the narrator, Tagata, compares himself and the malady he is dying from to Stevenson and his TB. And every day, while Tagata is dying at Moto'otua Hospital, he gazes up through his hospital window at Stevenson's grave on Mt Vaea.

In the 1970s, in the first documentary film I ever fronted, I'm filmed standing in front of Stevenson's home at Vailima and then climbing Mt Vaea through the lush tropical rainforest and, standing beside Stevenson's grave, reading 'Requiem' from the brass placard on the grave. My commentary in the film was mainly about my writing and the new literature being written by other indigenous Pacific writers. I'd like to imagine that Stevenson would have been a fan of our writing.

In the yet-unfinished novel, which I've been working on for about 16 years, Stevenson takes on the form of 'another' Papalagi writer who comes to Samoa to die, and becomes a major character and presence in the novel. My tribute to Stevenson? Yes. My taking the outsider literary myth of the writer/ artist adventuring in Paradise and reclaiming her/him for Samoa and myself? Yes, also.

Caught in the still huge mythology of Tusitala, we forget that Stevenson was in Samoa for only four years. So short a time yet it gave birth to such a large mythology! Ill, he'd chosen Samoa for his dying and burial. Heroic, decisive stuff of myth.

Stevenson lies "under the wide and starry sky", "glad did I live, and gladly die, and I laid me down with a will," smiling and gazing out at the Vasa Loloa and up to the atua and the heavens and into all the hearts and imaginations of those who continue to read his work, or see the films and television versions that make him a presence in even more lives.

Ia manuia!

Albert Wendt

Albert Wendt is author of *Flying Fox in a Freedom Tree, Pouliuli, Leaves of the Banyan Tree, Ola, Black Rainbow,* and several volumes of short fiction and poetry; he is editor of *Lali* and *Nuanua,* major collections of contemporary Pacific writing.

INTRODUCTION:

FROM IMAGINATION TO ACTION

The idea of the Pacific was first put into Robert Louis Stevenson's mind when he was in his twenties. A semi-invalid with suspected tuberculosis, he was drifting through his law studies at Edinburgh University while still living at home with his parents. In an 1890 letter, he recalled the visit of a distinguished and apparently self-assured New Zealander:

> In '74 or 5 there came to stay with my father and mother a certain Mr. Seed [Hon J.Seed], a prime minister or something of New Zealand. He spotted what my complaint was; told me, I had no business to stay in Europe; that I should find all I cared for, and all that was good for me, in the Navigator Islands [Samoa]; sat up till four in the morning persuading me, demolishing my scruples. And I resisted: I refused to go so far from my father and mother.

It was five years later that he first saw the Pacific, in August 1879. He had given up Scotland and his short-lived law career, and was now an aspiring but impoverished and still sickly writer of travel memoirs. He had published *An Inland Voyage* (1878), *Edinburgh. Picturesques Notes* (1879), and *Travels with a Donkey in the Cévennes* (1879). He was waiting out several months in the brawling seaport of San Francisco to marry Fanny Osbourne, the American he had fallen in love with at an artists' colony in France. To rejoin her in California, he had endured a rigorous journey by emigrant ship and cross-continental train (described later in *The Amateur Emigrant,* 1883), and now had to wait for her divorce to come through. Out for a walk in San Francisco, he met by chance another travel writer, Charles Warren Stoddard, who gave him a copy of his *South-Sea Idylls* (1873), together with Herman Melville's Pacific novel *Omoo* (1847). Often this is seen as the moment when the romantic imagination was caught and lured by the South Seas.

Turning imagination into action was still eight years away. Louis (as he was always called – pronounced Lewis) and Fanny Osbourne married in May 1880. Of resolute character and creative impulse, Fanny was almost eleven years older than him but always striking and vital. Her pioneering Indiana origins had equipped her to thrive on the hardships of their adventurous travelling life, and she was famous for her skill at creating domestic order in the most primitive wilderness conditions. While not always a compliant partner, she fully earned his tribute, "fellow-farer true through life", in the poem that is now her epitaph on their tomb in Samoa. They honeymooned colourfully in a derelict shack on a remote rattlesnake-infested abandoned silver mining camp in the mountains above Napa Valley. Stevenson's aching lungs and recurrent haemorrhages drove them always to seek clear air, and lack of money limited their choices. At Silverado, they could almost see the Pacific.

Then they lived itinerantly, travelling first to Edinburgh, where they were reconciled with his forgiving parents, and on to other places in Scotland, England and Europe, settling for a while (1884-87) at the seaside health resort of Bournemouth in southern England. He was beginning now to get income from his writing. However nomadic and spartan their life, and however great the pain in his throat and chest, he always wrote, habitually and compulsively, most often propped up in bed or on whatever could pass as a sofa (a miner's bunk during the Silverado honeymoon). Inventive and prolific, he published 16 books in that short period in Britain and Europe from 1881-88, including several of lasting popularity and literary importance. It is not possible now to conceive our culture's stock of shared narratives without *Treasure Island* (1883), *Kidnapped* (1886) or *The Strange Case of Dr Jekyll and Mr Hyde* (1886). *A Child's Garden of Verses* (1885) was prominent in the consciousness of English-speaking children throughout most of the 20th century, and is still often republished. In three years, he had produced four lasting masterpieces in different genres. His works of fiction, especially *Treasure Island* and *Jekyll and Hyde*, together with short stories like 'The Body Snatchers', continue to be re-read and re-made in all the new forms available to our own ingenious age –

cinema, TV serial, Broadway musical or theme-park spectacle. Dramatisations abound, and at least one Stevenson story, 'Markheim', has been adapted as an opera.

Stevenson's literary importance was even greater than this populist success might suggest. He brought realism, psychological insight and a sense of history's complexity to the old genre of period romance. With *Jekyll and Hyde*, he took both science fiction and the psychological horror story to a new level as serious genres. *A Child's Garden of Verses* freed children's poetry from Victorian moralising to deal with such real childhood feelings as insecurity, fear and the sense of exclusion. He moved the English short story in lasting new directions, especially in realism, in his collections *New Arabian Nights* (1882), *More New Arabian Nights* (1885) and *The Merry Men and Other Tales and Fables* (1887). He was idiosyncratic and influential as a travel writer and memoirist (*The Silverado Squatters*, 1883), and as an essayist (*Virginibus Puerisque*, 1881, *Memoirs and Portraits*, 1887). The range is as impressive as the quantity of important work, especially for an invalid propped on pillows and wracked with coughing fits.

So when Stevenson sailed into the Pacific in 1888, it was as a celebrity. He walked out on the élite literary world of Britain just as he became one of its most sought-after luminaries. In August 1887, with some money from his writing and the death of his father in 1886, he sailed again from Britain to America. Conditions were better than his previous crossing on an emigrant ship only one step up from steerage, and he was accompanied this time by a sizeable family party. Fanny, her teenage son Lloyd Osbourne, her French-Swiss maid Valentine Roch, and his own widowed mother Margaret Stevenson all went along. Mother and son were good sailors, unlike poor Fanny, who never escaped the misery of motion sickness, and the two hatched a scheme for Maggie to "likely hire a yacht for a month or so in the summer". This later turned into the Pacific venture.

In New York, Stevenson's books were hot, mostly in pirated editions, and a stage version of *Dr Jekyll and Mr Hyde* was about to open. (Two were running in New York 114 years later, as well as two recent film versions, and others on video.) He was besieged by journalists and pursued by publishers.

For an "irresistible sum", he signed as "a salaried party" for *Scribner's Magazine*, giving Scribner all his American rights, but that did not deter one vigorous rival syndicalist, a young Scot called S.S. McClure. In October the entourage moved on to the next of their many extraordinary habitations, Saranac Lake in the primitive Adirondack Wilderness, far up in upstate New York, near the Canadian border. Attracted by a new tuberculosis sanatorium there, they wintered in a hut in the mountains at temperatures well below zero Fahrenheit. There Stevenson wrote most of *The Master of Ballantrae* (1889), incorporating settings from the forests around him, though he was to finish that strange book in Tahiti and Hawaii. He also turned out his essays for *Scribner's* and ice-skated with McClure, who visited several times. When Stevenson once remarked how much better he always felt at sea, the nimble-minded publisher offered to cover the cost of hiring a yacht, plus author's fees, in exchange for travel essays or "stories of adventure and so forth." It was the adventure stories the world really wanted from Stevenson. He would soon provide some from his Pacific experiences, in unexpected and not wholly palatable forms.

Possible voyages were discussed during the icy evenings at Saranac – the Aegean, the Caribbean, or the Indian Ocean. But one recurred. Mrs Maggie Stevenson, surprisingly unperturbed at having exchanged Heriot Row, Edinburgh, for an Adirondack shack, and her stable engineer husband for her unpredictable son, wrote unflappably to her sister, "We may go and sail about the Pacific next winter." McClure sent books about the South Seas, and proposed a lecture tour to follow the cruise.

For his part, Stevenson was always fascinated by dualities, the contrasts in the human condition. It is his great underlying theme as a writer. His narratives (like *The Master of Ballantrae*) zigzag between extremes. So it is appropriate that he finally committed to undertake his South Sea idyll, contemplated for so long, while huddled in buffalo furs in a frozen Saranac hut with its doors and windows caulked against the blizzard.

As usual Fanny did the preparatory work. On a family visit to California in the spring of 1888, she was deputed to look out for a suitable yacht, and with her usual resourcefulness she found one. In May she telegraphed to her husband (now thawing out and messing about in boats at Manasquan, New Jersey), "Can secure splendid sea-going schooner yacht *Casco* for seven hundred and fifty a month with most comfortable accommodation for six aft and six forward. Can be ready for sea in ten days. Reply immediately. Fanny."

They were well matched in impulsive resolution. Stevenson sent the telegram boy back with the reply: "Blessed girl, take the yacht and expect us in ten days. Louis."

They sailed from San Francisco just over a month later. Skippered by an irascible American, the bizarre ship's company comprised one Russian, one Finnish, and two Swedish crewmen, a Chinese cook who pretended to be Japanese, and five totally inexperienced passengers: Robert Louis Stevenson, semi-invalid author, age 37; Fanny Stevenson, 48; Lloyd Osbourne, dropped-out Edinburgh law student of literary aspirations, 20; Margaret Stevenson, widow, dressed unfailingly in starched black, 59; and the French maid/cabin boy, Valentine Roch, about 24. Once Captain Otis set eyes on his famous but cadaverously thin passenger, he is reputed to have stowed gear for burial at sea. And when questioned about what he would do in an emergency such as the author's elderly mother being swept overboard, he is said to have replied, "Put it in the log."

Stevenson's enthusiasm was undampened. "This is an old dream of mine which actually seems to be coming true, and I am sun-struck," he wrote.

On 28 June 1888 the *Casco* sailed out of San Francisco Bay, setting course south-southwest for the Marquesas Islands, 5000 kilometres (more than 3000 miles) away, across the open, sketchily charted, and unpredictable Pacific Ocean.

DECIDING TO REMAIN:

SAMOA

The schooner Casco *was fast, built for racing, and they made landfall in the Marquesas, the north-east extremity of French Polynesia, after only a month, on 28 July 1888. The voyage from San Francisco was a time of "glad monotony" that Stevenson found stimulating. He felt "delightedly conscious... Day after day the air had the same indescribable liveliness and sweetness... I was aware of a spiritual change; or perhaps, a molecular reconstitution. My bones were sweeter to me."*

That autobiographical intimacy he put into The Wrecker, *a novel set primarily in the Pacific that he began to write the next year in collaboration with his stepson Lloyd Osbourne. The tone of* In the South Seas, *the travel book compiled partly from his articles for McClure's paper* The Sun, *and laboured over for three years, is even more personal. It is a strange and surprizing book from the start, for it opens with a farewell. Summarizing his three Pacific cruises, Stevenson then states unequivocally that "I decided to remain." He enthuses about the pleasure and interest, the "attractive power" and "sense of seduction", of a part of the world then almost unknown in Europe or America, and associated mainly with storms and savagery. This prologue makes it clear that the much-missed famous author will have no happy return in the near future to New York or Edinburgh. His cruises are for the time being completed, but the literary journey is still in process. "I must learn to address readers from the uttermost parts of the sea," he tells them. It is an unexpected and challenging way to begin a book of travels.*

FOR nearly ten years my health had been declining; and for some while before I set forth upon my voyage, I believed I was come to the afterpiece of life, and had only the nurse and undertaker to expect. It was suggested that I should try the South Seas; and I was not unwilling to visit like a ghost, and be carried like a bale, among scenes that had attracted me in youth and health. I chartered accordingly Dr. Merrit's schooner yacht, the *Casco*, seventy-four tons register; sailed from San Francisco towards the end of June 1888, visited the eastern islands, and was left early the next year at Honolulu. Hence, lacking courage to return to my old life of the house and sick-room, I set forth to leeward in a trading schooner, the *Equator*, of a little over seventy tons, spent four months among the atolls (low coral islands) of the Gilbert group, and reached Samoa towards the close of '89. By that time gratitude and habit were beginning to attach me to the islands; I had gained a competency of strength; I had made friends; I had learned new interests; the time of my voyages had passed like days in fairyland; and I decided to remain. I began to prepare these pages at sea, on a third cruise, in the trading steamer *Janet Nicoll*. If more days are granted me, they shall be passed where I have found life most pleasant and man most interesting; the axes of my black boys are already clearing the foundations of my future house; and I must learn to address readers from the uttermost parts of the sea.

That I should thus have reversed the verdict of Lord Tennyson's hero is less eccentric than appears. Few men who come to the islands leave them; they grow grey where they alighted; the palm shades and the trade-wind fans them till they die, perhaps cherishing to the last the fancy of a visit home, which is rarely made, more rarely enjoyed, and yet more rarely repeated. No part of the world exerts the same attractive power upon the visitor, and the task before me is to communicate to fireside travellers some sense of its seduction, and to describe the life, at sea and ashore, of many hundred thousand persons, some of our own blood and language, all our contemporaries, and yet as remote in thought and habit as Rob Roy or Barbarossa, the Apostles or the Caesars.

2

THE FIRST ISLAND:
NUKA-HIVA, MARQUESAS

No traveller in the Pacific ever forgets the sight of their first island. That land-fall is perhaps the quintessential Pacific experience, even for those born there, even (however inadequately) arriving by air. Stevenson's In the South Seas *account is unmatched in English narrative prose in capturing the magic, from the "silence of expectation" to the "explosions of surf", from "attenuating darkness" to "sparkling brightness", from "wrangling over charts" to admission into "a world of wonders"; and he writes of it with a vibrant subjectivity that in places becomes intense. It is as if, having just opened the book (1) by saying, "the task before me is to communicate to fireside travellers some sense of [the Pacific's] seduction", he promptly does it, and at the top of his form.*

ON the 28th of July 1888 the moon was an hour down by four in the morning. In the east a radiating centre of brightness told of the day; and beneath, on the skyline, the morning bank was already building, black as ink. We have all read of the swiftness of the day's coming and departure in low latitudes; it is a point on which the scientific and sentimental tourist are at one, and has inspired some tasteful poetry. The period certainly varies with the season; but here is one case exactly noted. Although the dawn was thus preparing by four, the sun was not up till six; and it was halfpast five before we could distinguish our expected islands from the clouds on the horizon. Eight degrees south, and the day two hours a-coming. The interval was passed on deck in the silence of expectation, the customary thrill of landfall heightened by the strangeness of the shores that we were then approaching. Slowly they

took shape in the attenuating darkness. Ua-huna, piling up to a truncated summit, appeared the first upon the starboard bow; almost abeam arose our destination, Nuka-hiva, whelmed in cloud; and betwixt and to the southward, the first rays of the sun displayed the needles of Ua-pu. These pricked about the line of the horizon; like the pinnacles of some ornate and monstrous church, they stood there, in the sparkling brightness of the morning, the fit signboard of a world of wonders.

Not one soul aboard the *Casco* had set foot upon the islands, or knew, except by accident, one word of any of the island tongues; and it was with something perhaps of the same anxious pleasure as thrilled the bosom of discoverers that we drew near these problematic shores. The land heaved up in peaks and rising vales; it fell in cliffs and buttresses; its colour ran through fifty modulations in a scale of pearl and rose and olive; and it was crowned above by opalescent clouds. The suffusion of vague hues deceived the eye; the shadows of clouds were confounded with the articulations of the mountains; and the isle and its unsubstantial canopy rose and shimmered before us like a single mass. There was no beacon, no smoke of towns to be expected, no plying pilot. Somewhere, in that pale phantasmagoria of cliff and cloud, our haven lay concealed; and somewhere to the east of it—the only sea-mark given —a certain headland, known indifferently as Cape Adam and Eve, or Cape Jack and Jane, and distinguished by two colossal figures, the gross statuary of nature. These we were to find; for these we craned and, stared, focussed glasses, and wrangled over charts; and the sun was overhead and the land close ahead before we found them. To a ship approaching, like the *Casco*, from the north, they proved indeed the least conspicuous features of a striking coast; the surf flying high above its base; strange, austere, and feathered mountains rising behind; and Jack and Jane, or Adam and Eve, impending, like a pair of warts above the breakers.

Thence we bore away along shore. On our port beam we might hear the explosions of the surf; a few birds flew fishing under the prow; there was no other sound or mark of life, whether of man or beast, in all that quarter of the island. Winged by her own impetus and the dying breeze, the *Casco* skimmed under cliffs, opened out a cove, showed us a beach and some green trees, and

(Left) "I believed I was come to the afterpiece of life, and had only the nurse and the undertaker to expect." RLS at sea in the Pacific, on the bowsprit, in sight of an island: "My bones were sweeter to me."

flitted by again, bowing to the swell. The trees, from our distance, might have been hazel; the beach might have been in Europe; the mountain forms behind modelled in little from the Alps, and the forest which clustered on their ramparts a growth no more considerable than our Scottish heath. Again the cliff yawned, but now with a deeper entry; and the *Casco*, hauling her wind, began to slide into the bay of Anaho. The cocoa-palm, that giraffe of vegetables, so graceful, so ungainly, to the European eye so foreign, was to be seen crowding on the beach, and climbing and fringing the steep sides of mountains. Rude and bare hills embraced the inlet upon either hand; it was enclosed to the landward by a bulk of shattered mountains. In every crevice of that barrier the forest harboured, roosting and nestling there like birds about a ruin; and far above, it greened and roughened the razor edges of the summit.

Under the eastern shore, our schooner, now bereft of any breeze, continued to creep in: the smart creature, when once under way, appearing motive in herself. From close aboard arose the bleating of young lambs; a bird sang in the hillside; the scent of a hundred fruits or flowers flowed forth to meet us; and presently, a house or two appeared, standing high upon the ankles of the hills, and one of these surrounded with what seemed a garden. These conspicuous habitations, that patch of culture, had we but known it, were a mark of the passage of whites; and we might have approached a hundred islands and not found their parallel. It was longer ere we spied the native village, standing (in the universal fashion) close upon a curve of beach, close under a grove of palms; the sea in front growling and whitening on a concave arc of reef. For the cocoa-tree and the island man are both lovers and neighbours of the surf. "The coral waxes, the palm grows, but man departs," says the sad Tahitian proverb; but they are all three, so long as they endure, co-haunters of the beach. The mark of anchorage was a blow-hole in the rocks, near the south-easterly corner of the bay. Punctually to our use, the blow-hole spouted; the schooner turned upon her heel; the anchor plunged. It was a small sound, a great event; my soul went down with these moorings whence no windlass may extract nor any diver fish it up; and I, and some part of my ship's company, were from that hour the bondslaves of the isles of Vivien.

A SENSE OF KINSHIP:

ANAHO, MARQUESAS

When his soul "went down with these moorings", it was not the only time Stevenson dropped spiritual anchor on a sea-shore. He came from a family of coastal engineers, builders of lighthouses and harbours, and was drawn in life and imagination to the point of encounter between land and sea. Treasure Island, Kidnapped, The Black Arrow, The Master of Ballantrae, The Wrecker, Catriona *and* The Ebb-Tide *(the last three written in the Pacific) all place powerful scenes on that turbulent margin. Seamen ashore like Long John Silver, Billy Bones, or Hoseason (in* Kidnapped*) are like incarnations of the violent conflict. Nowhere is the encounter more potent than in the Pacific surf. The* Flying Scud *(in* The Wrecker*) lies in the spray of the reef, the ominous ambivalent Attwater bestrides the lagoon (in* The Ebb-Tide*), and Kalamake in 'The Isle of Voices' is the giant wizard of an enchanted beach, and "the swell beat and burst upon his bosom, as it beats and breaks against a cliff."*

Once he dropped anchor at Nuka-Hiva, Stevenson would never again live more than walking distance from the ocean. He became a creature of the coast, and addicted to landfalls. Explaining to the disapproving Henry James why he was staying on in the Pacific, he wrote almost inarticulately, "to draw near a new island, I cannot say how much I like."

Sometimes these moments of arrival are imagined from the point of view of the residents ashore, as in the cinematic image seen from the Marquesas waterfront that opens The Wrecker, *"the appearance of a flying jib beyond the western islet", and the "magic cry of 'Ehippy' – ship." Rare among travel writing of the 19th century,* In the South Seas *and* A Footnote to History *reverse the European*

camera, oblige the American or English reader to imagine the frame of reference into which they had intruded. Many comparisons are made with Western culture and history; but the effect is the opposite of Eurocentric. Superiority and condescension are undermined when the reader, instead of being entertained by the exotic and inferior, is obliged to acknowledge how similar Polynesian practices are to their own, and how "insecure... is the pre-eminence of race."

And so, from the turbulence and then the magic of arrival at a strange shore, Stevenson moves, with an almost musical modulation of tone, to a serenely evoked sense of kinship and shared humanity.

THESE points of similarity between a South Sea people and some of my own folk at home ran much in my head in the islands; and not only inclined me to view my fresh acquaintances with favour, but continually modified my judgment. A polite Englishman comes to-day to the Marquesans and is amazed to find the men tattooed; polite Italians came not long ago to England and found our fathers stained with woad; and when I paid the return visit as a little boy, I was highly diverted with the backwardness of Italy: so insecure, so much a matter of the day and hour, is the pre-eminence of race. It was so that I hit upon a means of communication which I recommend to travellers. When I desired any detail of savage custom, or of superstitious belief, I cast back in the story of my fathers, and fished for what I wanted with some trait of equal barbarism: Michael Scott, Lord Derwentwater's head, the second-sight, the Water Kelpie—each of these I have found to be a killing bait; the black bull's head of Stirling procured me the legend of *Rahero*; and what I knew of the Cluny Macphersons, or the Appin Stewarts, enabled me to learn, and helped me to understand, about the *Tevas* of Tahiti. The native was no longer ashamed, his sense of kinship grew warmer, and his lips were opened. It is this sense of kinship that the traveller must rouse and share; or he had better content himself with travels from the blue bed to the brown. And the presence of one Cockney titterer will cause a whole party to walk in clouds of darkness.

The hamlet of Anaho stands on a margin of flat land between the west of the beach and the spring of the impending mountains. A grove of palms,

(Left) **"The Cruise of the Silver Ship": "Pahi Muni – the Silver Ship" was the Fakaravans' name for the schooner *Casco*.**

perpetually ruffling its green fans, carpets it (as for a triumph) with fallen branches, and shades it like an arbour. A road runs from end to end of the covert among beds of flowers, the milliner's shop of the community; and here and there, in the grateful twilight, in an air filled with a diversity of scents, and still within hearing of the surf upon the reef, the native houses stand in scattered neighbourhood.

The same word, as we have seen, represents in many tongues of Polynesia, with scarce a shade of difference, the abode of man. But although the word be the same, the structure itself continually varies; and the Marquesan, among the most backward and barbarous of islanders, is yet the most commodiously lodged. The grass huts of Hawaii, the birdcage houses of Tahiti, or the open shed, with the crazy Venetian blinds, of the polite Samoan—none of these can be compared with the Marquesan *paepae-hae*, or dwelling platform. The paepae is an oblong terrace built without cement of black volcanic stone, from twenty to fifty feet in length, raised from four to eight feet from the earth, and accessible by a broad stair. Along the back of this, and coming to about half its width, runs the open front of the house, like a covered gallery: the interior sometimes neat and almost elegant in its bareness, the sleeping space divided off by an endlong coaming, some bright raiment perhaps hanging from a nail, and a lamp and one of White's sewing-machines the only marks of civilization. On the outside, at one end of the terrace, burns the cooking-fire under a shed; at the other there is perhaps a pen for pigs; the remainder is the evening lounge and *al fresco* banquet hall of the inhabitants. To some houses water is brought down the mountains in bamboo pipes, perforated for the sake of sweetness. With the Highland comparison in my mind, I was struck to remember the sluttish mounds of turf and stone in which I have sat and been entertained in the Hebrides and the North Islands. Two things, I suppose, explain the contrast. In Scotland wood is rare, and with materials so rude as turf and stone the very hope of neatness is excluded. And in Scotland it is cold. Shelter and a hearth are needs so pressing that a man looks not beyond; he is out all day after a bare bellyful, and at night when he saith, 'Aha, it is warm!' he has not appetite for more. Or if for something else, then something higher; a fine school of poetry and song arose in these rough shelters, and an air like 'Lochaber no more' is an evidence of refinement more convincing, as well as more imperishable, than a palace.

To one such dwelling platform a considerable troop of relatives and dependants resort. In the hour of the dusk, when the fire blazes, and the scent of the cooked breadfruit fills the air, and perhaps the lamp glints already between the pillars and the house, you shall behold them silently assemble to this meal, men, women, and children; and the dogs and pigs frisk together up the terrace stairway, switching rival tails. The strangers from the ship were soon equally welcome: welcome to dip their fingers in the wooden dish, to drink cocoanuts, to share the circulating pipe, and to hear and hold high debate about the misdeeds of the French, the Panama Canal, or the geographical position of San Francisco and New Yo'ko. In a Highland hamlet, quite out of reach of any tourist, I have met the same plain and dignified hospitality.

4

DESPONDENCY AND DREAD:
ANAHO, MARQUESAS

*As visitors among the Marquesan people, who saw few Europeans, the whole party conducted themselves with an openness and courtesy that made them welcome and trusted. The pattern was repeated everywhere they called. Stevenson had a natural charm and attractive vitality. He was genuinely interested in the people he met. He took pains to learn their languages, and had a quick curiosity for indigenous oral literature: "I have had great fortune in finding old songs and ballads and stories." He began to write his own, initially the narrative poem that became 'The Feast of Famine' (**26**), which he called "a patchwork of details of manners and the impressions of a traveller."*

This eager engagement with the places and people he visited makes In the South Seas *an enticing travel book. Stevenson is immediately committed to them. The original scheme for the Pacific travel book planned a colourful introductory section of anecdotes about European smugglers, beachcombers, remittance men and other identities among the outcasts of the islands. Getting close to the islanders themselves made Stevenson realize that more important things were happening. So he changed the book's structure radically, opening with the summary of his personal situation, and the narrative of first landfall (see **1** and **2**), and then taking the reader into the people's own essential culture.*

He does not preach against colonization, but he makes uncomfortably clear the disastrous effects of early Spanish policies of genocide, the later depredations of disease, and the resentment against colonial (in this case French) intrusion. In one of his first letters from Nuka-Hiva he wrote: "I shouldn't wonder if there came trouble here some day... I could name a nation that is not beloved in certain islands – and does not know it! Strange: like ourselves, perhaps, in India!"

He also poignantly records the cultural trauma of being colonized. He perceived that for the Marquesans the loss of their cultural self-respect had taken away the will to live. Theirs is a society now of loss, lament, despondency and dread. The decline of the living race is made even more tragic by the ubiquitous presence of their population of ghosts. "Their life is beleaguered by the dead," he wrote in the notes to 'The Feast of Famine' (26). In writing of them, his traveller's record becomes a mourner's elegy.

IN their despondency there is an element of dread. The fear of ghosts and of the dark is very deeply written in the mind of the Polynesian; not least of the Marquesan. Poor Taipi, the chief of Anaho, was condemned to ride to Hatiheu on a moonless night. He borrowed a lantern, sat a long while nerving himself for the adventure, and when he at last departed, wrung the *Cascos* by the hand as for a final separation. Certain presences, called Vehinehae, frequent and make terrible the nocturnal roadside; I was told by one they were like so much mist, and as the traveller walked into them dispersed and dissipated; another described them as being shaped like men and having eyes like cats; from none could I obtain the smallest clearness as to what they did, or wherefore they were dreaded. We may be sure at least they represent the dead; for the dead, in the minds of the islanders, are all-pervasive. "When a native says that he is a man," writes Dr. Codrington, "he means that he is a man and not a ghost; not that he is a man and not a beast. The intelligent agents of this world are to his mind the men who are alive, and the ghosts the men who are dead." Dr. Codrington speaks of Melanesia; from what I have learned his words are equally true of the Polynesian. And yet more. Among cannibal Polynesians a dreadful suspicion rests generally on the dead; and the Marquesans, the greatest cannibals of all, are scarce likely to be free from similar beliefs. I hazard the guess that the Vehinehae are the hungry spirits of the dead, continuing their life's business of the cannibal ambuscade, and lying everywhere unseen, and eager to devour the living. Another superstition I picked up through the troubled medium of Tari Coffin's English. The dead, he told me, came and danced by night around the paepae of their former family; the family were thereupon overcome by some emotion (but whether of pious sorrow or of fear I could not gather), and must 'make a feast,' of which fish, pig, and popoi were indispensable ingredients. So far this is clear enough.

DESPONDENCY & DREAD

But here Tari went on to instance the new house of Toma and the housewarming feast which was just then in preparation as instances in point. Dare we indeed string them together, and add the case of the deserted ruin, as though the dead continually besieged the paepaes of the living: were kept at arm's-length, even from the first foundation, only by propitiatory feasts, and, so soon as the fire of life went out upon the hearth, swarmed back into possession of their ancient seat?

I speak by guess of these Marquesan superstitions. On the cannibal ghost I shall return elsewhere with certainty. And it is enough, for the present purpose, to remark that the men of the Marquesas, from whatever reason, fear and shrink from the presence of ghosts. Conceive how this must tell upon the nerves in islands where the number of the dead already so far exceeds that of the living, and the dead multiply and the living dwindle at so swift a rate. Conceive how the remnant huddles about the embers of the fire of life; even as old Red Indians, deserted on the march and in the snow, the kindly tribe all gone, the last flame expiring, and the night around populous with wolves.

CANNIBALS:

HATIHEU, MARQUESAS

In the South Seas *is the most neglected and misunderstood of Stevenson's books. Fanny Stevenson, usually a careful and constructive critic, dismissed it in progress as "a small treatise on the Polynesian races." She grumbled, in a May 1889 letter, that he was failing to use "the most enchanting material that anyone ever had in the whole world", and that instead, "He has taken it into his Scottish Presbyterian head, that a stern duty lies before him, and that his book must be a sort of scientific and historical impersonal thing, comparing the different languages (of which he knows nothing really) and the different peoples."*

This is the most quoted and influential critique of the book. It is a grave misrepresentation. There is no way of knowing, of course, whether Fanny's views helped add the highly personal tone that makes many passages so engaging (for instance, 1, 2, 3 above), but it is unlikely. The book's development clearly reflects Stevenson's response to the realities of the Pacific. He wrote in 1893 that he had seen it as a non-fiction "prose-epic" about the "unjust (yet I can see the inevitable) extinction of the Polynesian Islanders by our shabby civilization." Planning it in 1889, he had envisaged an ambitious sixty chapters, estimating 500 pages, and already wrote excitedly about the mixture of "wildness" and "beauty" he was aiming to recapture. Even in the reduced form it eventually took, with Tahiti, Hawaii and Samoa omitted from the original plan, it is confessional rather than historical, an often idiosyncratic travel book more than an impersonal treatise. Most important, and something that Fanny was perhaps unable to perceive, it moves from description to episode and from scene to discussion in an intensely-felt, tonally conscious, musical way, not a stern or scientific one.

But Fanny was discouraging, and McClure less than enthusiastic when the early articles arrived. The problem was their expectation. Fanny wanted "enchanting material", and McClure, remember, commissioned "stories of adventure and so forth", thinking he had hired the RLS of Treasure Island. *But Stevenson was not interested in swashbuckling his way around an enchanting South Seas of Western fantasy. Instead he gave them depopulation and despair. Then, almost defiantly, in Chapter 11, still in the Marquesas, he takes on a challenge even greater than tattooing, despondency or ghosts. He asks his civilized readers in Bournemouth and Brooklyn to think, in a careful, informed, open-minded way, about cannibalism.*

It was typical that he should require his readers to "look at both sides". He often demands that familiar judgments be suspended, and he challenges preconceptions. In 1894 he was carefully explaining the protocol of Samoan head-hunting to readers of the London Times. *He is said to have once written a sympathetic novel about a prostitute, which Fanny destroyed. Long John Silver and the Master of Ballantrae commit cold-blooded murder and treacherous robbery, but remain attractive and ambiguous as villains. 'Markheim', Jekyll and Hyde, 'The Bottle Imp' and 'The Isle of Voices' never merely condemn those who ally themselves even with the demonic. The human condition is complex and destructive violence is part of nature, his writing ubiquitously affirms. Suffering accompanies beauty, even in the alluring Pacific. Stevenson's romanticism is founded in a thoroughly pragmatic realism.*

The entire chapter follows below. McClure and Fanny should have reconsidered at least the penultimate paragraph (p. 38-39). In its complex mix of objectivity and repugnance, plain and evocative language, colour, movement, heat, sound, and the throbbing rhythm of the drums, Stevenson's imagined scene of the cannibal feast is vivid, horrific, and utterly compelling.

LONG-PIG – A CANNIBAL HIGH PLACE

NOTHING more strongly arouses our disgust than cannibalism, nothing so surely unmortars a society; nothing, we might plausibly argue, will so harden and degrade the minds of those that practise it. And yet we ourselves make much the same appearance in the eyes of the Buddhist and the vegetarian. We consume the carcasses of creatures of like appetites, passions, and organs with ourselves; we feed on babes, though not our own; and the slaughter-house resounds daily with screams of pain and fear. We distinguish, indeed; but the willingness of many nations to eat the dog, an animal with whom we live on terms of the next intimacy, shows how precariously the distinction is grounded. The pig is the main element of animal food among the islands; and I had many occasions, my mind being quickened by my cannibal surroundings, to observe his character and the manner of his death. Many islanders live with their pigs as we do with our dogs; both crowd around the hearth with equal freedom; and the island pig is a fellow of activity, enterprise, and sense. He husks his own cocoa-nuts, and (I am told) rolls them into the sun to burst; he is the terror of the shepherd. Mrs. Stevenson, senior, has seen one fleeing to the woods with a lamb in his mouth; and I saw another come rapidly (and erroneously) to the conclusion that the *Casco* was going down, and swim through the flush water to the rail in search of an escape. It was told us in childhood that pigs cannot swim; I have known one to leap overboard, swim five hundred yards to shore, and return to the house of his original owner.

I was once, at Tautira, a pig-master on a considerable scale; at first, in my pen, the utmost good feeling prevailed; a little sow with a belly-ache came and appealed to us for help in the manner of a child; and there was one shapely black boar, whom we called Catholicus, for he was a particular present from the Catholics of the village, and who early displayed the marks of courage and friendliness; no other animal, whether dog or pig, was suffered to approach him at his food, and for human beings he showed a full measure of that toadying fondness so common in the lower animals, and possibly their chief title to the name. One day, on visiting my piggery, I was amazed to see Catholicus draw back from my approach with cries of terror; and if I was amazed at the change, I was truly embarrassed when I learnt its reason. One of the pigs had been that morning killed; Catholicus had seen the murder, he had discovered he was dwelling in the shambles, and from that time his confidence and his delight in life were ended. We still reserved him a long while, but he could not endure the sight of any two-legged creature, nor could we, under the circumstances, encounter his eye without confusion. I have assisted besides, by the ear, at the act of butchery itself; the victim's cries of pain I think I could have borne, but the execution was mismanaged, and his expression of terror was contagious: that small heart moved to the same tune with ours. Upon such 'dread foundations' the life of the European reposes, and yet the European is among the less cruel of races. The paraphernalia of murder, the preparatory brutalities of his existence, are all hid away; an extreme sensibility reigns upon the surface; and ladies will faint at the recital of one tithe of what they daily expect of their butchers. Some will be even crying out upon me in their hearts for the coarseness of this paragraph. And so with the island cannibals. They were not cruel; apart from this custom, they are a race of the most kindly; rightly speaking, to cut a man's flesh after he is dead is far less hateful than to oppress him whilst he lives; and even the victims of their appetite were gently used in life and suddenly and painlessly despatched at last. In island circles of refinement it was doubtless thought bad taste to expatiate on what was ugly in the practice.

Cannibalism is traced from end to end of the Pacific, from the Marquesas to New Guinea, from New Zealand to Hawaii, here in the lively height of its exercise, there by scanty but significant survivals. Hawaii is the most doubtful. We find cannibalism chronicled in Hawaii, only in the history of a single war, where it seems to have been thought exception, as in the case of mountain outlaws, such as fell by the hand of Theseus. In Tahiti, a single circumstance survived, but that appears conclusive. In historic times, when human oblation was made in the marae, the eyes of the victim were formally offered to the chief: a delicacy to the leading guest. All Melanesia appears tainted. In Micronesia, in the Marshalls, with which my acquaintance is no more than that of a tourist, I could find no trace at all; and even in the Gilbert zone I long looked and asked in vain. I was told tales indeed of men who had been eaten in a famine; but these were nothing to my purpose, for the same thing is done under the same stress by all kindreds and generations of men. At last, in some manuscript notes of Dr. Turner's, which I was allowed to consult at Malua, I came on one damning evidence: on the island of Onoatoa the punishment for theft was to be killed and eaten. How shall we account for the universality of the practice over so vast an area, among people of such varying civilisation, and, with whatever intermixture, of such different blood? What circumstance is common to them all, but that they lived on islands destitute, or very nearly so, of animal food? I can never find it in my appetite that man was meant to live on vegetables only. When our stores ran low among the islands, I grew to weary for the recurrent day when economy allowed us to open another tin of miserable mutton. And in at least one ocean language, a particular word denotes that a man is 'hungry for fish,' having reached that stage when vegetables can no longer satisfy, and his soul, like those of the Hebrews in the desert, begins to lust after flesh-pots. Add to this the evidences of over-population and imminent famine already adduced, and I think we see some ground of indulgence for the island cannibal.

It is right to look at both sides of any question; but I am far from making the apology of this worse than bestial vice. The higher Polynesian races, such as the Tahitians, Hawaiians, and Samoans, had one and all outgrown, and some of them had in part forgot, the practice, before Cook or Bougainville had shown a top-sail in their waters. It lingered only in some low islands where life was difficult to maintain, and among inveterate savages like the New Zealanders or the Marquesans. The Marquesans intertwined man-eating with the whole texture of their lives; long-pig was in a sense their currency and sacrament; it formed the hire of the artist, illustrated public events, and was the occasion and attraction of a feast. To-day they are paying the penalty of this bloody commixture. The civil power, in its crusade against man-eating, has had to examine one after another all Marquesan arts and pleasures, has found them one after another tainted with a cannibal element, and one after another has placed them on the proscript list. Their art of tattooing stood by itself, the execution exquisite, the designs most beautiful and intricate; nothing more handsomely sets off a handsome man; it may cost some pain in the beginning, but I doubt if it be near so painful in the long-run, and I am sure it is far more becoming than the ignoble European practice of tight-lacing among women. And now it has been found needful to forbid the art. Their songs and dances were numerous (and the law has had to abolish them by the dozen). They now face empty-handed the tedium of their uneventful days; and who shall pity them? The least rigorous will say that they were justly served.

Death alone could not satisfy Marquesan vengeance: the flesh must be eaten. The chief who seized Mr. Whalon preferred to eat him; and he thought he had justified the wish when he explained it was a vengeance. Two or three years ago, the people of a valley seized and slew a wretch who had offended them. His offence, it is to be supposed, was dire; they could not bear to leave their vengeance incomplete, and, under the eyes of the French, they did not dare to hold a public festival. The body was accordingly divided; and every man retired to his own house to consummate the rite in secret, carrying his proportion of the dreadful meat in a Swedish match-box. The barbarous substance of the drama and the European properties employed offer a seizing contrast to the imagination. Yet more striking is another incident of the very year when I was there myself, 1888. In the spring, a man and woman skulked about the school-house in Hiva-oa till they found a particular child alone. Him they approached with honeyed words and carneying manners—'You are So-and-so, son of So-and-so?' they asked; and caressed and beguiled him deeper in the woods. Some instinct woke in the child's bosom, or some look betrayed the horrid purpose of his deceivers. He sought to break from them; he screamed; and they, casting off the mask, seized him the more strongly and began to run. His cries were heard; his schoolmates, playing not far off, came running to the rescue; and the sinister couple fled and vanished in the woods. They were never identified; no prosecution followed; but it was currently supposed they had some grudge against the boy's father, and designed to eat him in revenge. All over the islands, as at home among our own ancestors, it will be observed that the avenger takes no particular heed to strike an individual. A family, a class, a village, a whole valley or island, a whole race of mankind, share equally the guilt of any member. So, in the above story, the son was to pay the penalty for his father; so Mr. Whalon, the mate of an American whaler, was to bleed and be eaten for the misdeeds of a Peruvian slaver. I am reminded of an incident in Jaluit in the Marshall group, which was told me by an eye-witness, and which I tell here again for the strangeness of the scene. Two men had awakened the animosity of the Jaluit chiefs; and it was their wives who were selected to be punished. A single native served as executioner. Early in the morning, in the face of a large concourse of spectators, he waded out upon the reef between his victims. These neither complained nor resisted; accompanied their destroyer patiently; stooped down, when they had waded deep enough, at his command; and he (laying one hand upon the shoulders of each) held them under water till they drowned. Doubtless, although my informant did not tell me so, their families would be lamenting aloud upon the beach.

It was from Hatiheu that I paid my first visit to a cannibal high place.

The day was sultry and clouded. Drenching tropical showers succeeded bursts of sweltering sunshine. The green pathway of the road wound steeply upward. As we went, our little schoolboy guide a little ahead of us, Father Simeon had his portfolio in his hand, and named the trees for me, and read aloud from his notes the abstract of their virtues. Presently the road, mounting, showed us the vale of Hatiheu, on a larger scale; and the priest, with occasional reference to our guide, pointed out the boundaries and told me the names of the larger tribes that lived at perpetual war in the old days: one on the north-east, one along the beach, one behind upon the mountain. With a survivor of this latter clan Father Simeon had spoken; until the pacification he had never been to the sea's edge, nor, if I remember exactly, eaten of sea-fish. Each in its own district, the septs lived cantoned and beleaguered. One step without the boundaries was to affront death. If famine came, the men must out to the woods to gather chestnuts and small fruits; even as to this day, if the parents are backward in their weekly doles, school must be broken up and the scholars sent foraging. But in the old days, when there was trouble in one clan, there would be activity in all its neighbours; the woods would be laid full of ambushes; and he who went after vegetables for himself might remain to be a joint for his hereditary foes. Nor was the pointed occasion needful. A dozen different natural signs and social junctures called this people to the war-path and the cannibal hunt. Let one of chiefly rank have finished his tattooing, the wife of one be near upon her time, two of the debouching streams have deviated nearer on the beach of Hatiheu, a certain bird have been heard to sing, a certain ominous formation of cloud observed above the northern sea; and instantly the arms were oiled, and the man-hunters swarmed into the wood to lay their fratricidal ambuscades.

It appears besides that occasionally, perhaps in famine, the priest would shut himself in his house, where he lay for a stated period like a person dead. When he came forth it was to run for three days through the territory of the clan, naked and starving, and to sleep at night alone in the high place. It was now the turn of the others to keep the house, for to encounter the priest upon his rounds was death. On the eve of the fourth day the time of the running was over; the priest returned to his roof, the laymen came forth, and in the morning the number of the victims was announced. I have this tale of the priest on one authority—I think a good one—but I set it down with diffidence. The particulars are so striking that, had they been true, I almost think I must have heard them oftener referred to. Upon one point there seems to be no question: that the feast was sometimes furnished from within the clan. In times of scarcity, all who were not protected by their family connections—in the Highland expression, all the commons of the clan—had cause to tremble.

It was vain to resist, it was useless to flee. They were begirt upon all hands by cannibals; and the oven was ready to smoke for them abroad in the country of their foes, or at home in the valley of their fathers.

At a certain corner of the road our scholar-guide struck off to his left into the twilight of the forest. We were now on one of the ancient native roads, plunged in a high vault of wood, and clambering, it seemed, at random over boulders and dead trees; but the lad wound in and out and up and down without a check, for these paths are to the natives as marked as the king's highway is to us; insomuch that, in the days of the man-hunt, it was their labour rather to block and deface than to improve them. In the crypt of the wood the air was clammy and hot and cold; overhead, upon the leaves, the tropical rain uproariously poured, but only here and there, as through holes in a leaky roof, a single drop would fall, and make a spot upon my mackintosh. Presently the huge trunk of a banyan hove in sight, standing upon what seemed the ruins of an ancient fort; and our guide, halting and holding forth his arm, announced that we had reached the *paepae tapu*.

Paepae signifies a floor or platform such as a native house is built on; and even such a paepae—a paepae hae—may be called a paepae tapu in a lesser sense when it is deserted and becomes the haunt of spirits; but the public high place, such as I was now treading, was a thing on a great scale. As far as my eyes could pierce through the dark undergrowth, the floor of the forest was all paved. Three tiers of terrace ran on the slope of the hill; in front, a crumbling parapet contained the main arena; and the pavement of that was pierced and parcelled out with several wells and small enclosures. No trace remained of any superstructure, and the scheme of the amphitheatre was difficult to seize. I visited another in Hiva-oa, smaller but more perfect, where it was easy to follow rows of benches, and to distinguish isolated seats of honour for eminent persons; and where, on the upper platform, a single joist of the temple or dead-house still remained, its uprights richly carved.

In the old days the high place was sedulously tended. No tree except the sacred banyan was suffered to encroach upon its grades, no dead leaf to rot upon the pavement. The stones were smoothly set, and I am told they were kept bright with oil. On all sides the guardians lay encamped in their sub-sidiary huts to watch and cleanse it. No other foot of man was suffered to draw near; only the priest, in the days of his running, came there to sleep—perhaps to dream of his ungodly errand; but, in the time of the feast, the clan trooped to the high place in a body, and each had his appointed seat. There were places for the chiefs, the drummers, the dancers, the women, and the priests. The drums—perhaps twenty strong, and some of them twelve feet high—continuously throbbed in time. In time the singers kept up their long-drawn, lugubrious, ululating song; in time, too, the dancers, tricked out in singular finery, stepped, leaped, swayed, and gesticulated—their plumed fingers fluttering in the air like butterflies. The sense of time, in all these ocean races, is extremely perfect; and I conceive in such a festival that almost every sound and movement fell in one. So much the more unanimously must have grown the agitation of the feasters; so much the more wild must have been the scene to any European who could have beheld them there, in the strong sun and the strong shadow of the banyan, rubbed with saffron to throw in a more high relief the arabesque of the tattoo; the women bleached by days of confinement to a complexion almost European; the chiefs crowned with silver plumes of old men's beards and girt with kirtles of the hair of dead women. All manner of island food was meanwhile spread for the women and the commons; and, for those who were privileged to eat of it, there were carried up to the dead-house the baskets of long-pig. It is told that the feasts were long kept up; the people came from them brutishly exhausted with debauchery, and the chiefs heavy with their beastly food. There are certain sentiments which we call emphatically human—denying the honour of that name to those who lack them. In such feasts—particularly where the victim has been slain at home, and men banqueted on the poor clay of a comrade with whom they had played in infancy, or a woman whose favours they had shared—the whole body of these sentiments is outraged. To consider it too closely is to understand, if not to excuse, the fervours of self-righteous old ship-captains, who would man their guns, and open fire in passing, on a cannibal island.

And yet it was strange. There, upon the spot, as I stood under the high, dripping vault of the forest, with the young priest on the one hand, in his kilted gown, and the bright-eyed Marquesan schoolboy on the other, the whole business appeared infinitely distant, and fallen in the cold perspective and dry light of history. The bearing of the priest, perhaps, affected me. He smiled; he jested with the boy, the heir both of these feasters and their meat; he clapped his hands, and gave me a stave of one of the old, ill-omened choruses. Centuries might have come and gone since this slimy theatre was last in operation; and I beheld the place with no more emotion than I might have felt in visiting Stonehenge. In Hiva-oa, as I began to appreciate that the thing was still living and latent about my footsteps, and that it was still within the bounds of possibility that I might hear the cry of the trapped victim, my historic attitude entirely failed, and I was sensible of some repugnance for the natives. But here, too, the priests maintained their jocular attitude: rallying the cannibals as upon an eccentricity rather absurd than horrible; seeking, I should say, to shame them from the practice by good-natured ridicule, as we shame a child from stealing sugar. We may here recognise the temperate and sagacious mind of Bishop Dordillon.

6

DANGEROUS ATOLLS:
KAUEHI, PAUMOTUS

After two weeks at Anaho, they had moved to the capital, Tai-o-hae, and then crossed to Taakauku on the island of Hiva-Oa, six weeks in all among the volcanic mountains and dense bush of the Marquesas. Stevenson quickly noted the difference between volcanic "high islands" and coral "low islands". He chose next to sail south to the Paumotus, the "Low" or "Dangerous" Archipelago (now usually known as the Tuamotus; Stevenson's version is used here). He knew the five-day, 1200 km (750 mile) voyage into that region's treacherous winds and currents would be "difficult and dangerous", and one night an unsuspected atoll indeed brought them very close to destruction.

Stevenson's literary aspirations were undampened. He wrote to an old friend from the deck of the Casco, *"at sea, near the Paumotus… with a dreadful pen," that he had dreamed about their young days in Edinburgh, when he had held just the hope that "I should possibly write one little book." Now, with a blithe disregard for the dangers around him, he wrote in confident and quite literary-competitive terms about the book already shaping in his hand: "I shall have a fine book of travels, I feel sure; and will tell you more of the South Seas after a very few months than any other writer has done – except Herman Melville perhaps, who is a howling cheese."*

The landfall after this risky voyage was to be at Atuona in the Paumotus, but a series of near-collisions and mistaken identities intervened, and provide the opening of Part Two of In the South Seas. *This is a conscious contrast to the "first experience" and "world of wonders" that open Part 1 (see 2 above). Here he recreates the hazardous drama of sailing through complicated and ill-charted seas, full of uncertainty and unease, and at one moment of crisis suddenly breaks out into dialogue. It is a piece of travel narrative that in its sense of anxiety, disorientation, and unseen danger comes close to the best of his fiction – David Balfour's flight through the heather, say, or the search for the Master of Ballantrae in the Adirondack Wilderness. A year or two later, the literary imagination would return to this unsure landfall among the atolls, and enrich description with fictional character, drama and irony, in Keola's arrival there in 'The Isle of Voices' (24), and the superlative landfall episode that opens Chapter 7 of* The Ebb-Tide *(25). Herrick and Davis straining through the dark for "the voice of breakers" were shaped aboard the* Casco *in the same dangerous seas.*

IN the early morning of 4th September a whale-boat manned by natives dragged us down the green lane of the anchorage and round the spouting promontory. On the shore level it was a hot, breathless, and yet crystal morning; but high overhead the hills of Atuona were all cowled in cloud, and the ocean-river of the trades streamed without pause. As we crawled from under the immediate shelter of the land, we reached at last the limit of their influence. The wind fell upon our sails in puffs, which strengthened and grew more continuous; presently the *Casco* heeled down to her day's work; the whale-boat, quite outstripped, clung for a noisy moment to her quarter; the stipulated bread, rum, and tobacco were passed in; a moment more and the boat was in our wake, and our late pilots were cheering our departure.

This was the more inspiriting as we were bound for scenes so different, and though on a brief voyage, yet for a new province of creation. That wide field of ocean, called loosely the South Seas, extends from tropic to tropic, and from perhaps 123 degrees W. to 150 degrees E., a parallelogram of one hundred degrees by forty-seven, where degrees are the most spacious. Much of it lies vacant, much is closely sewn with isles, and the isles are of two sorts. No distinction is so continually dwelt upon in South Sea talk as that between the 'low' and the 'high' island, and there is none more broadly marked in nature. The Himalayas are not more different from the Sahara. On the one hand, and chiefly in groups of from eight to a dozen, volcanic islands rise above the sea; few reach an altitude of less than 4000 feet; one exceeds 13,000; their tops are often obscured in cloud, they are all clothed with various forests, all abound in food, and are all remarkable for picturesque and solemn scenery. On the other hand, we have the atoll; a thing of problematic origin and history, the reputed creature of an insect apparently unidentified; rudely annular in shape; enclosing a lagoon; rarely extending beyond a quarter of a mile at its chief width; often rising at its highest point to less than the stature of a man—man himself, the rat and the land crab, its chief inhabitants; not more variously supplied with plants; and offering to the eye, even when perfect, only a ring of glittering beach and verdant foliage, enclosing and enclosed by the blue sea.

In no quarter are the atolls so thickly congregated, in none are they so varied in size from the greatest to the least, and in none is navigation so beset with perils, as in that archipelago that we were now to thread. The huge system of the trades is, for some reason, quite confounded by this multiplicity of reefs; the wind intermits, squalls are frequent from the west and southwest, hurricanes are known. The currents are, besides, inextricably intermixed; dead reckoning becomes a farce; the charts are not to be trusted; and such is the number and similarity of these islands that, even when you have picked one up, you may be none the wiser. The reputation of the place is consequently infamous; insurance offices exclude it from their field, and it was not without misgiving that my captain risked the *Casco* in such waters. I believe, indeed, it is almost understood that yachts are to avoid this baffling archipelago; and it required all my instances—and all Mr. Otis's private taste for adventure—to deflect our course across its midst.

For a few days we sailed with a steady trade, and a steady westerly current setting us to leeward; and toward sundown of the seventh it was supposed we should have sighted Takaroa, one of Cook's so-called King George Islands. The sun set; yet a while longer the old moon—semi-brilliant herself, and with a silver belly, which was her successor—sailed among gathering clouds; she, too, deserted us; stars of every degree of sheen, and clouds of every variety of form disputed the sub-lustrous night; and still we gazed in vain for Takaroa. The mate stood on the bowsprit, his tall grey figure slashing up and down against the stars, and still

nihil astra praeter
Vidit et undas.

The rest of us were grouped at the port anchor davit, staring with no less assiduity, but with far less hope on the obscure horizon. Islands we beheld in plenty, but they were of "such stuff as dreams are made on," and vanished at a wink, only to appear in other places; and by and by not only islands, but refulgent and revolving lights began to stud the darkness; lighthouses of the mind or of the wearied optic nerve solemnly shining and winking as we passed. At length the mate himself despaired, scrambled on board again from his unrestful perch, and announced that we had missed our destination. He was the only man of practice in these waters, our sole pilot, shipped for that end at Tai-o-hae. If he declared we had missed Takaroa, it was not for us to quarrel with the fact, but if we could, to explain it. We had certainly run down our southing. Our canted wake upon the sea and our somewhat drunken-looking course upon the chart both testified with no less certainty to an impetuous westward current. We had no choice but to conclude we were again set down to leeward; and the best we could do was to bring the *Casco* to the wind, keep a good watch and expect morning.

I slept that night, as was then my somewhat dangerous practice, on deck upon the cockpit bench. A stir at last awoke me, to see all the eastern heaven dyed with faint orange, the binnacle lamp already dulled against the brightness of the day, and the steersman leaning eagerly across the wheel. "There it is, sir!" he cried, and pointed in the very eyeball of the dawn. For a while I could see nothing but the bluish ruins of the morning bank, which lay far along the horizon, like melting icebergs. Then the sun rose, pierced a gap in these *débris* of vapours, and displayed an inconsiderable islet, flat as a plate upon the sea, and spiked with palms of disproportioned altitude.

So far, so good. Here was certainly an atoll; and we were certainly got among the archipelago. But which? And where? The isle was too small for either Takaroa: in all our neighbourhood, indeed, there was none so inconsiderable, save only Tikei; and Tikei, one of Roggewein's so-called Pernicious Islands, seemed beside the question. At that rate, instead of drifting to the west, we must have fetched up thirty miles to windward. And how about the current? It had been setting us down, by observation, all these days: by the deflection of our wake, it should be setting us down that moment. When had it stopped? When had it begun again? and what kind of torrent was that which had swept us eastward in the interval? To these questions, so typical of navigation in that range of isles, I have no answer. Such were at least the facts; Tikei our island turned out to be; and it was our first experience of the dangerous archipelago, to make our landfall thirty miles out.

The sight of Tikei, thrown direct against the splendour of the morning, robbed of all its colour, and deformed with disproportioned trees like bristles

(Above) "A ring of white beach, green underwood, and tossing palms, gem-like in colour; of a fairy, of a heavenly prettiness." Fanny is carried ashore at an island landfall.

BY COURTESY OF EDINBURGH CITY LIBRARIES

on a broom, had scarce prepared us to be much in love with atolls. Later the same day, we saw under more fit conditions the island of Taiaro. *Lost in the Sea* is possibly the meaning of the name. And it was so we saw it; lost in blue sea and sky: a ring of white beach, green underwood, and tossing palms, gem-like in colour; of a fairy, of a heavenly prettiness. The surf ran all around it, white as snow, and broke at one point, far to seaward, on what seems an uncharted reef. There was no smoke, no sign of man; indeed, the isle is not inhabited, only visited at intervals. And yet a trader (Mr. Narii Salmon) was watching from the shore and wondering at the unexpected ship. I have spent since then long months upon low islands; I know the tedium of their undistinguished days; I know the burden of their diet. With whatever envy we may have looked from the deck on these green coverts, it was with a tenfold greater that Mr. Salmon and his comrades saw us steer, in our trim ship, to seaward.

The night fell lovely in the extreme. After the moon went down, the heaven was a thing to wonder at for stars. And as I lay in the cockpit and looked upon the steersman I was haunted by Emerson's verses:

And the lone seaman all the night
Sails astonished among stars.

By this glittering and imperfect brightness, about four bells in the first watch
we made our third atoll, Raraka. The low line of the isle lay straight along
the sky; so that I was at first reminded of a towpath, and we seemed to be
mounting some engineered and navigable stream. Presently a red star
appeared, about the height and brightness of a danger signal, and with that,
my simile was changed; we seemed rather to skirt the embankment of a
railway, and the eye began to look instinctively for the telegraph-posts, and the
ear to expect the coming of a train. Here and there, but rarely, faint tree-tops
broke the level. And the sound of the surf accompanied us, now in a drowsy
monotone, now with a menacing swing.

The isle lay nearly east and west, barring our advance on Fakarava. We
must, therefore, hug the coast until we gained the western end, where, through
a passage eight miles wide, we might sail southward between Raraka and the
next isle, Kauehi. We had the wind free, a lightish air; but clouds of an inky
blackness were beginning to arise, and at times it lightened—without thunder.
Something, I know not what, continually set us up upon the island. We lay
more and more to the nor'ard; and you would have thought the shore copied
our manoeuvre and outsailed us. Once and twice Raraka headed us again—
again, in the sea fashion, the quite innocent steersman was abused—and again
the *Casco* kept away. Had I been called on, with no more light than that of our
experience, to draw the configuration of that island, I should have shown a
series of bow-window promontories, each overlapping the other to the nor'ard,
and the trend of the land from the south-east to the north-west, and behold,
on the chart it lay near east and west in a straight line.

We had but just repeated our manoeuvre and kept away—for not more
than five minutes the railway embankment had been lost to view and the surf
to hearing—when I was aware of land again, not only on the weather bow, but
dead ahead. I played the part of the judicious landsman, holding my peace till
the last moment; and presently my mariners perceived it for themselves.

"Land ahead!" said the steersman.

"By God, it's Kauehi!" cried the mate.

And so it was. And with that I began to be sorry for cartographers. We
were scarce doing three and a half; and they asked me to believe that (in five

minutes) we had dropped an island, passed eight miles of open water, and run almost high and dry upon the next. But my captain was more sorry for himself to be afloat in such a labyrinth; laid the *Casco* to, with the log line up and down, and sat on the stern rail and watched it till the morning. He had enough of night in the Paumotus.

By daylight on the 9th we began to skirt Kauehi and had now an opportunity to see near at hand the geography of atolls. Here and there, where it was high, the farther side loomed up; here and there the near side dipped entirely and showed a broad path of water into the lagoon; here and there both sides were equally abased, and we could look right through the discontinuous ring to the sea horizon on the south. Conceive, on a vast scale, the submerged hoop of the duck-hunter, trimmed with green rushes to conceal his head—water within, water without—you have the image of the perfect atoll. Conceive one that has been partly plucked of its rush fringe; you have the atoll of Kauehi. And for either shore of it at closer quarters, conceive the line of some old Roman highway traversing a wet morass, and here sunk out of view and there re-arising, crowned with a green tuft of thicket; only instead of the stagnant waters of a marsh, the live ocean now boiled against, now buried the frail barrier. Last night's impression in the dark was thus confirmed by day, and not corrected. We sailed indeed by a mere causeway in the sea, of nature's handiwork, yet of no greater magnitude than many of the works of man.

The isle was uninhabited; it was all green brush and white sand, set in transcendently blue water; even the cocoa-palms were rare, though some of these completed the bright harmony of colour by hanging out a fan of golden yellow. For long there was no sign of life beyond the vegetable, and no sound but the continuous grumble of the surf. In silence and desertion these fair shores slipped past, and were submerged and rose again with clumps of thicket from the sea. And then a bird or two appeared, hovering and crying; swiftly these became more numerous, and presently, looking ahead, we were aware of a vast effervescence of winged life. In this place the annular isle was mostly under water, carrying here and there on its submerged line a wooded islet. Over one of these the the birds hung and flew with an incredible density like that of gnats or hiving bees; the mass flashed white and black, and heaved and quivered, and the screaming of the creatures rose over the voice of the surf in a shrill clattering whirr. As you descend some inland valley a not dissimilar sound announces the nearness of a mill and pouring river. Some stragglers, as

I said, came to meet our approach; a few still hung about the ship as we departed. The crying died away, the last pair of wings was left behind, and once more the low shores of Kauehi streamed past our eyes in silence like a picture. I supposed at the time that the birds lived, like ants or citizens, concentred where we saw them. I have been told since (I know not if correctly) that the whole isle, or much of it, is similarly peopled; and that the effervescence at a single spot would be the mark of a boat's crew of egg-hunters from one of the neighbouring inhabited atolls. So that here at Kauehi, and the day before at Taiaro, the *Casco* sailed by under the fire of unsuspected eyes. And one thing is surely true, that even on these ribbons of land an army might be hid and no passing mariner divine its presence.

GRAVEYARD STORIES:
FAKARAVA, PAUMOTUS

Stevenson wrote in a letter: "these landfalls at dawn; new islands peaking from the morning bank... the whole tale of my life is better to me than any poem." Among the people of the Paumotus, as in the Marquesas, his sympathetic mind was engaged and exhilarated. From Fakarava he wrote, "the interest, indeed, has been incredible: *I did not dream there were such places or such races."* The Fakaravans called the Casco *"Pahi Muni", the "Silver Ship", and he joked he might name his book of Pacific travels "The Cruise of the Silver Ship — so there will be one poetic page at least — the title." As that implies, he was most interested in the reality within the poem.*

Fakarava is little more than a narrow curving sandbank 130 km (80 miles) long: a "ring of... land, with its string of palm trees", he would describe it in 'The Isle of Voices' (24). But the Stevenson party promptly settled in, won friends, and lived among the people in a small beach shack — a "little bare one-twentieth furnished house, surrounded by mangoes," he called it. He caught a cold, wrote, smoked, swam, gathered shells, and at night listened to stories. Fanny wrote later that she could never read Island Nights' Entertainments *"without a mental picture rising before me of the lagoon, and the cocoa palms, and the wonderful moonlight of Fakarava."*

Again, the stories were all of death, hauntings and the occult, literal and realistic renderings of the busy life led by the Pacific's spirits. Often the stories were told by "a man with a genius for such narrations", the half-French M. Donat-Rimarau. Among the listeners on the sandy floor was a man who was already one of the Western world's greatest writers of the supernatural. Following Poe instead

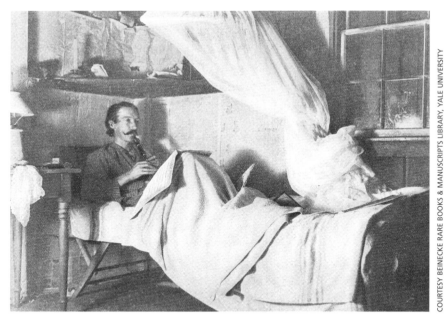

(Above) **"The whole tale of my life is better to me than any poem." RLS relaxing in Waikiki with his flageolet.**

of Dickens, he had broken from Victorian whimsy and Gothic terror to give the supernatural a ghoulish-psychological credibility. He had drawn into supernatural fiction the new mystery of science, and at the same time taken it back to its folklore roots – think of Jekyll *and* Hyde, *'Markheim', 'Thrawn Janet' and 'The Body Snatchers'. Now he found himself in a society where the supernatural was not confined to occasions of the exceptionally macabre, but was simply pervasive, inevitable; always feared and never in doubt.*

In time he became deeply conversant with the different supernatural lore of various Pacific cultures. When he came to summarize them for In the South Seas, *he located the chapter in the Paumotu section, in recognition of "a particular quality in Paumotuan superstitions." As with cannibalism (5), he writes without condescension, inviting sympathy rather than scorn from readers in Christian civilization.*

GRAVEYARD STORIES

WITH my superstitious friend, the islander, I fear I am not wholly frank, often leading the way with stories of my own, and being always a grave and sometimes an excited hearer. But the deceit is scarce mortal, since I am as pleased to hear as he to tell, as pleased with the story as he with the belief; and, besides, it is entirely needful. For it is scarce possible to exaggerate the extent and empire of his superstitions; they mould his life, they colour his thinking; and when he does not speak to me of ghosts, and gods, and devils, he is playing the dissembler and talking only with his lips. With thoughts so different, one must indulge the other; and I would rather that I should indulge his superstition than he my incredulity. Of one thing, besides, I may be sure: Let me indulge it as I please, I shall not hear the whole; for he is already on his guard with me, and the amount of the lore is boundless.

I will give but a few instances at random, chiefly from my own doorstep in Upolu, during the past month (October 1890). One of my workmen was sent the other day to the banana patch, there to dig; this is a hollow of the mountain, buried in woods, out of all sight and cry of mankind; and long before dusk Lafaele was back again beside the cook-house with embarrassed looks; he dared not longer stay alone, he was afraid of "spilits in the bush." It seems these are the souls of the unburied dead, haunting where they fell, and wearing woodland shapes of pig, or bird, or insect; the bush is full of them, they seem to eat nothing, slay solitary wanderers apparently in spite, and at times, in human form, go down to villages and consort with the inhabitants undetected. So much I learned a day or so after, walking in the bush with a very intelligent youth, a native. It was a little before noon; a grey day and squally; and perhaps I had spoken lightly. A dark squall burst on the side of the mountain; the woods shook and cried; the dead leaves rose from the ground in clouds, like butterflies; and my companion came suddenly to a full stop. He was afraid, he said, of the trees falling; but as soon as I had changed the subject of our talk he proceeded with alacrity. A day or two before a messenger came up the mountain from Apia with a letter; I was in the bush, he must await my return, then wait till I had answered: and before I was done his voice sounded shrill with terror of the coming night and the long forest road. These are the commons. Take the chiefs. There has been a great coming and going of signs and omens in our group. One river ran down blood; red eels were captured in another; an unknown fish was thrown upon the coast, an ominous word found written on its scales. So far we might be reading in a monkish chronicle; now we come on a fresh note, at once modern and Polynesian. The gods of Upolu and Savaii, our two chief islands, contended recently at cricket. Since then they are at war. Sounds of battle are heard to roll along the coast. A woman saw a man swim from the high seas and plunge direct into the bush; he was no man of that neighbourhood; and it was known he was one of the gods, speeding to a council. Most perspicuous of all, a missionary on Savaii, who is also a medical man, was disturbed late in the night by knocking; it was no hour for the dispensary, but at length he woke his servant and sent him to inquire; the servant, looking from a window, beheld crowds of persons, all with grievous wounds, lopped limbs, broken heads, and bleeding bullet-holes; but when the door was opened all had disappeared. They were gods from the field of battle. Now these reports have certainly significance; it is not hard to trace them to political grumblers or to read in them a threat of coming trouble; from that merely human side I found them ominous myself. But it was the spiritual side of their significance that was discussed in secret council by my rulers. I shall best depict this mingled habit of the Polynesian mind by two connected instances. I once lived in a village, the name of which I do not mean to tell. The chief and his sister were persons perfectly intelligent: gentlefolk, apt of speech. The sister was very religious, a great church-goer, one that used to reprove me if I stayed away; I found afterwards that she privately worshipped a shark. The chief himself was somewhat of a free-thinker; at the least, a latitudinarian: he was a man, besides, filled with European knowledge and accomplishments; of an impassive, ironical habit; and I should as soon have expected superstition in Mr. Herbert Spencer. Hear the sequel. I had discovered by unmistakable signs that they buried too shallow in the village graveyard, and I took my friend, as the responsible authority, to task. "There is something wrong about your graveyard," said I, "which you must attend to, or it may have very bad results." "Something wrong? What is it?" he asked, with an emotion that surprised me. "If you care to go along there any evening about nine o'clock you can see for yourself," said I. He stepped backward. "A ghost!" he cried.

In short, in the whole field of the South Seas, there is not one to blame another. Half blood and whole, pious and debauched, intelligent and dull, all men believe in ghosts, all men combine with their recent Christianity fear of and a lingering faith in the old island deities. So, in Europe, the gods of Olympus slowly dwindled into village bogies; so to-day, the theological Highlander sneaks from under the eye of the Free Church divine to lay an offering by a sacred well.

I try to deal with the whole matter here because of a particular quality in Paumotuan superstitions. It is true I heard them told by a man with a genius for such narrations. Close about our evening lamp, within sound of the island surf, we hung on his words, thrilling. The reader, in far other scenes, must listen close for the faint echo.

This bundle of weird stories sprang from the burial and the woman's selfish conjuration. I was dissatisfied with what I heard, harped upon questions, and struck at last this vein of metal. It is from sundown to about four in the morning that the kinsfolk camp upon the grave; and these are the hours of the spirits' wanderings. At any time of the night—it may be earlier, it may be later—a sound is to be heard below, which is the noise of his liberation; at four sharp, another and a louder marks the instant of the re-imprisonment; between-whiles, he goes his malignant rounds. "Did you ever see an evil spirit?" was once asked of a Paumotuan. "Once." "Under what form?" "It was in the form of a crane." "And how did you know that crane to be a spirit?" was asked. "I will tell you," he answered; and this was the purport of his inconclusive narrative. His father had been dead nearly a fortnight; others had wearied of the watch; and as the sun was setting, he found himself by the grave alone. It was not yet dark, rather the hour of the afterglow, when he was aware of a snow-white crane upon the coral mound; presently more cranes came, some white, some black; then the cranes vanished, and he saw in their place a white cat, to which there was silently joined a great company of cats of every hue conceivable; then these also disappeared, and he was left astonished.

This was an anodyne appearance. Take instead the experience of Rua-a-mariterangi on the isle of Katiu. He had a need for some pandanus, and crossed the isle to the sea-beach, where it chiefly flourishes. The day was still, and Rua was surprised to hear a crashing sound among the thickets, and then the fall of a considerable tree. Here must be some one building a canoe; and he entered the margin of the wood to find and pass the time of day with this chance neighbour. The crashing sounded more at hand; and then he was aware of something drawing swiftly near among the tree-tops. It swung by its heels downward, like an ape, so that its hands were free for murder; it depended safely by the slightest twigs; the speed of its coming was incredible; and soon Rua recognised it for a corpse, horrible with age, its bowels hanging as it came. Prayer was the weapon of Christian in the Valley of the Shadow, and it is to prayer that Rua-a-mariterangi attributes his escape. No merely human expedition had availed.

This demon was plainly from the grave; yet you will observe he was abroad by day. And inconsistent as it may seem with the hours of the night watch and the many references to the rising of the morning star, it is no singular exception. I could never find a case of another who had seen this ghost, diurnal and arboreal in its habits; but others have heard the fall of the tree, which seems the signal of its coming. Mr. Donat was once pearling on the uninhabited isle of Haraiki. It was a day without a breath of wind, such as alternate in the archipelago with days of contumelious breezes. The divers were in the midst of the lagoon upon their employment; the cook, a boy of ten, was over his pots in the camp. Thus were all souls accounted for except a single native who accompanied Donat into the wood in quest of sea-fowls' eggs. In a moment, out of the stillness, came the sound of the fall of a great tree. Donat would have passed on to find the cause. "No," cried his companion, "that was no tree. It was something *not right*. Let us go back to camp." Next Sunday the divers were turned on, all that part of the isle was thoroughly examined, and sure enough no tree had fallen. A little later Mr. Donat saw one of his divers flee from a similar sound, in similar unaffected panic, on the same isle. But neither would explain, and it was not till afterwards, when he met with Rua, that he learned the occasion of their terrors.

But whether by day or night, the purpose of the dead in these abhorred activities is still the same. In Samoa, my informant had no idea of the food of the bush spirits; no such ambiguity would exist in the mind of a Paumotuan. In that hungry archipelago, living and dead must alike toil for nutriment; and the race having been cannibal in the past, the spirits are so still. When the living ate the dead, horrified nocturnal imagination drew the shocking inference that the dead might eat the living. Doubtless they slay men, doubtless even mutilate them, in mere malice. Marquesan spirits sometimes tear out the eyes of travellers; but even that may be more practical than appears, for the eye is a cannibal dainty. And certainly the root idea of the dead, at least in the far eastern islands, is to prowl for food. It was as a dainty morsel for a meal that the woman denounced Donat at the funeral. There are spirits besides who prey in particular not on the bodies but on the souls of the dead. The point is clearly made in a Tahitian story. A child fell sick, grew swiftly worse, and at last showed signs of death. The mother hastened to the house of a sorcerer, who lived hard by. "You are yet in time," said he; "a spirit has just run past my door carrying the soul of your child wrapped in the leaf of a purao; but I have a spirit stronger and swifter who will run him down ere he has time to eat it." Wrapped in a leaf: like other things edible and corruptible.

Or take an experience of Mr. Donat's on the island of Anaa. It was a night of a high wind, with violent squalls; his child was very sick, and the father, though he had gone to bed, lay wakeful, hearkening to the gale. All at once a fowl was violently dashed on the house wall. Supposing he had forgot to put it in shelter with the rest, Donat arose, found the bird (a cock) lying on the verandah, and put it in the hen-house, the door of which he securely fastened. Fifteen minutes later the business was repeated, only this time, as it was being dashed against the wall, the bird crew. Again Donat replaced it, examining the hen-house thoroughly and finding it quite perfect; as he was so engaged the wind puffed out his light, and he must grope back to the door a good deal shaken. Yet a third time the bird was dashed upon the wall; a third time Donat set it, now near dead, beside its mates; and he was scarce returned before there came a rush, like that of a furious strong man, against the door, and a whistle as loud as that of a railway engine rang about the house. The sceptical reader may here detect the finger of the tempest; but the women gave up all for lost and clustered on the beds lamenting. Nothing followed, and I must suppose the gale somewhat abated, for presently after a chief came visiting. He was a bold man to be abroad so late, but doubtless carried a bright lantern. And he was certainly a man of counsel, for as soon as he heard the details of these disturbances he was in a position to explain their nature. "Your child," said he, "must certainly die. This is the evil spirit of our island who lies in wait to eat the spirits of the newly dead." And then he went on to expatiate on the strangeness of the spirit's conduct. He was not usually, he explained, so open of assault, but sat silent on the house-top waiting, in the guise of a bird, while within the people tended the dying and bewailed the dead, and had no thought of peril. But when the day came and the doors were opened, and men began to go abroad, blood-stains on the wall betrayed the tragedy.

This is the quality I admire in Paumotuan legend. In Tahiti the spirit-eater is said to assume a vesture which has much more of pomp, but how much less of horror. It has been seen by all sorts and conditions, native and foreign; only the last insist it is a meteor. My authority was not so sure. He was riding with his wife about two in the morning; both were near asleep, and the horses not much better. It was a brilliant and still night, and the road wound over a mountain, near by a deserted marae (old Tahitian temple). All at once the appearance passed above them: a form of light; the head round and greenish; the body long, red, and with a focus of yet redder brilliancy about the midst. A buzzing hoot accompanied its passage; it flew direct out of one marae, and direct for another down the mountain side. And this, as my informant argued, is suggestive. For why should a mere meteor frequent the altars of abominable gods? The horses, I should say, were equally dismayed with their riders. Now I am not dismayed at all—not even agreeably. Give me rather the bird upon the house-top and the morning blood-gouts on the wall.

But the dead are not exclusive in their diet. They carry with them to the grave, in particular, the Polynesian taste for fish, and enter at times with the living into a partnership in fishery. Rua-a-mariterangi is again my authority; I feel it diminishes the credit of the fact, but how it builds up the image of this inveterate ghost-seer! He belongs to the miserably poor island of Taenga, yet his father's house was always well supplied. As Rua grew up he was called at last to go a-fishing with this fortunate parent. They rowed into the lagoon at dusk, to an unlikely place, and the boy lay down in the stern, and the father began vainly to cast his line over the bows. It is to be supposed that Rua slept; and when he awoke there was the figure of another beside his father, and his father was pulling in the fish hand over hand. "Who is that man, father?" Rua asked. "It is none of your business," said the father; and Rua supposed the stranger had swum off to them from shore. Night after night they fared into the lagoon, often to the most unlikely places; night after night the stranger would suddenly be seen on board, and as suddenly be missed; and morning after morning the canoe returned laden with fish. "My father is a very lucky man," thought Rua. At last, one fine day, there came first one boat party and then another, who must be entertained; father and son put off later than usual into the lagoon; and before the canoe was landed it was four o'clock, and the morning star was close on the horizon. Then the stranger appeared seized with some distress; turned about, showing for the first time his face, which was that of one long dead, with shining eyes; stared into the east, set the tips of his fingers to his mouth like one a-cold, uttered a strange, shuddering sound between a whistle and a moan—a thing to freeze the blood; and, the day-star just rising from the sea, he suddenly was not. Then Rua understood why his father prospered, why his fishes rotted early in the day, and why some were always carried to the cemetery and laid upon the graves. My informant is a man not certainly averse to superstition but he keeps his head, and takes a certain superior interest, which I may be allowed to call scientific. The last point reminding him of some parallel practice in Tahiti, he asked Rua if the fish were left, or carried home again after a formal dedication. It appears old Mariterangi practised both methods; sometimes treating his shadowy partner to a mere oblation, sometimes honestly leaving his fish to rot upon the grave.

It is plain we have in Europe stories of a similar complexion; and the Polynesian *varua ino* or *aitu o le vao* is clearly the near kinsman of the Transylvanian vampire. Here is a tale in which the kinship appears broadly marked. On the atoll of Penrhyn, then still partly savage, a certain chief was long the salutary terror of the natives. He died, he was buried; and his late neighbours had scarce tasted the delights of licence ere his ghost appeared about the village. Fear seized upon all; a council was held of the chief men and sorcerers; and with the approval of the Rarotongan missionary, who was as frightened as the rest, and in the presence of several whites—my friend Mr. Ben Hird being one—the grave was opened, deepened until water came, and the body re-interred face down. The still recent staking of suicides in England and the decapitation of vampires in the east of Europe form close parallels.

So in Samoa only the spirits of the unburied awake fear. During the late war many fell in the bush; their bodies, sometimes headless, were brought back by native pastors and interred; but this (I know not why) was insufficient, and the spirit still lingered on the theatre of death. When peace returned a singular scene was enacted in many places, and chiefly round the high gorges of Lotoanuu, where the struggle was long centred and the loss had been severe. Kinswomen of the dead came carrying a mat or sheet and guided by survivors of the fight. The place of death was earnestly sought out; the sheet was spread upon the ground; and the women, moved with pious anxiety, sat about and watched it. If any living thing alighted it was twice brushed away; upon the third coming it was known to be the spirit of the dead, was folded in, carried home and buried beside the body; and the aitu rested. The rite was practised beyond doubt in simple piety; the repose of the soul was its object: its motive, reverent affection. The present king disowns indeed all knowledge of a dangerous aitu; he declares the souls of the unburied were only wanderers in limbo, lacking an entrance to the proper country of the dead, unhappy, nowise hurtful. And this severely classic opinion doubtless represents the views of the enlightened. But the flight of my Lafaele marks the grosser terrors of the ignorant.

This belief in the exorcising efficacy of funeral rites perhaps explains a fact, otherwise amazing, that no Polynesian seems at all to share our European horror of human bones and mummies. Of the first they made their cherished ornaments; they preserved them in houses or in mortuary caves; and the watchers of royal sepulchres dwelt with their children among the bones of generations. The mummy, even in the making, was as little feared. In the Marquesas, on the extreme coast, it was made by the household with continual unction and exposure to the sun; in the Carolines, upon the farthest west, it is still cured in the smoke of the family hearth. Head-hunting, besides, still lives around my doorstep in Samoa. And not ten years ago, in the Gilberts, the widow must disinter, cleanse, polish, and thenceforth carry about her, by day and night, the head of her dead husband. In all these cases we may suppose the process, whether of cleansing or drying, to have fully exorcised the aitu.

But the Paumotuan belief is more obscure. Here the man is duly buried, and he has to be watched. He is duly watched, and the spirit goes abroad in spite of watches. Indeed, it is not the purpose of the vigils to prevent these wanderings; only to mollify by polite attention the inveterate malignity of the dead. Neglect (it is supposed) may irritate and thus invite his visits, and the aged and weakly sometimes balance risks and stay at home. Observe, it is the dead man's kindred and next friends who thus deprecate his fury with nocturnal watchings. Even the placatory vigil is held perilous, except in company, and a boy was pointed out to me in Rotoava, because he had watched alone by his own father. Not the ties of the dead, nor yet their proved character, affect the issue. A late Resident, who died in Fakarava of sunstroke, was beloved in life and is still remembered with affection; none the less his spirit went about the island clothed with terrors, and the neighbourhood of Government House was still avoided after dark. We may sum up the cheerful doctrine thus: All men become vampires, and the vampire spares none. And here we come face to face with a tempting inconsistency. For the whistling spirits are notoriously clannish; I understood them to wait upon and to enlighten kinsfolk only, and that the medium was always of the race of the communicating spirit. Here, then, we have the bonds of the family, on the one hand, severed at the hour of death; on the other, helpfully persisting.

The child's soul in the Tahitian tale was wrapped in leaves. It is the spirits of the newly dead that are the dainty. When they are slain, the house is stained with blood. Rua's dead fisherman was decomposed; so—and horribly—was his arboreal demon. The spirit, then, is a thing material; and it is by the material ensigns of corruption that he is distinguished from the living man. This opinion is widespread, adds a gross terror to the more ugly Polynesian tales, and sometimes defaces the more engaging with a painful and incongruous touch. I will give two examples sufficiently wide apart, one from Tahiti, one from Samoa.

And first from Tahiti. A man went to visit the husband of his sister, then some time dead. In her life the sister had been dainty in the island fashion, and went always adorned with a coronet of flowers. In the midst of the night the brother awoke and was aware of a heavenly fragrance going to and fro in the dark house. The lamp I must suppose to have burned out; no Tahitian would have lain down without one lighted. A while he lay wondering and delighted; then called upon the rest. "Do none of you smell flowers?" he asked. "O," said his brother-in-law, "we are used to that here." The next morning these two men went walking, and the widower confessed that his dead wife came about the house continually, and that he had even seen her. She was shaped and dressed and crowned with flowers as in her lifetime; only she moved a few inches above the earth with a very easy progress, and flitted dryshod above the surface of the river. And now comes my point: It was always in a back view that she appeared; and these brothers-in-law, debating the affair, agreed that this was to conceal the inroads of corruption.

Now for the Samoan story. I owe it to the kindness of Dr. F. Otto Sierich, whose collection of folktales I expect with a high degree of interest. A man in Manu'a was married to two wives and had no issue. He went to Savaii, married there a third, and was more fortunate. When his wife was near her time he remembered he was in a strange island, like a poor man; and when his child was born he must be shamed for lack of gifts. It was in vain his wife dissuaded him. He returned to his father in Manu'a seeking help; and with what he could get he set off in the night to re-embark. Now his wives heard of his coming; they were incensed that he did not stay to visit them; and on the beach, by his canoe, intercepted and slew him. Now the third wife lay asleep in Savaii; her babe was born and slept by her side; and she was awakened by the spirit of her husband. "Get up," he said, "my father is sick in Manu'a and we must go to visit him." "It is well," said she; "take you the child, while I carry its mats." "I cannot carry the child," said the spirit; "I am too cold from the sea." When they were got on board the canoe the wife smelt carrion. "How is this?" she said. "What have you in the canoe that I should smell carrion?" "It is nothing in the canoe," said the spirit. "It is the land-wind blowing down the mountains, where some beast lies dead." It appears it was still night when they reached Manu'a—the swiftest passage on record—and as they entered the reef the bale-fires burned in the village. Again she asked him to carry the child; but now he need no more dissemble. "I cannot carry your child," said he, "for I am dead, and the fires you see are burning for my funeral."

The curious may learn in Dr. Sierich's book the unexpected sequel of the tale. Here is enough for my purpose. Though the man was but new dead, the ghost was already putrefied, as though putrefaction were the mark and of the essence of a spirit. The vigil on the Paumotuan grave does not extend beyond two weeks, and they told me this period was thought to coincide with that of the resolution of the body. The ghost always marked with decay—the danger seemingly ending with the process of dissolution—here is tempting matter for the theorist. But it will not do. The lady of the flowers had been long dead, and her spirit was still supposed to bear the brand of perishability. The Resident had been more than a fortnight buried, and his vampire was still supposed to go the rounds.

Of the lost state of the dead, from the lurid Mangaian legend, in which infernal deities hocus and destroy the souls of all, to the various submarine and aerial limbos where the dead feast, float idle, or resume the occupations of their life on earth, it would be wearisome to tell. One story I give, for it is singular in itself, is well-known in Tahiti, and has this of interest, that it is post-Christian, dating indeed from but a few years back. A princess of the reigning house died; was transported to the neighbouring isle of Raiatea; fell there under the empire of a spirit who condemned her to climb cocoa-palms all day and bring him the nuts; was found after some time in this miserable servitude by a second spirit, one of her own house; and by him, upon her lamentations, reconveyed to Tahiti, where she found her body still waked, but already swollen with the approaches of corruption. It is a lively point in the tale that, on the sight of this dishonoured tabernacle, the princess prayed she might continue to be numbered with the dead. But it seems it was too late, her spirit was replaced by the least dignified of entrances, and her startled family beheld the body move. The seemingly purgatorial labours, the helpful kindred spirit, and the horror of the princess at the sight of her tainted body, are all points to be remarked.

The truth is, the tales are not necessarily consistent in themselves; and they are further darkened for the stranger by an ambiguity of language. Ghosts, vampires, spirits, and gods are all confounded. And yet I seem to perceive that (with exceptions) those whom we would count gods were less maleficent. Permanent spirits haunt and do murder in corners of Samoa; but those legitimate gods of Upolu and Savaii, whose wars and cricketings of late convulsed society, I did not gather to be dreaded, or not with a like fear. The spirit of Aana that ate souls is certainly a fearsome inmate; but the high gods, even of the archipelago, seem helpful. Mahinui—from whom our convict-catechist had been named—the spirit of the sea, like a Proteus endowed with endless avatars, came to the assistance of the shipwrecked and carried them ashore in the guise of a ray fish. The same divinity bore priests from isle to isle about the archipelago, and by his aid, within the century, persons have been seen to fly. The tutelar deity of each isle is likewise helpful, and by a particular form of wedge-shaped cloud on the horizon announces the coming of a ship.

To one who conceives of these atolls, so narrow, so barren, so beset with sea, here would seem a superfluity of ghostly denizens. And yet there are more. In the various brackish pools and ponds, beautiful women with long red hair are seen to rise and bathe; only (timid as mice) on the first sound of feet upon the coral they dive again for ever. They are known to be healthy and harmless living people, dwellers of an underworld; and the same fancy is current in Tahiti, where also they have the hair red. *Tetea* is the Tahitian name; the Paumotuan, *Mokurea*.

8

GARDEN OF THE WORLD:

TAUTIRA, TAHITI

After three weeks on the beach at Fakarava, Stevenson's cold "took a very bad turn", and Fanny hurried the party away to Papeete, on Tahiti, the capital of French Polynesia, where there would be a doctor. Lung or throat haemorrhage was Stevenson's usual reaction to viral infection. The conclusion has always been that he had consumption (tuberculosis), although the length of his survival with those symptoms and the lack of any transmission to those who lived in such close contact with him make that seem unlikely. More probably it was hereditary haemorrhagic rupturing of the blood vessels (HHT) (as Alan Guttmacher suggested in the American Journal of Genetics, *2000). He continued to chain-smoke through all these adventures.*

Tahiti, in the Society Islands, was 1000 km (600 miles) west of the Pau-motus, a near neighbour by Pacific standards. The house they at first lived in, "opposite the British Consul's", would be used in 'The Bottle Imp' (22), but more significantly Stevenson would draw on his own condition and the Papeete waterfront for images of illness, apathy and dereliction in the squalid opening of The Ebb-Tide.

In search of clear air as always, they soon moved across the island to the isolated village of Tautira, settling at first in a simple "bird-cage" house. They were received with even more Polynesian warmth than before. Princess Moë, a grandmother of royal class, great beauty and speaking perfect English, called several times a day with a specially-prepared dish of raw fish in lime juice and cocoanut milk for the invalid. He recovered. Fanny believed Moë saved his life. Stevenson wrote a poem in praise of her (27). The local chief, Ori o Ori, invited

(Above) **"I threw one look to either hand/And knew I was in Fairyland."** Tautira, **"the Garden of the World... mere Heaven."**

BY COURTESY OF EDINBURGH CITY LIBRARIES

*them to share his home, and became such a close friend that he and Stevenson exchanged names – "Rui" and "Terii-Tera". The ballad 'Song of Rahero' (see **26**) is dedicated to him, "my brother in the island mode". Their stay was extended when the* Casco's *spars were found to be crumbling with dry rot, but nobody minded. "We are in heaven here," Stevenson wrote. In other letters he called Tautira "The Garden of the World", "Hans-Christian-Andersen-ville", "mere Heaven", and "first chop".*

His high-spirited enjoyment of the place and its hospitable people is well caught in a letter to a friend's small son, Thomas Archer. He had earlier given "Tomarcher" an Erewhonian account of Tahitian society's tolerance for children: "their parents obey them... The children beat their parents here; it does not make their parents any better; so do not try it."

The letter is included here as a reminder that the versatile Stevenson was one of the best of all children's writers (Virginibus Puerisque, A Child's Garden of Verses, Treasure Island); *which means that with his keenly sympathetic mind he could imagine a young reader's interest and response, and make those part of his text.*

Tautira, Island of Tahiti [November 1888].

DEAR Tomarcher, — This is a pretty state of things! seven o'clock and no word of breakfast! And I was awake a good deal last night, for it was full moon, and they had made a great fire of cocoa-nut husks down by the sea, and as we have no blinds or shutters, this kept my room very bright. And then the rats had a wedding or a school-feast under my bed. And then I woke early, and I have nothing to read except Virgil's *Æneid*, which is not good fun on an empty stomach, and a Latin dictionary, which is good for naught, and by some humorous accident, your dear papa's article on Skerryvore. And I read the whole of that, and very impudent it is, but you must not tell your dear papa I said so, or it might come to a battle in which you might lose either a dear papa or a valued correspondent, or both, which would be prodigal. And still no breakfast; so I said "Let's write to Tomarcher."

This is a much better place for children than any I have hitherto seen in these seas. The girls (and sometimes the boys) play a very elaborate kind of hopscotch. The boys play horses exactly as we do in Europe; and have very good fun on stilts, trying to knock each other down, in which they do not often succeed. The children of all ages go to church and are allowed to do what they please, running about the aisles, rolling balls, stealing mama's bonnet and publicly sitting on it, and at last going to sleep in the middle of the floor. I forgot to say that the whips to play horses, and the balls to roll about the church — at least I never saw them used elsewhere — grow ready made on trees; which is rough on toy-shops. The whips are so good that I wanted to play horses myself; but no such luck! my hair is grey, and I am a great, big, ugly man. The balls are rather hard, but very light and quite round. When you grow up and become offensively rich, you can charter a ship in the port of London, and have it come back to you entirely loaded with these balls; when you could satisfy your mind as to their character, and give them away when done with to your uncles and aunts. But what I really wanted to tell you was this: besides the tree-top toys (Hush-a-by, toy-shop, on the tree-top!), I have seen some real made toys, the first hitherto observed in the South Seas.

This was how. You are to imagine a four-wheeled gig; one horse; in the front seat two Tahiti natives, in their Sunday clothes, blue coat, white shirt, kilt (a little longer than the Scotch) of a blue stuff with big white or yellow flowers, legs and feet bare; in the back seat me and my wife, who is a friend of yours; under our feet, plenty of lunch and things: among us a great deal of fun in broken Tahitian, one of the natives, the sub-chief of the village, being a great ally of mine. Indeed we have exchanged names; so that he is now Rui, the nearest they can come to Louis, for they have no *l* and no *s* in their language. Rui is six feet three in his stockings, and a magnificent man. We all have straw hats, for the sun is strong. We drive between the sea, which makes a great noise, and the mountains; the road is cut through a forest mostly of fruit trees, the very creepers, which take the place of our ivy, heavy with a great and delicious fruit, bigger than your head and far nicer, called Barbedine. Presently we came to a house in a pretty garden, quite by itself, very nicely kept, the doors and windows open, no one about, and no noise but that of the sea. It looked like a house in a fairy-tale, and just beyond we must ford a river, and there we saw the inhabitants. Just in the mouth of the river, where it met the sea waves, they were ducking and bathing and screaming together like a covey of birds: seven or eight little naked brown boys and girls as happy as the day was long; and on the banks of the stream beside them, real toys—toy ships, full rigged, and with their sails set, though they were lying in the dust on their beam ends. And then I knew for sure they were all children in a fairy-story, living alone together in that lonely house with the only toys in all the island; and that I had myself driven, in my four-wheeled gig, into a corner of the fairy-story, and the question was, should I get out again? But it was all right; I guess only one of the wheels of the gig had got into the fairy-story; and the next jolt the whole thing vanished, and we drove on in our sea-side forest as before, and I have the honour to be Tomarcher's valued correspondent, TERIITERA, which he was previously known as

ROBERT LOUIS STEVENSON

BEST HAND AT THE WHEEL:
HONOLULU, HAWAII

Empathy, enthusiasm, self-dramatization, charm – however we explain him, there is no doubting that Stevenson had an extraordinary gift for making friends, responding to others on their own terms whatever the circumstances, yet remaining naturally himself. At Tautira, while the Casco *was under repair, the party became short of food and money, but the hospitality was unstinted. Princess Moë arranged feasts, and displays of singing and dancing that caused his Scottish mother Maggie to remark, "the more one sees and hears of what goes on here, the more one can understand the Indian system of early marriages."*

Stevenson was worrying more about money than morals – he could only hope that some funds from his writing were waiting in Honolulu. Yet through anxiety, illness and distraction, his capacity for work never faltered. At Tautira he went close to finishing The Master of Ballantrae, *worked on 'The Song of Rahero' (see* 26*), based on a story told by Princess Moë, and "got wonderful materials for my book* [In the South Seas]*". He "collected songs and legends on the spot... legends, on which I have seen half a dozen seniors sitting in conclave and debating what came next." This remark suggests that Stevenson did not share the tendency common among 19th-century collectors of Polynesian myths and legends to delimit and 'fossilize' them, concealing the diversity and vitality of indigenous traditions. On the contrary, Stevenson witnesses the living process of oral narrative, and makes a friendly joke of it.*

When the Casco *was finally ready to collect them, after two months at Tautira, there was another emotional farewell ceremony, and on Christmas Day 1888 they sailed north for Hawaii. More time was lost during 5000 km (3000 miles) of "calms, squalls, head sea, waterspouts of rain, hurricane weather all about", including times when they could only run before the storm with the crew lashed to the deck. Then they were becalmed for two days within sight of Oahu, and the scant provisions of "decayed beef and stale biscuit" ran seriously low. A last-minute headwind off Honolulu added further drama.*

Having travelled hopefully and arrived late, Stevenson caught the spirit of the whole adventure – his own spirit, at least – in a colourful and witty letter to his cousin Bob. It conjures the dangers, and his roguish disregard for them, his admiration for the people he had met on visits "more like dreams than realities", his interest in their oral culture, and his unflagging zest for the sheer eccentricity of it all. The advice the New Zealander Mr. Seed had given all those years ago to the sickly youth in Edinburgh had been proved right. In the freshness, literary challenge and cultural diversity of the Pacific, Stevenson had already found "all that was good for me."

Honolulu, Hawaiian Islands, February 1889.

MY Dear Rob, – My extremely foolhardy venture is practically over. How foolhardy it was I don't think I realised. We had a very small schooner, and, like most yachts, over-rigged and over-sparred, and like many American yachts on a very dangerous sail plan. The waters we sailed in are, of course, entirely unlighted, and very badly charted; in the Dangerous Archipelago, through which we were fools enough to go, we were perfectly in ignorance of where we were for a whole night and half the next day, and this in the midst of invisible islands and rapid and variable currents; and we were lucky when we found our whereabouts at last. We have twice had all we wanted in the way of squalls: once, as I came on deck, I found the green sea over the cockpit and running down the companion like a brook to meet me; at that same moment the foresail sheet jammed and the captain had no knife; this was the only occasion on the cruise that ever I set a hand to a rope, but I worked like a Trojan, judging the possibility of haemorrhage better than the certainty of drowning. Another time I saw a rather singular thing: our whole ship's company as pale as paper from the captain to the cook; we had a black squall astern on the port side and a white squall ahead to starboard; the complication passed off innocuous, the black squall only fetching us with its tail, and the white one slewing off somewhere else. Twice we were a long while (days) in the close vicinity of hurricane weather, but again luck prevailed, and we saw none of it. These are dangers incident to these seas and small craft. What was an amazement, and at the same time a powerful stroke of luck, both our masts were rotten, and we found it out—I was going to say in time, but it was stranger and luckier than that. The head of the main-mast hung over so that hands were afraid to go to the helm; and less than three weeks before—I am not sure it was more than a fortnight—we had been nearly twelve hours beating off the lee shore of Eimeo (or Moorea, next island to Tahiti) in half a gale of wind with a violent head sea: she would neither tack nor wear once, and had to be boxed off with the mainsail—you can imagine what an ungodly show of kites we carried—and yet the mast stood. The very day after that, in the southern bight of Tahiti, we had a near squeak, the wind suddenly coming calm; the reefs were close in with, my eye! what a surf! The pilot thought we were gone, and the captain had a boat cleared, when a lucky squall came to our rescue. My wife, hearing the order given about the boats, remarked to my mother, "Isn't that nice? We shall soon be ashore!" Thus does the female mind unconsciously skirt along the verge of eternity. Our voyage up here was most disastrous—calms, squalls, head sea, waterspouts of rain, hurricane weather all about, and we in the midst of the hurricane season, when even the hopeful builder and owner of the yacht had pronounced these seas unfit for her. We ran out of food, and were quite given up for lost in Honolulu: people had ceased to speak to Belle about the *Casco*, as a deadly subject.

But the perils of the deep were part of the programme; and though I am very glad to be done with them for a while and comfortably ashore, where a squall does not matter a snuff to any one, I feel pretty sure I shall want to get to sea again ere long...

From my point of view, up to now the cruise has been a wonderful success. I never knew the world was so amusing. On the last voyage we had grown so used to sea-life that no one wearied, though it lasted a full month, except Fanny, who is always ill. All the time our visits to the islands have been more like dreams than realities: the people, the life, the beachcombers, the old stories and songs I have picked up, so interesting; the climate, the scenery, and (in some places) the women, so beautiful. The women are handsomest in Tahiti, the men in the Marquesas; both as fine types as can be imagined...

One stirring day was that in which we sighted Hawaii. It blew fair, but very strong; we carried jib, foresail, and mainsail, all single-reefed, and she carried her lee rail under water and flew. The swell, the heaviest I have ever been out in—I tried in vain to estimate the height, *at least* fifteen feet—came tearing after us about a point and a half off the wind. We had the best hand— old Louis—at the wheel; and really, he did nobly, and had noble luck, for it never caught us once. At times it seemed we must have it; Louis would look over his shoulder with the queerest look and dive down his neck into his shoulders; and then it missed us somehow, and only sprays came over our quarter, turning the little outside lane of deck into a mill race as deep as the cockpit coamings. I never remember anything more delightful and exciting.

10

MELANCHOLY LANDING:

MOLOKAI, HAWAII

They were welcomed to Honolulu by Fanny's daughter Belle, who had almost given them up. She was living there with her charming but unstable artist husband Joe Strong, and their young son Austin. All three would soon become extra commitments for Stevenson to support. He and Fanny took a "grim little wooden shanty" among the scattered beach houses at Waikiki. The time in Hawaii was used in 'The Bottle Imp' and 'The Isle of Voices' (22, 24). He finished his two Pacific verse narratives, and contemplated a book to be called South Sea Ballads *(26). He was working hard to make literary contact with the culture.*

Social contact came through Belle and Joe, who introduced them to the lively high life of the enterprising but beleaguered little kingdom. The half-Scottish heir to the throne, Princess Kaiulani, became a favourite friend (see the poem in 27). Stevenson became drawn into political matters. King Kalakaua, described by Stevenson as "a fine intelligent fellow, but... what a crop for the drink!" had aspirations to lead a pan-Pacific federation. Though out-manoeuvered and vastly out-budgeted by vested interests, his idea was a visionary one. Stevenson wrote letters of support to the London Times. *He was revealing a knight-errant tendency in political affairs, and his sympathies were always with the oppressed and displaced, unusually so at that apogee of the colonial era. In America in 1879, he wrote (in* The Amateur Emigrant): *"If oppression drives a wise man mad, what should be raging in the heart of those poor tribes, who have been driven back, step after step?"*

In 1886 he had been narrowly dissuaded from moving his family into the thick of Ireland's Home Rule troubles, even seriously envisaging his own

(Above) **King Kalakaua of Hawaii. RLS vigorously supported his vision of a pan-Pacific federation independent of Western dominion.**

martyrdom. In Hawaii he set himself against the powerful church and commercial interests that were promoting annexation by the United States, and then alienated them even more by publishing a passionate defence of a Belgian Catholic priest, Father Damien, who had recently died amid controversy over his conduct of the leper colony on the Hawaiian island of Molokai.

Though his assault on Damien's Protestant detractors was overstated, Stevenson made better use of the visit he made to the Molokai colony in May 1889. Letters he wrote at the time show how moving he found it (and see also the poem 'To Mother Maryanne', in 27); but strong emotion became tempered into a finely cadenced compassion in the account he published (not included in In the South Seas*). Its subtle shades are built on two images, both recurrent in his fiction: the experience of arrival, and the ideal of a just society. Around these he weaves a piece of reportage that is also a poignant narrative of the decline and survival of a victimized community. Landfall here is evoked in sorrowful falling cadences – "In the chronicle of man there is perhaps no more melancholy landing than this of the leper immigrants..." Yet his stories of the colony's history are full of human interest and vitality set against reminders of disfigurement and approaching death.*

Extraordinarily, an account of dismal rejection and doomed exile becomes an affirmation of "the gusto of existence".

THE LAZARETTO

THE windward coast of Molokai is gloomy and abrupt. A wall of cliff of from two to three thousand feet in height extends the more part of the length (some forty miles) from east to west. Wood clusters on its front like ivy; and in the wet season streams descend in waterfalls and play below on the surface of the ocean. For in almost the whole of its length the cliff, without the formality of any beach, plunges in the Pacific. Bold water follows the coast; ships may almost everywhere approach within a trifling distance of the towering shore; and immediately in front of Molokai surveyors have found some of the deepest soundings of that ocean. This unusual depth of water, the continuity of the Trade, and the length of which *fetch* extends unbroken from the shores of California, magnify the sea. The swell is nursed by the steady wind, it grows in that long distance, it draws near through the deep soundings without combing, and spends itself undiminished on the cliffs of Molokai.

Toward the eastern end a river in a winding glen descends from the interior; the barrier is quite broken here, and a beach is formed and makes a place of call, Wailau. A few miles farther east, the cove of Pelekunu offers a doubtful chance of landing, and is also visited by steamers. The third and last place of approach is at the Lazaretto. A shelf of undercliff here borders the precipice, expanding toward its western end in a blunt promontory, a little more than a mile square. The lee of this precipice offers unusual facilities for landing, and in favourable states of wind and sea ships may anchor. But these facilities to seaward are more than counterbalanced by the uncompromising character of the barrier behind. The *Pali* (as the precipice is called) in the extent of this strip of undercliff makes three recesses, Waihanau, Waialeia, and Waikolu—as their names imply, three gutters of the mountain. These are clothed in wood; from a distance they show like verdant niches and retreats for lovers; but the face of the rock is so precipitous that only in the first, Waihanau, is there a practicable path. The rains continually destroy it; it must be renewed continually; to ride there is impossible; to mount without frequent falls seems unexpected; and even the descent exhausts a powerful man. The existence of another path more to the westward was affirmed to me by some, denied by others. At the most, therefore, in two points, the cliff is scantly passable upward. Passage coastwise is beyond expectation to any creature without wings. To the west, the strip of undercliff simply discontinues. To the east, the wall itself thrusts forth a huge protrusion, and the way is barred except to fish and sea-birds. Here, then, is a prison fortified by nature, a place where thousands may be quartered and a pair of sentinels suffice to watch and hold the only issues.

The undercliff is in itself narrow; it is widened on one hand by the recesses of the cliff; and on the other by the expansion of the foreland; and the last contains (for a guess) two-thirds of the whole territory. It rises in the midst to a low hill enclosing a dead crater, like a quarry hole; the interior sides clothed with trees; at the foot a salt pool, unsoundable, at least unsounded. Hence the land slopes to the sea's edge and upward toward the Pali in grassy downs. A single sick pandanus breaks, or broke while I was there, that naked heath; except in man's enclosures, I can recall nowhere else one switch of timber. The foreland is grazed by some 1,500 head of stock, 700 of them horses, for the patients are continual and furious riders; the rest cows and asses. These all do excellently well. The horrid pest to which the place is sacred spares them, being man's prerogative. It was strange to see those droves of animals feeding and sporting in exuberant health by the sea margin, and to reflect upon their destiny, brought from so far, at so much cost and toil, only to be ridden to and fro upon and eaten by the defeatured and dying.

The shaven down, the scattered boulders, the cry of the wind in the grass, the frequent showers of rain, the bulk of the Pali, the beating of the near sea, all the features and conditions strike the mind as northern, and to the Northerner the scene is in consequence grateful, like one of his native minor tunes. It is stirring to look eastward and see the huge viridescent mountain front sunder the settlement from the next habitations of clean men at Pelekunu—at its foot, in the sea, two tilted islets. It is pleasant in the early morning to ride by the roots of the Pali, when the low sun and the cool breeze are in your face, and from above, in the cliffside forest, falls a perpetual chirruping of birds. It is pleasant, above all, to wander by the margin of the sea. The heath breaks down, like Helicon, in cliffs. A narrow fringe of emerald edges the precipitous shore; close beyond the blue show the bold soundings; the wanderer stands plainly on a mere buttress of the vast cathedral front of the island, and above and below him, in the air and in the water, the precipice continues. Along the brink, rock architecture and sea music please the senses, and in that tainted place the thought of the cleanness of the antiseptic ocean is welcome to the mind.

Yet this is but one side of the scenery of the Lazaretto: and I received an impression strongly contrasted when I entered the recess of Waialeia. The sides were niched and channelled with dry tracks of torrents, grass clung on the sheer precipice, forest clustered on the smallest vantage of a shelf. The floor of the amphitheatre was piled with shattered rock, detritus of the mountain, with which in the time of the rains, the torrents had maintained a cannonade. Vigorously black themselves, these were spotted with snow-white lichen and shaded and intermingled with plants and trees of a vivid green. The day was overcast; clouds ran low about the edges of the basin; and yet the colours glowed as though immersed in sunshine. On the downs the effect is of some bleak, noble coast of Scotland or Scandinavia; here in the recess I felt myself transported to the tropics.

There are two villages, Kalaupapa, on the western shore of the promontory, Kalawao, toward the east upon the strip of undercliff; and along the road which joins them, each reaches forth scattered habitations.

Kalaupapa, the most sheltered in prevailing winds, is the customary landing-place. When the run of the sea inclines the other way, ships pass far to the eastward near the two islets, and passengers are landed with extreme difficulty, and I was assured not without danger, on a spur of rock. Kalaupapa, being quite upon the downs, is the more bleak; a long, bare, irregular, ungardened village of unsightly houses. Here are two churches, Protestant and Catholic, and the Bishop Home for Girls. Kalawao is even beautiful; pleasant houses stand in gardens of flowers; the Pali rises behind; in front, across the sea, the eye commands the islets and the huge green face of cliff excluding Pelekunu. This is the view from the window of the lay brother, Mr. Dutton, and he assured me he found its beauty far more striking than the deformations of the sick. The passing visitor can scarce attain to such philosophy. Here is Damien's Home for Boys. Close behind is a double graveyard, where some of the dead retain courtesy titles, and figure in their epitaphs as 'Mr.' or as 'Mrs.' The inevitable twin churches complete the village. A fifth church, the church of the Mormons, exists somewhere in the settlement; but I could never find it. On the westward end of Kalawao what we may call the official quarter stretches toward the promontory. The main feature is the enclosure of the hospital and prison, where bad cases and bad characters are kept in surveill-ance; a green in a stockade with a few papaias and one flowering oleander, surrounded on three sides by low white houses. A little way off, enclosed in walls and hedges, stands the Guest House of Kalawao, and, beyond that again, the quarters of the doctor.

The Guest House is kept ready for the visits of members of the Board. I arrived there early in the day, opened the gate, turned my horse loose, and entered in possession of the vacant house. I wandered through its chambers, visited the bathroom and the kitchen, and at last, throwing myself upon a bed, I fell asleep. Not before the hour of dinner, Dr. Swift, returning from his duties, wakened me and introduced himself. A similar arrival may be read of in the tale of the Three Bears; and that is well called a guest house where there is no host. Singular indeed is the isolation of the visitor in the Lazaretto. No patient is suffered to approach his place of residence. His room is tidied out by a clean helper during the day and while he is abroad. He returns at night to solitary walls. For a while a bell sounds at intervals from the hospital; silence succeeds, only pointed by the humming of the surf or the chirp of crickets. He steps to his door; perhaps a light still shines in the hospital; all else is dark. He returns and sits by his lamp and the crowding experiences besiege his memory; sights of pain in a land of disease and disfigurement, bright examples of fortitude and kindness, moral beauty, physical horror, intimately knit. He must be a man very little impressionable if he recall not these hours with an especial poignancy; he must be a man either very virtuous or very dull, if they were not hours of self-review and vain aspirations after good.

When the Hawaiian Government embraced the plan of segregation they were doubtless (as is the way of Governments) unprepared, and the constitut-ion of the Lazaretto, as it now exists, was approached by blunder and reached by accident. There was no design to pauperise; the lepers were to work, and in whole or part be self-supporting; and when a site fell to be chosen, some extent of cultivable soil was first required. In this, as in other conditions, Kalawao was wholly fitted for the purpose. In the old days, when Molokai swarmed with population, the foreland must have been a busy and perhaps a holy place; and thirty years ago it was covered with the ruins of heiaus, but still inhabited and still in active cultivation. Terms of sale were easily agreed upon. Unhappily, the Government coquetted; the farmers were held for months under suspense; for months, in consequence, their houses were left unrepaired; their fields untilled, and the property was already much deteriorated before the purchase was confirmed and the clean inhabitants ejected from the foreland. The history of misgovernment by Board followed the common course to the customary end; *too late* was coupled as usual with *too early;* the Government had procrastinated to its loss, yet even then it was unready, and for another period of months the deserted farms lay idle. At length the first shipment of lepers landed (1865) with a small kit of blankets, tin dishes, and the like, but neither food nor money, to find the roofs fallen from the houses and the taro rotting in the ground.

They were strangers to each other, collected by common calamity, disfigured, mortally sick, banished without sin from home and friends. Few would understand the principle on which they were thus forfeited in all that makes life dear; many must have conceived their ostracism to be grounded in malevolent caprice; all came with sorrow at heart, many with despair and rage. In the chronicle of man there is perhaps no more melancholy landing than this of the leper immigrants among the ruined houses and dead harvests of Molokai. But the spirit of our race is finely tempered and the business of life engrossing to the last. As the spider, when you have wrecked its web, begins immediately to spin fresh strands, so these exiles, widowed, orphaned, unchilded, legally dead and physically dying, struck root in their new place. By a culpable neglect in the authorities they were suffered to divide among themselves the whole territory of the settlement; fell to work with growing hope, repaired the houses, replanted the fields, and began to look about them with the pride of the proprietor. Upon this scene of reviving industry a second deportation arrived, and the first were called upon to share and subdivide their lots. They did so, not without complaint, which the authorities disregarded; a third shipment followed shortly after in the same conditions, and a further redistribution of the land was imposed upon the early settlers. Remuneration was demanded; Government demurred upon the price; the lepers were affronted, withdrew their offer, and stood upon their rights, and a new regimen arose of necessity. The two first companies continued to subsist upon their farms; but the third, and all subsequent shipments, must be fed by Government. Pauperism had begun, and the original design miscarried. To-day all are paupers; the single occasion of healthy interest and exercise subducted, and the country at large saddled with the support of many useless mouths.

The lepers, cast out from society and progressively deprived of employ-ment, swiftly decivilised. *"Aole Kanawai ma Keia Wahi!"* —"There is no law in this place"—was their word of salutation to newcomers; cards, dancing, and debauch were the diversions; the women served as prostitutes, the children as drudges; the dying were callously uncared for; heathenism revived; *okolehau* was brewed and in their orgies the disfigured sick ran naked by the sea. This is Damien's picture; these traits were viewed through the tarnish of missionary spectacles; but they seem all true to the human character in that unnatural and gloomy situation, nor is there one that need surprise a student of his fellow men. What may, indeed, surprise him—and what Damien, true to the clerical prevention, neglected to commemorate—is the lack of crime. Since 1865, the year of the landing, blood has been shed but once in the precinct; and the chief difficulty felt by successive rulers has been one inevitable in a colony of paupers, that of administration.

There has been but one chief luna (or overseer) from the first—Mr. Meyer, a man of much sagacity and force of character. But Mr. Meyer dwells in his own house on the top of the Pali; comes to the settlement only at fixed intervals or upon some emergency, and even then approaches it with pre-cautions, which I could not but admire, and to which, in all likelihood, he owes his long immunity from the disease. He may thus be rather regarded as a visiting inspector, and the subluna resident among the lepers and most frequently a leper himself, as the proper ruler of Kalawao. No less than ten persons have held this post in little more than twenty years, a fact which gives a measure at once of the difficulty of the office and the brevity of leper life.

The first was a Frenchman of the name of Lepart, a capable, high-spirited man; he was calumniated to the Government, justified himself and resigned. A British officer of the name of Walsh succeeded, soon died, and on his death-bed prayed to have the office continued to his wife. As this lady suffered from some deficiency of sight, and spoke no Hawaiian, there was conjoined with her an old ship Captain, "a rough, honest, bawling good fellow," as ignorant of Hawaiian as herself. This unpromising Ministry fell at last, not by its own weakness, but the fault of others. The Board of Health was already giving a ration of butcher's meat, so many pounds a week to every patient; and the Ministry of the Interior, alarmed at the growing expense, issued an order limiting the number of cattle to be slaughtered. The figures were inconsistent; Mrs. Walsh quite properly obeyed the last command; the ration was in consequence reduced, and the lepers, under the lead of an able half-white, took out more cattle and killed them for themselves. A ship with police was despatched from Honolulu to quell this horrid rising; the half-white was imprisoned, and Mrs. Walsh and the skipper removed. A full-blood Hawaiian, who had been Captain of the King's guard, was chosen to succeed. He was a good man, a very bad luna; stood in fear of every one; always supposed he should be "prayed to death" and did, in fact, whether from the result of enchantments or the fear of them, die within the year. The next appointment was equally daring and successful. The ablest man in the lazaretto, the half-white who had killed the cattle, was installed as ruler—from the prison to the throne. He was one of those who must either rule or rebel, and as soon as he held the chief place and till death removed him the settlement was quiet.

Another half-white followed, the famous Billy Ragsdale, who had left a broad mark on the traditions of the colony. They tell that he sat in his porch and suitors approached him on their knees; that he sent his glove to the store or the butcher's for a token, and that Mrs. Ragsdale went to church on Sunday with two boys bearing her train and a third holding her umbrella. Mr. Meyer (I am aware) denies these scandals; he might have been the last to hear of them, had they existed, and man, though he delights in making myths, is usually inspired by some original in fact. That Ragsdale was arrogant is, besides, undoubted, for his arrogance came near plunging the settlement in war. Hawaiians readily obey a half-white, still more readily a man of chiefly caste. Now there lived in the settlement, in Ragsdale's day, a brother of Queen Emma, Prince Peter Kaiu. Of a sudden Mr. Meyer received (by a messenger coming breathless up the Pali) a curt, civil, menacing note from Prince Peter. If Ragsdale were going on in this way—the way not specified—Prince Peter would show him which had the most friends in the settlement. Some minutes later a second note came from Ragsdale, breathing wrath and consternation, but not more explicit than the first. Mr. Meyer put a bottle of claret in his pocket, hastened down the cliff, and came to the house of the Prince. A crowd of men surrounded it, the friends referred to, or their van; it seems not known if they were armed, but their looks were martial. Prince Peter himself, although incensed, proved malleable in debate, owned it was disgraceful for the two best-educated men in Kalawao to quarrel, and consented to leave his friends behind and go alone with Mr. Meyer to the luna's. Ragsdale lived in a grass house on the foreland; it was garrisoned by some score of men with guns, axes, shovels, and fish spears. Ragsdale himself was on the watch but the sight of two men coming empty-handed made him ashamed of his preparations and he received them civilly. A conversation followed; some misunderstandings were explained away; an apology handsomely offered by Ragsdale was handsomely accepted by the Prince; the bottle of claret was drunk in company, and the friends on either side disbanded. Thus ended the alarm of war, and the opponents continued in a serviceable alliance until death divided them.

It was in the reign of Ragsdale that Father Damien arrived, May, '73. He draws no very favourable picture of the society that paid homage to King Billy; but the reign was efficient, and save for the episode of Prince Peter, quiet. So much could not be said for that of his critic and successor, Damien himself, whose term of office served only to publish the weakness of a noble man. He was rough in his ways and he had no control; authority was relaxed, the luna's life was threatened, and he was soon eager to resign. Two more conclude the list: Mr. Strahan, who was still alive at the time of my visit, and Mr. Ambrose Hutchinson, who still held the reins of office.

Mr. Strahan, born of Scottish parents in Philadelphia, ran away to sea in a whaler and deserted in Tahiti. He learned carpentering, coopering, and seamanship; sailed mate in ships, made copra in the Palmyras, worked on the guano islands, and led in all ways the career of the South Sea adventurer. For two years he lived in Easter Island, the isle of nameless gods and forgotten pieties. A mysterious sickness, brought from the mainland by labour slaves, struck and prostrated the population. Mr. Strahan was seen sometimes alone to go out fishing, and he made with his own hands a barrow to convey the corpses to the grave, and crutches on which the native clergyman might accompany the funerals. "That was my best time," said the old gentleman, regretfully. At last, when he was mate of a schooner, he chanced one day to be shaving, as I have received the story, in the cabin. "Good God, Strahan!" cried the Captain, "you have cut off a piece of your ear." He had cut off a piece of his ear and did not know it; the plague, long latent in his blood, was now declared, and the wanderer found a home in Kalawao. As a luna he did well, reducing at once the previous discontents. He claims to have introduced coffee shops, sewing-machines, musical instruments—"I wanted to put some life in the thing," says he—and the system of medals by which the drawing of double rations was at length prevented. Some of his claims are called in question; it is said he must certainly be under illusion as to the sewing-machines and the musical instruments; but all agree as to the efficiency of his administration. His worst trouble arose by accident, and depicts well the jealous suspicion and the vain and passing agitations of a pauperised society. From a chance boat he purchased a load of native food which (as it had not been made expressly for the settlement) was packed in bundles larger than the regulation size. These he set his assistants to break up and weigh out afresh. Word of it got abroad; it was rumoured that Strahan was secretly diminishing the rations; and he was suddenly surrounded as he rode by some fifty or a hundred horsemen menacing his life. "I sat right in my saddle like this. Says I: 'You may kill me; I'll be the sooner through with this leprosy. Why don't you do it?' I says: 'Barking dogs don't bite.' I was a hard old coon," added the ex-luna. In the progress of the disease blindness at last unfitted him for further duty, and he now dwells in a cottage by the hospital, delighting to receive visitors, to recall his varied experiences, and to recite his poetry. "It's dogg'rel, that's what it is," he says. "I'm not an educated man, but the idea's there. You see," he adds, "I've got nothing to do but to sit here and think." The surroundings of his later life have lent a colour to these musings, and he awaits death in his clean cottage, sightless; after so many joyous and so many rude adventures, so much plough-ing the sea, so much frequentation of fair islands, one subject inspires and occupies his verse; he will speak to you gladly of old comrades or old days of pleasure and peril; but when he takes his pen it is to treat, with womanly tenderness, of the child that is a leper.

One incident remains—that of the murder. The Kapiolani Home was founded in Oahu for clean children born within the precinct, and Mr. Meyer was instructed to obtain the consent of the parents. It was given (to their honour be it said) by all, and the condition made, that one of the parents should accompany each child upon a visit of inspection, was naturally granted. There was an old leper in the settlement, a widower, with a leper son and two clean daughters, children. He was himself too far advanced to be allowed beyond the precinct, and he asked and obtained leave for his son to accom-pany the children in his place. The steamer came late, about 6 at night, and the children and their friends were bundled on board with extreme, perhaps indecent, haste. The Harbour Master came breathing hurry, to a shed after the baggage, and found the old man sitting in despair upon his children's trunk. He bid him rise; was unanswered, possibly unheard; and roughly plucked the trunk from below the sitter. In a moment, and for the only time in the story of the lazaretto, savage instinct woke; a knife was drawn, the Harbour Master was slain, and before the pitiable homicide could be disarmed two more were wounded. Even justice feared to approach the settlement; the trial was held at a safe distance, on the island of Lanai, and the criminal sentenced to ten years in prison. Outside, the tale was used to infamous purpose, and, whether from political intrigue or in the wantonness of sentimentalism, magnified as a case of inhumanity to lepers.

The murder stands alone, as I have said, in the criminal annals of Kalawao. Brewing *okolehau* or potato spirit is the common offence, and occurs, or is discovered, about once in the two years; there have been besides a burglary or two, and occasional assaults, always about women. For even here, in the anteroom of the grave and among so marred a company, the ancient forces of humanity prevail. And from Ragsdale and Prince Peter, when the collision of their vanities embroiled the foreland, the partisans who gathered at their cry, filled with the ineradicable human readiness to shed blood upon a public difference; the horsemen who surrounded Strahan, calling for his life; Strahan himself, when he sat in the saddle and defied them; and the men who brawled, and the poor pair for whom they quarrelled—all were lepers, maimed, defeatured, seated by an open grave. Yet upon this sheaf of anecdotes the influence of pauperism is plainly to be traced, while they might all be told, all understood, and leprosy not mentioned. Our normal forces, our whole limbs, even that expectation of days which we collate from actuarial tables— it seems there is nothing of which we may not be deprived, and still retain the gusto of existence. But perhaps mankind have scarce yet learned how mechanical, how involuntary, how fatal, or (if the reader pleases) how divine, is their immixture in the interests and the affairs of life.

Such is the story, such the Newgate calendar, of this scarce paralleled society, where all are lepers, stripped of their lands and families, prisoners without offence, sick unto death, already dead in law, and denied that chief regulator and moderator of men's lives, a daily task; where so many have besides been caught like bandits, lurking armed in woods, resisting to the blood, hauled in with violence; scarce sooner taken than tamed. They claimed to be outside the law; it seems they were men that did not want it, and without judges and police could do better than ourselves surrounded with protection and restraint.

11

RIOT AND DANCE:
GREAT vs LITTLE MAKIN, GILBERT ISLANDS

After six months in Honolulu, the original plan to return to Britain had faded. Stevenson felt "oppressed by civilisation" there. He needed the ocean again, and some new islands. He even talked of buying one. So he contracted for his party to sail aboard the Equator, *a new trading schooner bound initially for the Gilbert Islands in Micronesia (in what is now Kiribati). It was a less equable touring party. Maggie Stevenson had returned to Scotland for a visit, and Valentine the long-serving maid had left for America. The wastrel Joe Strong, after various misdemeanours, was included, in hopes the voyage might rehabilitate him.*

They sailed, fifteen men and Fanny (see poem 7 in **27***), on a ship with no real passenger quarters, on 24 June 1889, under an amiable Scot, Captain Denis Reid. Stevenson and his stepson Lloyd Osbourne, now 21, began to sketch the plot of a collaborative novel based on a castaway episode they had encountered in Hawaii; it became* The Wrecker. *They planned to do the proper writing in Samoa, where the regular steamer connections to New Zealand, Sydney and Hawaii would make serial publication possible.*

This was a pleasant crossing, apart from the improvised quarters, 5000 km (3000 miles) southwest in fair winds. They landed on 14 July at Butaritari on Great Makin Island, to find the people rowdy and dangerous. A communal drinking spree to celebrate 4th July, and boost the takings of the two American trading posts, had turned ugly. When the Stevensons moved into a rented bungalow near one of the bars, stones were thrown. They responded eloquently by holding target practice with their revolvers on the beach (Fanny the best shot, from her pioneering origins). Stevenson used his mana and diplomatic skills to persuade the rival stores to withhold liquor supplies, and the king was able to restore the usual licensing tapu.

As things were settling, a party arrived from the neighbouring island of Little Makin for a song and dance contest. Stevenson wrote an engaging account for In the South Seas. *Never claiming to be more than an uninformed bystander, he manages to be both sympathetic and discriminating in evoking this expression of an essentially communal culture.*

Thursday, July 25

THE street was this day much enlivened by the presence of the men from Little Makin; they average taller than Butaritarians, and being on a holiday, went wreathed with yellow leaves and gorgeous in vivid colours. They are said to be more savage, and to be proud of the distinction. Indeed, it seemed to us they swaggered in the town, like plaided Highlanders upon the streets of Inverness, conscious of barbaric virtues.

In the afternoon the summer parlour was observed to be packed with people; others standing outside and stooping to peer under the eaves, like children at home about a circus. It was the Makin company, rehearsing for the day of competition. Karaiti sat in the front row close to the singers, where we were summoned (I suppose in honour of Queen Victoria) to join him. A strong breathless heat reigned under the iron roof, and the air was heavy with the scent of wreaths. The singers, with fine mats about their loins, cocoa-nut feathers set in rings upon their fingers, and their heads crowned with yellow leaves, sat on the floor by companies. A varying number of soloists stood up for different songs; and these bore the chief part in the music. But the full force of the companies, even when not singing, contributed continuously to the effect, and marked the ictus of the measure, mimicking, grimacing, casting up their heads and eyes, fluttering the feathers on their fingers, clapping hands, or beating (loud as a kettledrum) on the left breast; the time was exquisite, the music barbarous, but full of conscious art. I noted some devices constantly employed. A sudden change would be introduced (I think of key) with no break of the measure, but emphasised by a dramatic heightening of the voice and a swinging, general gesticulation. The voices of the soloists would begin far apart in a rude discord, and gradually draw together to a unison; which, when they had reached, they were joined and drowned by the full chorus. The ordinary, hurried, barking unmelodious movement of the voices would at times be broken and glorified by a psalm-like strain of melody, often well constructed, or seeming so by contrast. There was much variety of measure, and towards the end of each piece, when the fun became fast and furious, a recourse to this figure—

$$\frac{2}{4} \mid \flat \flat \; \downarrow \mid \flat \flat \; \downarrow \mid \flat \flat \; \downarrow \mid$$

It is difficult to conceive what fire and devilry they get into these hammering finales; all go together, voices, hands, eyes, leaves, and fluttering finger-rings; the chorus swings to the eye, the song throbs on the ear; the faces are convulsed with enthusiasm and effort.

Presently the troop stood up in a body, the drums forming a half-circle for the soloists, who were sometimes five or even more in number. The songs that followed were highly dramatic; though I had none to give me any explanation, I would at times make out some shadowy but decisive outline of a plot; and I was continually reminded of certain quarrelsome concerted scenes in grand operas at home; just so the single voices issue from and fall again into the general volume; just so do the performers separate and crowd together, brandish the raised hand, and roll the eye to heaven—or the gallery. Already this is beyond the Thespian model; the art of this people is already past the embryo: song, dance, drums, quartette and solo—it is the drama full developed although still in miniature. Of all so-called dancing in the South Seas, that which I saw in Butaritari stands easily the first. The *hula*, as it may be viewed by the speedy globe-trotter in Honolulu, is surely the most dull of man's inventions, and the spectator yawns under its length as at a college lecture or a parliamentary debate. But the Gilbert Island dance leads on the mind; it thrills, rouses, subjugates; it has the essence of all art, an unexplored imminent significance. Where so many are engaged, and where all must make (at a given moment) the same swift, elaborate, and often arbitrary movement, the toil of rehearsal is of course extreme. But they begin as children. A child and a man may often be seen together in a maniap': the man sings and gesticulates, the child stands before him with streaming tears and tremulously copies him in act and sound; it is the Gilbert Island artist learning (as all artists must) his art in sorrow.

12

SEX, MARRIAGE AND NAKED VIRTUE:
BUTARITARI

They stayed about six weeks at Butaritari, while the Equator *was away cruising the Micronesian islands for trade. Mixing with traders this time, as well as local people, Stevenson's account of the visit exemplifies how hard he worked to get into the complexities of the Pacific's multicultural world as he actually found it. He knew by now that the Pacific peoples are as different from each other as the Europeans, and joked about the Hawaiians, "with their Italian* brio *and their ready friendliness." The whites, too, are various, morally as well as ethnically, "many of them good, kind, pleasant fellows; others quite the lowest I have ever seen in the slums of cities."*

Stevenson continued to make friends, mixing with sailors and traders as readily as with the islands' royalty, and he was now seeing the copra business in its acrid reality. His understanding of the dirty ground-level workings of colonialism at its most far-flung would make The Ebb-Tide *and 'The Beach of Falesá' so insightful as critiques of the imperial enterprise. He personally knew three probable murderers, he said, and conjured a wonderfully bizarre scene from the ménage of one of them, "in his big home out of a wreck, with his New Hebrides wife in her savage turban of hair and yet a perfect lady, and his adorable little girls in Rob Roy McGregor dresses, dancing to the hand organ, performing circus on the floor with startling effects of nudity, and curling up together on a mat to sleep, three sizes, three attitudes, three Rob Roy dresses, and six little clenched fists: the murderer meanwhile brooding and gloating over his chicks, till your whole heart went out to him." Dickens never drew a stranger scene, and the devoted rogues Wiltshire and Davis are in the making.*

Time and again Stevenson surprizes his reader, goes under first impressions, and interweaves anecdote, character, dialogue and drama into his descriptions, always the lively and engaging travel writer rather than anthropologist. The chapter about Micronesian gender relations and politics is a good example.

HUSBAND AND WIFE

THE trader accustomed to the manners of Eastern Polynesia has a lesson to learn among the Gilberts. The *ridi* is but a spare attire; as late as thirty years back the women went naked until marriage; within ten years the custom lingered; and these facts, above all when heard in description, conveyed a very false idea of the manners of the group. A very intelligent missionary described it (in its former state) as a 'Paradise of naked women' for the resident whites. It was at least a platonic Paradise, where Lothario ventured at his peril. Since 1860, fourteen whites have perished on a single island, all for the same cause, all found where they had no business, and speared by some indignant father of a family; the figure was given me by one of their contemporaries who had been more prudent and survived. The strange persistence of these fourteen martyrs might seem to point to monomania or a series of romantic passions; gin is the more likely key. The poor buzzards sat alone in their houses by an open case; they drank; their brain was fired; they stumbled towards the nearest houses on chance; and the dart went through their liver. In place of a Paradise the trader found an archipelago of fierce husbands and of virtuous women. "Of course if you wish to make love to them, it's the same as anywhere else," observed a trader innocently; but he and his companions rarely so choose.

The trader must be credited with a virtue: he often makes a kind and loyal husband. Some of the worst beachcombers in the Pacific, some of the last of the old school, have fallen in my path, and some of them were admirable to their native wives, and one made a despairing widower. The position of a trader's wife in the Gilberts is, besides, unusually enviable. She shares the immunities of her husband. Curfew in Butaritari sounds for her in vain. Long after the bell is rung and the great island ladies are confined for the night to their own roof, this chartered libertine may scamper and giggle through the deserted streets or go down to bathe in the dark. The resources of the store are at her hand; she goes arrayed like a queen, and feasts delicately every day upon tinned meats. And she who was perhaps of no regard or station among natives sits with captains, and is entertained on board of schooners. Five of these privileged dames were some time our neighbours. Four were handsome skittish lasses, gamesome like children, and like children liable to fits of pouting. They wore dresses by day, but there was a tendency after dark to strip these lendings and to career and squall about the compound in the aboriginal *ridi*. Games of cards were continually played, with shells for counters; their course was much marred by cheating; and the end of a round (above all if a man was of the party) resolved itself into a scrimmage for the counters. The fifth was a matron. It was a picture to see her sail to church on a Sunday, a parasol in hand, a nursemaid following, and the baby buried in a trade hat and armed with a patent feeding-bottle. The service was enlivened by her continual supervision and correction of the maid. It was impossible not to fancy the baby was a doll, and the church some European playroom. All these women were legitimately married. It is true that the certificate of one, when she proudly showed it, proved to run thus, that she was "married for one night," and her gracious partner was at liberty to "send her to hell" the next morning; but she was none the wiser or the worse for the dastardly trick. Another, I heard, was married on a work of mine in a pirated edition; it answered the purpose as well as a Hall Bible. Notwithstanding all these allurements of social distinction, rare food and raiment, a comparative vacation from toil, and legitimate marriage contracted on a pirated edition, the trader must sometimes seek long before he can be mated. While I was in the group one had been eight months on the quest, and he was still a bachelor.

Within strictly native society the old laws and practices were harsh, but not without a certain stamp of high-mindedness. Stealthy adultery was punished with death; open elopement was properly considered virtue in comparison, and compounded for a fine in land. The male adulterer alone seems to have been punished. It is correct manners for a jealous man to hang himself; a jealous woman has a different remedy—she bites her rival. Ten or twenty years ago it was a capital offence to raise a woman's *ridi*; to this day it is still punished with a heavy fine, and the garment itself is still symbolically sacred. Suppose a piece of land to be disputed in Butaritari, the claimant who shall first hang a *ridi* on the tapu-post has gained his cause, since no one can remove or touch it but himself.

The *ridi* was the badge not of the woman but the wife, the mark not of her sex but of her station. It was the collar on the slave's neck, the brand on merchandise. The adulterous woman seems to have been spared; were the husband offended, it would be a poor consolation to send his draught cattle to the shambles. Karaiti, to this day, calls his eight wives his "horses," some trader having explained to him the employment of these animals on farms; and Nanteitei hired out his wives to do mason-work. Husbands, at least when of high rank, had the power of life and death; even whites seem to have possessed it; and their wives, when they had transgressed beyond forgiveness, made haste to pronounce the formula of deprecation—*I Kana Kim*. This form of words had so much virtue that a condemned criminal repeating it on a particular day to the king who had condemned him, must be instantly released. It is an offer of abasement, and, strangely enough, the reverse—the imitation—is a common vulgar insult in Great Britain to this day. I give a scene between a trader and his Gilbert Island wife, as it was told me by the husband, now one of the oldest residents, but then a freshman in the group.

"Go and light a fire," said the trader, "and when I have brought this oil I will cook some fish."

The woman grunted at him, island fashion.

"I am not a pig that you should grunt at me," said he.

"I know you are not a pig," said the woman, "neither am I your slave."

"To be sure you are not my slave, and if you do not care to stop with me, you had better go home to your people," said he. "But in the mean time go and light the fire; and when I have brought this oil I will cook some fish."

She went as if to obey; and presently when the trader looked she had built a fire so big that the cookhouse was catching in flames.

"I Kana Kim!" she cried, as she saw him coming; but he recked not, and hit her with a cooking-pot. The leg pierced her skull, blood spouted, it was thought she was a dead woman, and the natives surrounded the house in a menacing expectation. Another white was present, a man of older experience. "You will have us both killed if you go on like this," he cried. "She had said *I Kana Kim!*" If she had not said *I Kana Kim* he might have struck her with a caldron. It was not the blow that made the crime, but the disregard of an accepted formula.

Polygamy, the particular sacredness of wives, their semi-servile state, their seclusion in kings' harems, even their privilege of biting, all would seem to indicate a Mohammedan society and the opinion of the soullessness of woman. And not so in the least. It is a mere appearance. After you have studied these extremes in one house, you may go to the next and find all reversed, the woman the mistress, the man only the first of her thralls. The authority is not with the husband as such, nor the wife as such. It resides in the chief or the chief-woman; in him or her who has inherited the lands of the clan, and stands to the clansman in the place of parent, exacting their service, answerable for their fines. There is but the one source of power and the one ground of dignity—rank. The king married a chief-woman; she became his menial, and must work with her hands on Messrs. Wightman's pier. The king divorced her; she regained at once her former state and power. She married the Hawaiian sailor, and behold the man is her flunkey and can be shown the door at pleasure. Nay, and such low-born lords are even corrected physically, and, like grown but dutiful children, must endure the discipline.

We were intimate in one such household, that of Nei Takauti and Nan Tok'; I put the lady first of necessity. During one week of fool's paradise, Mrs. Stevenson had gone alone to the sea-side of the island after shells. I am very sure the proceeding was unsafe; and she soon perceived a man and woman watching her. Do what she would, her guardians held her steadily in view; and when the afternoon began to fall, and they thought she had stayed long enough, took her in charge, and by signs and broken English ordered her home. On the way the lady drew from her earring-hole a clay pipe, the husband lighted it, and it was handed to my unfortunate wife, who knew not how to refuse the incommodious favour; and when they were all come to our house, the pair sat down beside her on the floor, and improved the occasion with prayer. From that day they were our family friends; bringing thrice a day the beautiful island garlands of white flowers, visiting us any evening, and frequently carrying us down to their own maniap' in return, the woman leading Mrs. Stevenson by the hand like one child with another.

Nan Tok', the husband, was young, extremely handsome, of the most approved good humour, and suffering in his precarious station from suppressed high spirits. Nei Takauti, the wife, was getting old; her grown son by a former marriage had just hanged himself before his mother's eyes in despair at a well-merited rebuke. Perhaps she had never been beautiful, but her face was full of character, her eye of sombre fire. She was a high chief-woman, but by a strange exception for a person of her rank, was small, spare, and sinewy, with lean small hands and corded neck. Her full dress of an evening was invariably a white chemise—and for adornment, green leaves (or sometimes white blossoms) stuck in her hair and thrust through her huge earring-holes. The husband on the contrary changed to view like a kaleidoscope. Whatever pretty thing my wife might have given to Nei Takauti—a string of beads, a ribbon, a piece of bright fabric—appeared the next evening on the person of Nan Tok'. It was plain he was a clothes-horse; that he wore livery; that, in a word, he was his wife's wife. They reversed the parts indeed, down to the least particular; it was the husband who showed himself the ministering angel in the hour of pain, while the wife displayed the apathy and heartlessness of the proverbial man.

When Nei Takauti had a headache Nan Tok' was full of attention and concern. When the husband had a cold and a racking toothache the wife heeded not, except to jeer. It is always the woman's part to fill and light the pipe; Nei Takauti handed hers in silence to the wedded page; but she carried it herself, as though the page were not entirely trusted. Thus she kept the money, but it was he who ran the errands, anxiously sedulous. A cloud on her face dimmed instantly his beaming looks; on an early visit to their maniap' my wife saw he had cause to be wary. Nan Tok' had a friend with him, a giddy young thing, of his own age and sex; and they had worked themselves into that stage of jocularity when consequences are too often disregarded. Nei Takauti mentioned her own name. Instantly Nan Tok' held up two fingers, his friend did likewise, both in an ecstasy of slyness. It was plain the lady had two names; and from the nature of their merriment, and the wrath that gathered on her brow, there must be something ticklish in the second. The husband pronounced it; a well-directed cocoa-nut from the hand of his wife caught him on the side of the head, and the voices and the mirth of these indiscreet young gentlemen ceased for the day.

The people of Eastern Polynesia are never at a loss; their etiquette is absolute and plenary; in every circumstance it tells them what to do and how to do it. The Gilbertines are seemingly more free, and pay for their freedom (like ourselves) in frequent perplexity. This was often the case with the topsy-turvy couple. We had once supplied them during a visit with a pipe and tobacco; and when they had smoked and were about to leave, they found themselves confronted with a problem: should they take or leave what remained of the tobacco? The piece of plug was taken up, it was laid down again, it was handed back and forth, and argued over, till the wife began to

(Above) "Her face was full of character, her eye of sombre fire... her pride in her young husband it seemed that she dissembled, fearing possibly to spoil him." RLS and Fanny with "our family friends", Nan Tok' (left) and Nei Takauti.

look haggard and the husband elderly. They ended by taking it, and I wager were not yet clear of the compound before they were sure they had decided wrong. Another time they had been given each a liberal cup of coffee, and Nan Tok' with difficulty and disaffection made an end of his. Nei Takauti had taken some, she had no mind for more, plainly conceived it would be a breach of manners to set down the cup unfinished, and ordered her wedded retainer to dispose of what was left. "I have swallowed all I can, I cannot swallow more, it is a physical impossibility," he seemed to say; and his stern officer reiterated her commands with secret imperative signals. Luckless dog! but in mere humanity we came to the rescue and removed the cup.

I cannot but smile over this funny household; yet I remember the good souls with affection and respect. Their attention to ourselves was surprising. The garlands are much esteemed, the blossoms must be sought far and wide; and though they had many retainers to call to their aid, we often saw themselves passing afield after the blossoms, and the wife engaged with her own hands in putting them together. It was no want of heart, only that disregard so incident to husbands, that made Nei Takauti despise the sufferings of Nan Tok'. When my wife was unwell she proved a diligent and kindly nurse; and the pair, to the extreme embarrassment of the sufferer, became fixtures in the sick-room. This rugged, capable, imperious old dame, with the wild eyes, had deep and tender qualities: her pride in her young husband it seemed that she dissembled, fearing possibly to spoil him; and when she spoke of her dead son there came something tragic in her face. But I seemed to trace in the Gilbertines a virility of sense and sentiment which distinguishes them (like their harsh and uncouth language) from their brother islanders in the east.

13

A MIGHTY MONARCH:

APEMAMA

The Equator *dropped them next at Apemama, the subject of the fourth and final part of* In the South Seas. *Or rather, the dominant and despotic subject is Apemama's King Tembinoka. This talented, eccentric tyrant brings a Henry VIII gusto to the closing chapters, by his larger than life love of power, parties, gourmandizing, bad brandy, gadgets, wives, cheating at cards, capital punishment, his own poetry, collecting consumer goods, shooting his subjects at random, flamboyant clothes, cross-dressing, and, eventually, the Stevensons. Sidney Colvin, editor of Stevenson's letters, thought that "the character of the king is far the most interesting and attractive part of...* In the South Seas." *Of course, Stevenson knew how to end a book. But "attractive" is not the right word; it is too close to the "enchanting material" that Fanny wanted her husband to use for the travel book (see* 5). *The romantic Pacific adventure they and McClure and the market expected could certainly find room for some rollicking caricature among the native potentates. In the grotesque comedy of absolute power, Stevenson's King Tembinoka is a match for W.S. Gilbert's Mikado, who first snarled out his hit-list for execution only four years earlier, in 1885. But there is another dimension to Stevenson's tyrant. He is much nastier. While it is an engaging portrait in some ways, allowing us to enjoy the king's gargantuan excesses, and giving full credit to his political and dramatic skills, and the orderliness of his kingdom, Stevenson also shows that he is brutish, egotistic, and lacking the slightest sense of justice or responsibility beyond his own gratification. "I kill plenty men," he boasted, in between "embarrassing details" about how his ancestral house was founded in a coition between a woman and a shark. Tembinoka is as attractive and repugnant as Long John Silver.*

Stevenson well knew how charismatic evil can be. He would show it again in his own island tyrant, Attwater in The Ebb-Tide.

The extracts that follow are selected from the seven chapters given to the monarchy and its ruler in In the South Seas.

WE were scarce yet moored, however, before distant and busy figures appeared upon the beach, a boat was launched, and a crew pulled out to us bringing the king's ladder. Tembinok' had once an accident; has feared ever since to intrust his person to the rotten chandlery of South Sea traders; and devised in consequence a frame of wood, which is brought on board a ship as soon as she appears, and remains lashed to her side until she leave. The boat's crew, having applied this engine, returned at once to shore. They might not come on board; neither might we land, or not without danger of offence; the king giving pratique in person. An interval followed, during which dinner was delayed for the great man; the prelude of the ladder, giving us some notion of his weighty body and sensible, ingenious character, had highly whetted our curiosity; and it was with something like excitement that we saw the beach and terrace suddenly blacken with attendant vassals, the king and party embark, the boat (a man-of-war gig) come flying towards us dead before the wind, and the royal coxswain lay us cleverly aboard, mount the ladder with a jealous diffidence, and descend heavily on deck.

Not long ago he was overgrown with fat, obscured to view, and a burthen to himself. Captains visiting the island advised him to walk; and though it broke the habits of a life and the traditions of his rank, he practised the remedy with benefit. His corpulence is now portable; you would call him lusty rather than fat; but his gait is still dull, stumbling, and elephantine. He neither stops nor hastens, but goes about his business with an implacable deliberation. We could never see him and not be struck with his extraordinary natural means for the theatre: a beaked profile like Dante's in the mask, a mane of long black hair, the eye brilliant, imperious, and inquiring: for certain parts, and to one who could have used it, the face was a fortune. His voice matched it well, being shrill, powerful, and uncanny, with a note like a sea-bird's. Where there are no fashions, none to set them, few to follow them if they were set, and none to criticise, he dresses as Sir Charles Grandison lived—"to his own heart." Now he wears a woman's frock, now a naval uniform; now (and more usually) figures in a masquerade costume of his own design: trousers and a singular jacket with shirt tails, the cut and fit wonderful for island work-manship, the material always handsome, sometimes green velvet, sometimes cardinal red silk. This masquerade becomes him admirably. In the woman's frock he looks ominous and weird beyond belief. I see him now come pacing towards me in the cruel sun, solitary, a figure out of Hoffmann...

HE is greedy of things new and foreign. House after house, chest after chest, in the palace precinct, is already crammed with clocks, musical boxes, blue spectacles, umbrellas, knitted waist-coats, bolts of stuff, tools, rifles, fowling-pieces, medicines, European foods, sewing-machines, and, what is more extraordinary, stoves: all that ever caught his eye, tickled his appetite, pleased him for its use, or puzzled him with its apparent inutility. And still his lust is unabated. He is possessed by the seven devils of the collector. He hears a thing spoken of, and a shadow comes on his face. "I think I no got him," he will say; and the treasures he has seem worthless in comparison. If a ship be bound for Apemama, the merchant racks his brain to hit upon some novelty. This he leaves carelessly in the main cabin or partly conceals in his own berth, so that the king shall spy it for himself. "How much you want?" inquires Tembinok', passing and pointing. "No, king; that too dear," returns the trader. "I think I like him," says the king. This was a bowl of gold-fish. On another occasion it was scented soap. "No, king; that cost too much," said the trader; "too good for a Kanaka." "How much you got? I take him all," replied his majesty, and became the lord of seventeen boxes at two dollars a cake...

TEMBINOK', like most tyrants, is a conservative; like many conserv-atives, he eagerly welcomes new ideas, and, except in the field of politics, leans to practical reform. When the missionaries came, professing a knowledge of the truth, he readily received them; attended their worship, acquired the accomplishment of public prayer, and made himself a student at their feet. It is thus—it is by the cultivation of similar passing chances—that he has learned to read, to write, to cipher, and to speak this queer, personal English, so different from ordinary "Beach de Mar," so much more obscure, expressive, and condensed. His education attended to, he found time to become critical of the new inmates. Like Nakaeia of Makin, he is an admirer of silence in the island; broods over it like a great ear; has spies who report daily; and had rather his subjects sang than talked. The service, and in particular the sermon, were thus sure to become offences: "Here, in my island, *I* 'peak," he once observed to me. "My chiefs no 'peak—do what I talk." He looked at the missionary,

(Above) **"He looks up with a smile and reminds you, 'I got power.'"** RLS and Fanny intent on the conversation of King Tembinoka (right).

and what did he see? "See Kanaka 'peak in big outch!" he cried, with a strong ring of sarcasm. Yet he endured the subversive spectacle, and might even have continued to endure it, had not a fresh point arisen. He looked again, to employ his own figure; and the Kanaka was no longer speaking, he was doing worse—he was building a copra-house. The king was touched in his chief interests; revenue and prerogative were threatened. He considered besides (and some think with him) that trade is incompatible with the missionary claims. "Tuppoti mitonary think 'good man': very good. Tuppoti he think 'cobra': no good. I send him away ship." Such was his abrupt history of the evangelist in Apemama.

Similar deportations are common: "I send him away ship" is the epitaph of not a few, his majesty paying the exile's fare to the next place of call. For instance, being passionately fond of European food, he has several times added to his household a white cook, and one after another these have been deported...

HERE is a household unlike, indeed, to one of ours; more unlike still to the Oriental harem: that of an elderly childless man, his days menaced, dwelling alone amid a bevy of women of all ages, ranks, and relationships—the mother, the sister, the cousin, the legitimate wife, the concubine, the favourite, the eldest born, and she of yesterday; he, in their midst, the only master, the only male, the sole dispenser of honours, clothes, and luxuries, the sole mark of multitudinous ambitions and desires. I doubt if you could find a man in Europe so bold as to attempt this piece of tact and government. And seemingly Tembinok' himself had trouble in the beginning. I hear of him shooting at a wife for some levity on board a schooner. Another, on some more serious offence, he slew outright; he exposed her body in an open box, and (to make the warning more memorable) suffered it to putrefy before the palace gate. Doubtless his growing years have come to his assistance for upon so large a scale it is more easy to play the father than the husband. And to-day, at least to the eye of a stranger, all seems to go smoothly, and the wives to be proud of their trust, proud of their rank, and proud of their cunning lord...

IN THE background figured a multitude of ladies, the lean, the plump, and the elephantine, some in sacque frocks, some in the hairbreadth *ridi;* high-born and low, slave and mistress; from the queen to the scullion, from the favourite to the scraggy sentries at the palisade. Not all of these of course are of "my pamily"—many are mere attendants; yet a surprising number shared the responsibility of the king's trust. These were key-bearers, treasurers, wardens of the armoury, the napery, and the stores. Each knew and did her part to admiration. Should anything be required—a particular gun, perhaps, or a particular bolt of stuff—the right queen was summoned; she came bringing the right chest, opened it in the king's presence, and displayed her charge in perfect preservation—the gun cleaned and oiled, the goods duly folded. Without delay or haste, and with the minimum of speech, the whole great establishment turned on wheels like a machine. Nowhere have I seen order more complete and pervasive. And yet I was always reminded of Norse tales of trolls and ogres who kept their hearts buried in the ground for the mere safety, and must confide the secret to their wives. For these weapons are the life of Tembinok'. He does not aim at popularity; but drives and braves his subjects, with a simplicity of domination which it is impossible not to admire, hard not to sympathise with. Should one out of so many prove faithless, should the armoury be secretly unlocked, should the crones have dozed by the palisade and the weapons find their way unseen into the village, revolution would be nearly certain, death the most probable result, and the spirit of the tyrant of Apemama flit to rejoin his predecessors of Mariki and Tapituea. Yet those whom he so trusts are all women, and all rivals...

[After Stevenson had problems with a royal cook:]

AS SOON as I left, it seems the king called for a Winchester and strolled outside the palisade, awaiting the defaulter. That day Tembinok' wore the woman's frock; as like as not, his make-up was completed by a pith helmet and blue spectacles. Conceive the glaring stretch of sandhills, the dwarf palms with their noonday shadows, the line of the palisade, the crone sentries (each by a small clear fire) cooking syrup on their posts—and this chimæra waiting with his deadly engine. To him, enter at last the cook, strolling down the sandhill from Equator Town, listless, vain, and graceful; with no thought of alarm. As soon as he was well within range, the travestied monarch fired the six shots over his head, at his feet, and on either hand of him: the second Apemama warning, startling in itself, fatal in significance, for the next time his majesty will aim to hit. I am told the king is a crack shot; that when he aims to kill, the grave may be got ready; and when he aims to miss, misses by so near a margin that the culprit tastes six times the bitterness of death...

THUS all things on the island, even the priests of the gods, obey the word of Tembinok'. He can give and take, and slay, and allay the scruples of the conscientious, and do all things (apparently) but interfere in the cookery of a turtle. "I got power" is his favourite word; it interlards his conversation; the thought haunts him and is ever fresh; and when he has asked and meditates of foreign countries, he looks up with a smile and reminds you, *"I got power."* Nor is his delight only in the possession, but in the exercise. He rejoices in the crooked and violent paths of kingship like a strong man to run a race, or like an artist in his art. To feel, to use his power, to embellish his island and the picture of the island life after a private ideal, to milk the island vigorously, to extend his singular museum—these employ delightfully the sum of his abilities. I never saw a man more patently in the right trade.

14

BLUE WATER:

SAMOA, AUCKLAND, ARUNUKA, NOUMEA, SYDNEY

At last even Tembinoka the mighty monarch dips below the horizon, and Stevenson's South Seas book ends as it began, at sea on the Pacific: "The king took us on board in his own gig, dressed for the occasion in the naval uniform. He had little to say, he refused refreshments, shook us briefly by the hand, and went ashore again. That night the palm-tops of Apemama had dipped behind the sea, and the schooner sailed solitary under the stars."

During their two months at Apemama, Stevenson had worked on his travel book, on ballads (one about Tembinoka), and with Lloyd on The Wrecker *and 'The Pearl Fisher', that later became* The Ebb-Tide. *The task of imaginatively writing about the Pacific's disparate cultures and the encounters between them had begun.*

The Equator *traded from island to island. The dull diet of the low islands made Stevenson write, "I think I could shed tears over a dish of turnips", and he longed, he said, for "an island with a profile." Eventually, on 7 December 1889, after a 26-day voyage south-east into Polynesia, he found one – Upolu, Samoa. He had arrived at Mr. Seed's beneficent Navigator Islands at long last. Upolu is hilly and densely bushed, and the profile behind Apia Harbour is topped by Mount Vaea, where soon he would gladly live, and quite soon die. His first impression was of "a tamer force of nature" than the Marquesas or Tahiti, a view aided, as he said in a letter, by the great symmetrical German plantations, "with their countless regular avenues of palms." But he liked the many rivers and waterfalls, and their "great volume of sound", and he neatly evoked "the sudden angry splash and roar of the Pacific on the reef."*

Harry J. Moors, an enterprising American store manager with his ear close to the ground locally, befriended the party and proved invaluable, providing them accommodation in his home and giving Stevenson some of the information he wanted about recent local history. Stevenson worked hard, interviewing people, writing up notes for what became A Footnote to History *(17-19), and writing 'The Bottle Imp' (22).*

When they thought of buying land as a domestic base for future Pacific travels, Moors found them some, ideal and affordable, four kilometres up behind Apia, at the foot of Mount Vaea, "314¼ acres of beautiful land in the bush," as Stevenson wrote. It has fresh air, ample water, land for agriculture, fertile climate, and the necessary view of the ocean and its shore – "really a noble place." They called it Vailima, for its "five waters", or springs; or for the local story of a girl who carried water (vai) to a dying chief in her folded fingers (lima).

There was no intention yet to renounce Europe. A trip by the S.S. Lübeck *to Sydney in February 1890 was intended as a stopover, but the cooler weather got into Stevenson's frail and pitted lungs again, and the fits of coughing blood returned. Fanny the indomitable overcame a maritime strike and secured them berths out on an iron-screw rigged steamer, the* Janet Nicholl, *with a Melanesian, non-union crew, bound for Polynesia. They sailed on 11 April 1890.*

A brief call at Auckland on 19 April almost put an explosive end to the whole story, when a stock of fireworks and cartridges, illicitly loaded by another passenger, somehow ignited as the ship was leaving port. In "gorgeous flames and the most horrible chemical stench", and general alarm and confusion, the helmsman deserted the wheel, the ship drifted and burned, the captain crawled heroically into the fire with a blanket, Stevenson stood "muddled with the smoke", and Fanny peremptorily stopped a crew member from tossing overboard a smouldering trunk that was packed with her husband's manuscripts. They lost clothes, and, more seriously for the future, including this book, a great many photographs.

By chance the Janet Nicholl *called early at Apia, so the party could ride up the newly cleared track to where Vailima was taking shape – a temporary wooden house in a clearing in the bush. The voyage then followed a wide arc north of Samoa, touching thirty-three small "low islands" in a little over three months.*

The Janet Nicholl *was notoriously unstable – "the worst roller I was ever aboard of," remarked the normally seaworthy Stevenson. One night he was "shied out of the berth." The cabin where he worked (as, of course, he did, assiduously) was "heated like the Babylonian furnace", and an uncongenial fellow passenger* (the one who brought the fireworks aboard) burdened them with what Fanny called his "incessant and inconsequent conversation." The steamer's trading calls at innumerable low islands may also have come to seem inconsequent: "hackney cabs have more variety than atolls", Stevenson grumbled, though in his more characteristic sanguine mood he found "some extremely entertaining; some also were old acquaintances and pleasant to revisit."

One such old acquaintance was Apemama, where they were rapturously received by the jovial monster King Tembinoka. Fanny presented the kingdom with a new national flag, made in Sydney to her own design. She was also a hit with the harem.

In July 1890, Stevenson started "the blood-spitting" again, the first time he had been afflicted at sea. Being on a stifling steamship may have been a factor. Laid up on the Gilbert Island of Aranuka, he still kept at "savage hard work", "waist-deep in my big book on the South Seas", and well into "two huge novels" that became The Wrecker and The Ebb-Tide. He wrote little directly about this voyage, and the main account is Fanny's Cruise of the Janet Nichol among the South Sea Islands, A Diary, published in 1915. (The ship's spelling is as unstable as her sailing.)

After a rowdy visit to the convalescent by Tembinoka and his retinue, the Janet Nicholl went south to New Caledonia, their first contact with Melanesia. Stevenson stayed on alone in Noumea when the ship sailed for Sydney, feeling "utterly fatigued". On the depressing waterfront of the French penal colony he gathered material that supplemented the Papeete setting of the opening of The Ebb-Tide. He also acquired plentiful supplies of good French wine for Vailima.

When he moved on to Sydney, despite its congenial Union Club there was yet another severe congestive illness. This seems to have sealed the decision to return home, not to Edinburgh, Bournemouth or San Francisco, but to Vailima. His first announcement of this, in a letter to Henry James, is frequently quoted in extract, but worth reading in full, for its mastery of warm and lively epistolary converse with a literary peer, as well as for its biographical significance.

Union Club, Sydney, August 1890

MY DEAR HENRY JAMES,—Kipling is too clever to live. The *Bête Humaine* I had already perused in Noumea, listening the while to the strains of the convict band. He is a Beast; but not human, and, to be frank, not very interesting. 'Nervous maladies: the homicidal ward,' would be the better name: O, this game gets very tedious.

Your two long and kind letters have helped to entertain the old familiar sickbed. So has a book called *The Bondman*, by Hall Caine; I wish you would look at it. I am not half-way through yet. Read the book, and communicate your views. Hall Caine, by the way, appears to take Hugo's view of History and Chronology. (*Later;* the book doesn't keep up; it gets very wild.)

I must tell you plainly—I can't tell Colvin—I do not think I shall come to England more than once, and then it'll be to die. Health I enjoy in the tropics; even here, which they call sub- or semi-tropical, I come only to catch cold. I have not been out since my arrival; live here in a nice bedroom by the fireside, and read books and letters from Henry James, and send out to get his *Tragic Muse*, only to be told they can't be had as yet in Sydney, and have altogether a placid time. But I can't go out! The thermometer was nearly down to 50° the other day—no temperature for me, Mr. James: how should I do in England? I fear not at all. Am I very sorry? I am sorry about seven or eight people in England, and one or two in the States. And outside of that, I simply prefer Samoa. These are the words of honesty and soberness. (I am fasting from all but sin, coughing, *The Bondman*, a couple of eggs and a cup of tea.) I was never fond of towns, houses, society, or (it seems) civilisation. Nor yet it seems was I ever very fond of (what is technically called) God's green earth. The sea, islands, the islanders, the island life and climate, make and keep me truly happier. These last two years I have been much at sea, and I have *never wearied;* sometimes I have indeed grown impatient for some destination; more often I was sorry that the voyage drew so early to an end; and never once did I lose my fidelity to blue water and a ship. It is plain, then, that for me my exile to the place of schooners and islands can be in no sense regarded as a calamity.

Good-bye just now: I must take a turn at my proofs.

N.B.—Even my wife has weakened about the sea. She wearied, the last time we were ashore, to get afloat again.—Yours ever,

R.L.S.

15

A HARD AND INTERESTING AND BEAUTIFUL LIFE:

VAILIMA, SAMOA

Back in Britain they tended to blame Fanny for the loss of their famous friend (presumably on the grounds that she was American) but that seems unjust. Her role and skills were always in operations, turning his imaginings into action. His statement that opens In the South Seas *(1) is entirely personal, and he was markedly consistent in explaining in his letters the decision to stay. His reasons were medical, financial, temperamental and literary.*

Medically, he needed warmth and clear air for his lungs; even in Sydney he complained of "the extreme cold", cheerfully admitting the incongruity of that for someone from Edinburgh.

Financially, he needed an investment, "an endowment for the survivors", somewhere "with a livelihood assured."

Temperamentally, Stevenson needed both the shore and the sea, a sense of secure refuge and also a sense of infinite horizons. The last long paragraph of his letter to James (14) restates in the Pacific context one of the best-known of all his lines, "To travel hopefully is a better thing than to arrive." One early poem describes his attraction to Fanny in the image of a sailor approaching a foreign island that offers refuge if he can pass the danger: "...the mysterious islet, and behold/ Surf and great mountains and loud river-bars/ And from the shore hear inland voices call." He liked to be laird and paterfamilias *but also to be something of a bohemian vagabond, an exile, travelling dangerously. A Pacific island like Upolu satisfied all these contrary impulses.*

He was writing at the top of his literary game in the Pacific, stimulated by the new material, "exulting in the knowledge of a new world", and the challenge of lifting it above "romance... sugar candy sham epic" (as he put it later). He had at least seven important Pacific books on the brew that were integral to the decision to live in Samoa: In the South Seas, The Wrecker, The Ebb-Tide, A Footnote to History, Island Nights' Entertainments, *a volume of verse ballads and a collection of songs and legends. "I have a whole world in my head, a whole new society to work," he wrote. His last Scottish books, too,* Catriona *and* Weir of Hermiston, *seem only to have gained from these new Pacific insights.*

Mundanely, it is worth remembering that Apia had regular steamer services that kept him globally aware. He kept almost as promptly up to date with new writing by Kipling, Zola, James, Hardy, Barrie and others as he could have done in Bournemouth. Furniture and friends made the voyage successfully.

Stevenson and Fanny moved into their new home in September 1890, when it was only an unfurnished temporary cottage in a clearing at the end of a rough track through the bush. A letter gives the best insight into his life in the early months, literary, social and agricultural; and into his light, bright, witty, dramatic, impressionistic skill at conveying its essence.

In the Mountain, Apia, Samoa,
Monday, November 2nd, 1890

MY DEAR COLVIN,—This is a hard and interesting and beautiful life that we lead now. Our place is in a deep cleft of Vaea Mountain, some six hundred feet above the sea, embowered in forest, which is our strangling enemy, and which we combat with axes and dollars. I went crazy over outdoor work, and had at last to confine myself to the house, or literature must have gone by the board. *Nothing* is so interesting as weeding, clearing, and path-making; the oversight of labourers becomes a disease; it is quite an effort not to drop into the farmer; and it does make you feel so well. To come down covered with mud and drenched with sweat and rain after some hours in the bush, change, rub down, and take a chair in the verandah, is to taste a quiet conscience. And the strange thing that I mark is this: If I go out and make sixpence, bossing my labourers and plying the cutlass or the spade, idiot conscience applauds me; if I sit in the house and make twenty pounds, idiot conscience wails over my neglect and the day wasted. For near a fortnight I did not go beyond the verandah; then I found my rush of work run out, and went down for the night to Apia; put in Sunday afternoon with our consul, "a nice

(Above) **"Our place is in a deep cleft of Vaea Mountain... embowered in forest, which is our strangling enemy." Vailima, with family and staff.**

young man," dined with my friend H.J. Moors in the evening, went to church—no less—at the white and half-white church—I had never been before, and was much interested; the woman I sat next *looked* a full-blood native, and it was in the prettiest and readiest English that she sang the hymns; back to Moors', where we yarned of the islands, being both wide wanderers, till bedtime; bed, sleep, breakfast, horse saddled; round to the mission, to get Mr. Clarke to be my interpreter; over with him to the King's whom I have not called on since my return; received by that mild old gentleman; have some interesting talk with him about Samoan superstitions and my land—the scene of a great battle in his (Malietoa Laupepa's) youth—the place which we have cleared the platform of his fort—the gulley of the stream full of dead bodies— the fight rolled off up Vaea mountain-side; back with Clarke to the mission; had a bit of lunch and consulted over a queer point of missionary policy just arisen, about our new Town Hall and the balls there—too long to go into, but a quaint example of the intricate questions which spring up daily in the missionary path.

Then off up the hill; Jack very fresh, the sun (close on noon) staring hot, the breeze very strong and pleasant; the ineffable green country all round— gorgeous little birds (I think they are hummingbirds, but they say not) skirmishing in the wayside flowers. About a quarter way up I met a native coming down with the trunk of a cocoa palm across his shoulder; his brown breast glittering with sweat and oil: "Talofa"—"Talofa, alii—You see that white man? He speak for you." "White man he gone up here ?"—"Ioe" (Yes) "Tofa, alii"—"Tofa, soifua!" I put on Jack up the steep path, till he is all as white as shaving stick—Brown's euxesis, wish I had some—past Tanuga-manono, a bush village—see into the houses as I pass—they are open sheds scattered on a green—see the brown folk sitting there, suckling kids, sleeping on their stiff wooden pillows—then on through the wood path—and here I find the mysterious white man (poor devil!) with his twenty years' certificate of good behaviour as a book-keeper, frozen out by the strikes in the colonies, come up here on a chance, no work to be found, big hotel bill, no ship to leave in—and come up to beg twenty dollars because he heard I was a Scotchman, offering to leave his portmanteau in pledge. Settle this, and on again; and here my house comes in view, and a war whoop fetches my wife and Henry (or Simelé), our Samoan boy, on the front balcony; and I am home again, and only sorry that I shall have to go down again to Apia this day week. I could, and would, dwell here unmoved, but there are things to be attended to.

Never say I don't give you details and news. That is a picture of a letter.

I have been hard at work since I came; three chapters of *The Wrecker*, and since that, eight of the South Sea book, and, along and about and in between, a hatful of verses. Some day I'll send the verse to you, and you'll say if any of it is any good. I have got in a better vein with the South Sea book, as I think you will see; I think these chapters will do for the volume without much change. Those that I did in the *Janet Nicoll*, under the most ungodly circum-stances, I fear will want a lot of suppling and lightening, but I hope to have your remarks in a month or two upon that point. It seems a long while since I have heard from you. I do hope you are well. I am wonderful, but tired from so much work; 'tis really immense what I have done; in the South Sea book I have fifty pages copied fair, some of which has been four times, and all twice written; certainly fifty pages of solid scriving inside a fortnight, but I was at it by seven a.m. till lunch, and from two till four or five every day; between whiles, verse and blowing on the flageolet; never outside. If you could see this place! but I don't want any one to see it till my clearing is done, and my house built. It will be a home for angels.

So far I wrote after my bit of dinner, some cold meat and bananas, on arrival. Then out to see where Henry and some of the men were clearing the garden; for it was plain there was to be no work to-day indoors, and I must set in consequence to farmering. I stuck a good while on the way up, for the path there is largely my own handiwork, and there were a lot of sprouts and saplings and stones to be removed. Then I reached our clearing just where the streams join in one; it had a fine autumn smell of burning, the smoke blew in the woods, and the boys were pretty merry and busy. Now I had a private design—

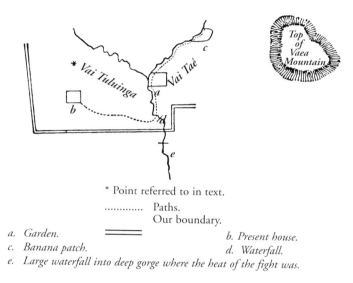

* Point referred to in text.

.... Paths.

Our boundary.

a. *Garden.*
c. *Banana patch.*
b. *Present house.*
d. *Waterfall.*
e. *Large waterfall into deep gorge where the heat of the fight was.*

The Vaita'e I had explored pretty far up; not yet the other stream, the Vaituliga (g=nasal n, as ng in sing); and up that, with my wood knife, I set off alone. It is here quite dry; it went through endless woods; about as broad as a Devonshire lane, here and there crossed by fallen trees; huge trees overhead in the sun, dripping lianas and tufted with orchids, tree ferns, ferns depending with air roots from the steep banks, great arums—I had not skill enough to say if any of them were the edible kind, one of our staples here!—hundreds of bananas—another staple—and alas! I had skill enough to know all of these for the bad kind that bears no fruit. My Henry moralised over this the other day; how hard it was that the bad banana flourished wild, and the good must be weeded and tended; and I had not the heart to tell him how fortunate they were here, and how hungry were other lands by comparison. The ascent of this lovely lane of my dry stream filled me with delight. I could not but be reminded of old Mayne Reid, as I have been more than once since I came to the tropics; and I thought, if Reid had been still living, I would have written to tell him that, for me, *it had come true;* and I thought, forbye, that, if the great powers go on as they are going, and the Chief Justice delays, it would come truer still; and the war-conch will sound in the hills, and my home will be inclosed in camps, before the year is ended. And all at once—mark you, how Mayne-Reid is on the spot—a strange thing happened. I saw a liana stretch across the bed of the brook about breast-high, swung up my knife to sever it, and—behold! it was a wire! On either hand it plunged into thick bush; to-morrow I shall see where it goes and get a guess perhaps of what it means. To-day I know no more than—there it is. A little higher the brook began to trickle, then to fill. At last, as I meant to do some work upon the homeward trail, it was time to turn. I did not return by the stream; knife in hand, as long as my endurance lasted, I was to cut a path in the congested bush.

At first it went ill with me; I got badly stung as high as the elbows by the stinging plant; I was nearly hung in a tough liana—a rotten trunk giving way under my feet; it was deplorable bad business. And an axe—if I dared swing one—would have been more to the purpose than my cutlass. Of a sudden things began to go strangely easier; I found stumps, bushing out again; my body began to wonder, then my mind; I raised my eyes and looked ahead; and, by George, I was no longer pioneering, I had struck an old track overgrown, and was restoring an old path. So I laboured till I was in such a state that Carolina Wilhelmina Skeggs could scarce have found a name for it. Thereon desisted, returned to the stream; made my way down that stony track to the garden, where the smoke was still hanging and the sun was still in the high treetops, and so home. Here, fondly supposing my long day was over, I rubbed down; exquisite agony; water spreads the poison of these weeds; I got it all over my hands, on my chest, in my eyes, and presently, while eating an orange, *à la* Rarotonga, burned my lip and eye with orange juice. Now all day, our three small pigs had been adrift, to the mortal peril of our corn, lettuce, onions, etc., and as I stood smarting on the back verandah, behold the three piglings issuing from the wood just opposite. Instantly I got together as many boys as I could—three, and got the pigs penned against the rampart of the sty, till the others joined; whereupon we formed a cordon, closed, captured the deserters, and dropped them, squeaking amain, into their strengthened barracks where, please God, they may now stay!

Perhaps you may suppose the day now over; you are not the head of a plantation, my juvenile friend. Politics succeeded: Henry got adrift in his English, Bene was too cowardly to tell me what he was after: result, I have lost seven good labourers, and had to sit down and write to you to keep my temper. Let me sketch my lads.—Henry—Henry has gone down to town or I could not be writing to you—this were the hour of his English lesson else, when he learns what he calls 'long explesions' or 'your chief's language' for the matter of an hour and a half—Henry is a chiefling from Savaii; I once loathed, I now like and—pending fresh discoveries—have a kind of respect for Henry. He does good work for us; goes among the labourers, bossing and watching; helps Fanny, is civil, kindly, thoughtful; *O si sic semper!* But will he be 'his sometime self throughout the year'? Anyway, he has deserved of us, and he must disappoint me sharply ere I give him up.—Bene—or Peni—Ben, in plain English—is supposed to be my ganger; the Lord love him! God made a truckling coward, there is his full history. He cannot tell me what he wants; he dares not tell me what is wrong; he dares not transmit my orders or translate my censures. And with all this, honest, sober, industrious, miserably smiling over the miserable issue of his own unmanliness.—Paul—a German cook and steward—a glutton of work—a splendid fellow; drawbacks, three: (1) no cook; (2) an inveterate bungler; a man with twenty thumbs, continually falling in the dishes, throwing out the dinner, preserving the garbage; (3) a dr—, well, don't let us say that—but we daren't let him go to town, and he—poor, good soul—is afraid to be let go.—Lafaele (Raphael), a strong, dull, deprecatory man; splendid with an axe, if watched; the better for a rowing, when he calls me 'Papa' in the most wheedling tones; desperately afraid of ghosts, so that he dare not walk alone up in the banana patch—see map. The rest are changing labourers; and tonight, owing to the miserable cowardice of Peni, who did not venture to tell me what the men wanted—and which was no more than fair— all are gone—and my weeding in the article of being finished! Pity the sorrows of a planter.

I am, Sir, yours, and be jowned to you, The Planter,

R.L.S.

16

OUR FOREST HOUSE,
OUR ISLAND HELPERS:
VAILIMA, SAMOA

The four years at Vailima have become a literary legend. They are described in Stevenson's letters, like the one in 15, in first-hand accounts by Fanny, Belle, Maggie, Austin, Graham Balfour (a visiting cousin), and H.J. Moors, and in almost innumerable biographies and travel books. The present selection's purpose is primarily literary, seeking to illustrate how well Stevenson wrote about the Pacific rather than explain in detail how he lived there. Two general biographical comments relevant to that writing are offered, however.

1. It was a considerable achievement and a huge amount of work to transform Vailima into the gracious and vital home and social centre that it quickly became. Fanny was a home-maker and gardener of genius, and the house and estate still reflect her skills. They sent Lloyd to sell up Skerryvore, their Bournemouth house, and ship the contents to Samoa, crystal, china, sofas and all. The story of how the piano was carried from Apia Harbour through the bush to Vailima is worth a film. They imported chickens and pigs, the latter as compulsively nomadic as their owners, and were soon almost self-sufficient in food. Many letters, like 15 above, speak of being "crazy over outdoor work", and half jokingly complain about "all the myriad misfortunes of the planter's life."

The house itself was ambitious, designed by a Sydney architect, impressive with its great hall, stairways, and redwood ceilings, yet appropriate to its setting, too, only two-storeyed, with a low sloping roof that matches the surrounding hills, and deep trellised balcony/verandahs that shade the windows and link indoors with outdoors much like a Samoan fale. The furnishings reflect the same sense of place, mahogany furniture sitting below tapa hangings, imported carpets mixed with native mats, bookcases everywhere, some decorated with Pacific souvenirs. Even the would-be baronial stone and brick fireplace, famously unique in that climate, is a homely joke more than an imperial imposition. Louis and Fanny had "shed real tears" over the details of the house, he wrote from the Janet Nicholl, and should have felt rewarded.

2. The house, the estate, every letter, every photograph, and every account of life there from 1890-94, testify to a natural, comfortable and affectionate relationship between the family and staff, and between the household and the wider community, settler and Samoan. Distinctions were preserved, and the hierarchical social patterns of Britain and Samoa melded, but humanely and respectfully, not with rigidity or hauteur (See 21). Sometimes Stevenson resolved disputes in the Samoan way, listening to extended discussion of the issue. He gave "serious, respectful attention to... all native formalities", Belle Strong reported. Fanny's determined energy won the admiration of workmen twice her size and half her age, who named her Aolele, the little flying cloud. All the family were known by Samoan names, which helped in creating new kinds of employer relationships: Tusitala, the writer of tales; Tamaitai, Madam, or Aolele, Flying Cloud; Loia for Lloyd; and Teuila, the adorner, for Fanny's daughter Belle. An amusing poem describes Belle's busy activity among the staff and children (27). The family soon comprised four generations, with Maggie Stevenson rejoining them (with her Edinburgh furniture), and Belle and her son Austin. Belle's artist husband Joe Strong lasted a year, until even Stevenson's bohemian tolerance was exhausted by his drunkenness, promiscuity, deceit, thefts and slanders, and Joe was divorced and repatriated to California where he would be less conspicuous.

The house became a centre for spirited hospitality. Stevenson was known for his impulsive dinner invitations and was an engaging host. Moors called the family "great dancing people", and the three women put in time helping Samoan and part-Samoan wives and daughters acquire European social skills for their frequent "private balls". These were far from exclusive, invitations issued "without regard for social station... wives and daughters, white, half-caste or wholly Polynesian", reported Graham Balfour. They played tennis and rode horseback paper-chases, all with the same social and racial mix. Stevenson was playing tennis with a friend's Samoan wife one day in August 1893 when he began to cough blood. Fanny banned him from playing again, but the tennis parties continued. It took generosity and enlightened race attitudes to create a community like Vailima from scratch in the 1890s.

Communal rituals played an important role in this, satisfying needs on both sides, especially meals and weekly prayers. Stevenson wrote many of the prayers himself, and delivered them in his role as head of the family. They thus linked the life of the house, family and staff, with his inner life as a writer.

VAILIMA PRAYERS

For Success

LORD, behold our family here assembled. We thank Thee for this place in which we dwell; for the love that unites us; for the peace accorded us this day; for the hope with which we expect the morrow; for the health, the work, the food, and the bright skies, that make our lives delightful; for our friends in all parts of the earth, and our friendly helpers in this foreign isle. Let peace abound in our small company. Purge out of every heart the lurking grudge.

(Above) **"Lord, behold our family here assembled. We thank Thee for this place in which we dwell; for the love that unites us." The verandah at Vailima: (Back row) Joe Strong (in lava-lava, with parrot); Margaret Stevenson; Lloyd Osbourne; RLS; Fanny; Simi. (Middle row) Mary Carter (maid, in white); Talolo (chief cook); Austin Strong; Belle Strong; Lafoele (cattleman); Tomasi (assistant cook, with axe). (Front row) Auvea (ground staff); Elena (laundress); Arrick (pantry boy).**

Give us grace and strength to forbear and to persevere. Offenders, give us the grace to accept and to forgive offenders. Forgetful ourselves, help us to bear cheerfully the forgetfulness of others. Give us courage and gaiety and the quiet mind. Spare to us our friends, soften to us our enemies. Bless us, if it may be, on all our innocent endeavours. If it may not, give us the strength to encounter that which is to come, that we be brave in peril, constant in tribulation, temperate in wrath, and in all changes of fortune and down to the gates of death, loyal and loving one to another. As the clay to the potter, as the windmill to the wind, as children of their sire, we beseech of Thee this help and mercy, for Christ's sake.

In Time Of Rain

WE thank Thee, Lord, for the glory of the late days and the excellent face of Thy sun. We thank Thee for good news received. We thank Thee for the pleasures we have enjoyed and for those we have been able to confer. And now, when the clouds gather and the rain impends over the forest and our house, permit us not to be cast down; let us not lose the savour of past mercies and past pleasures but, like the voice of a bird singing in the rain, let grateful memory survive in the hour of darkness. If there be in front of us any painful duty, strengthen us with the grace of courage; if any act of mercy, teach us tenderness and patience.

For The Family

AID us, if it be Thy will, in our concerns. Have mercy on this land and innocent people. Help them who this day contend in disappointment with their frailties. Bless our family, bless our forest house, bless our island helpers. Thou who hast made for us this place of ease and hope, accept and inflame our gratitude; help us to repay, in service one to another, the debt of Thine unmerited benefits and mercies, so that when the period of our stewardship draws to a conclusion, when the windows begin to be darkened, when the bond of the family is to be loosed, there shall be no bitterness of remorse in our farewells.

Help us to look back on the long way that Thou hast brought us, on the

(Above) **"Folk of many families and nations": Vailima's American mistress (Fanny/Aolele), Samoan maid, North American bear rug, Pacific woven matting, Scottish fireplace, English coal scuttle, Polynesian kava bowl, and international ornaments.**

long days in which we have been served not according to our deserts but our desires; on the pit and the miry clay, the blackness of despair, the horror of misconduct, from which our feet have been plucked out. For our sins forgiven or prevented, for our shame unpublished, we bless and thank Thee, O God. Help us yet again and ever. So order events, so strengthen our frailty, as that day by day we shall come before Thee with this song of gratitude, and in the end we be dismissed with honour. In their weakness and their fear, the vessels of Thy handiwork so pray to Thee, so praise Thee. Amen.

Another In Time Of Rain

LORD, Thou sendest down rain upon the uncounted millions of the forest, and givest the trees to drink exceedingly. We are here upon this isle a few handfuls of men, and how many myriads upon myriads of stalwart trees! Teach us the lesson of the trees. The sea around us, which this rain recruits, teems with the race of fish: teach us, Lord, the meaning of the fishes. Let us see ourselves for what we are, one out of the countless number of the clans of Thy handiwork. When we would despair, let us remember that these also please and serve Thee.

Sunday

WE beseech Thee, Lord, to behold us with favour, folk of many families and nations gathered together in the peace of this roof, weak men and women subsisting under the covert of Thy patience. Be patient still; suffer us yet awhile longer; with our broken purposes of good, with our idle endeavours against evil, suffer us awhile longer to endure and (if it may be) help us to do better. Bless to us our extraordinary mercies; if the day come when these must be taken, brace us to play the man under affliction. Be with our friends, be with ourselves. Go with each of us to rest; if any awake, temper to them the dark hours of watching; and when the day returns, return to us, our sun and comforter, and call us up with morning faces and with morning hearts—eager to labour—eager to be happy, if happiness shall be our portion—and, if the day be marked for sorrow, strong to endure it.

We thank Thee and praise Thee; and in the words of Him to whom this day is sacred, close our oblation.

17

CONTEMPORARY HISTORY, GOLIATH'S HEAD, AND CEASELESS SONG:
SAMOA

In the first two years at Vailima, Stevenson continued to work on his new kind of travel writing with In the South Seas, *struggling, he wrote once, to find the right "style"; and on his new kind of fiction. He was conscious of being innovative, speaking repeatedly of his last novels and stories in terms like "the first realistic South Sea story" ('The Beach of Falesá'), "peculiarity about this tale"* (The Ebb-Tide), *"something different"* (Weir of Hermiston). *In 1891 he also began work on a new kind of history, "a piece of contemporary history in the most exact sense", pioneering the 20th century idea that history can be written as it happens.*

Stevenson often said that he hoped this book, A Footnote to History *(1892), would "help" the Samoan people, but this does not mean he simplified it in any facile way. Its main weakness, in fact, at least for non-Samoan readers, is that it becomes too complicated and esoteric. It explains a complex dispute that involved several Samoan factions (and that European word is not adequate to describe their subtle and shifting shades); three partly but not wholly rivalrous colonial nations, Germany, Great Britain and USA, all operating almost blind at that distance; and commercial, political, territorial and religious interests. This led to a military conflict fought partly with machetes and head-taking, partly by rifle-fire, and partly by the most destructive high-tech weaponry yet invented, the shell power of iron-clad steam warships.*

The point is that the reader is required to make the effort. This history begins, not with the arrival in the Pacific of the British or the Germans, but with Samoan "ideas and manners", that date back "before the Roman Empire". It explains Samoan systems of governance, custom, ceremony and language, stressing their *sophistication, long pedigree, and right to be respected. European ideas, he says, are neither absolute nor innately right (see also **21**). They are conditioned by their own history, especially their "memories of feudalism." To say, "Let us... conceive that etiquette and morals differ in one country and another" is to affirm an egalitarian principle not widely practised in 19th-century colonialism. It is made more provocative when rubbed in by the adroit suggestion that ritual head-taking originated with David and Goliath.*

THE ELEMENTS OF DISCORD: NATIVE

THE story I have to tell is still going on as I write; the characters are alive and active; it is a piece of contemporary history in the most exact sense. And yet, for all its actuality and the part played in it by mails and telegraphs and iron war-ships, the ideas and the manners of the native actors date back before the Roman Empire. They are Christians, church-goers, singers of hymns at family worship, hardy cricketers; their books are printed in London by Spottiswoode, Trübner, or the Tract Society; but in most other points they are the contemporaries of our tattooed ancestors who drove their chariots on the wrong side of the Roman wall. We have passed the feudal system; they are not yet clear of the patriarchal. We are in the thick of the age of finance; they are in a period of communism. And this makes them hard to understand.

To us, with our feudal ideas, Samoa has the first appearance of a land of despotism. An elaborate courtliness marks the race alone among Polynesians; terms of ceremony fly thick as oaths on board a ship; commoners my-lord each other when they meet—and urchins as they play marbles. And for the real noble a whole private dialect is set apart. The common names for an axe, for blood, for bamboo, a bamboo knife, a pig, food, entrails, and an oven are taboo in his presence, as the common names for a bug and for many offices and members of the body are taboo in the drawing-rooms of English ladies. Special words are set apart for his leg, his face, his hair, his belly, his eyelids, his son, his daughter, his wife, his wife's pregnancy, his wife's adultery, adultery with his wife, his dwelling, his spear, his comb, his sleep, his dreams, his anger, the mutual anger of several chiefs, his food, his pleasure in eating, the food and eating of his pigeons, his ulcers, his cough, his sickness, his recovery, his death, his being carried on a bier, the exhumation of his bones and his skull after death. To address these demigods is quite a branch of knowledge, and he who goes to visit a high chief does well to make sure of the competence of his interpreter. To complete the picture, the same word signifies the watching of a virgin and the warding of a chief; and the same word means to cherish a chief and to fondle a favourite child.

Men like us, full of memories of feudalism, hear of a man so addressed, so flattered, and we leap at once to the conclusion that he is hereditary and absolute. Hereditary he is; born of a great family, he must always be a man of mark; but yet his office is elective and (in a weak sense) is held on good behaviour. Compare the case of a Highland chief: born one of the great ones of his clan, he was sometimes appointed its chief officer and conventional father; was loved and respected and served and fed and died for implicitly, if he gave loyalty a chance; and yet, if he sufficiently outraged clan sentiment, was liable to deposition. As to authority, the parallel is not so close. Doubtless the Samoan chief, if he be popular, wields a great influence; but it is limited. Important matters are debated in a fono, or native parliament, with its feasting and parade, its endless speeches and polite genealogical allusions. Debated, I say—not decided; for even a small minority will often strike a clan or a province impotent. In the midst of these ineffective councils the chief sits usually silent: a kind of a gagged audience for village orators. And the deliverance of the fono seems (for the moment) to be final. The absolute chiefs of Tahiti and Hawaii were addressed as plain John and Thomas; the chiefs of Samoa are surfeited with lip-honour, but the seat and extent of their actual authority is hard to find.

It is so in the members of the state, and worse in the belly. The idea of a sovereign pervades the air. The name we have; the thing we are not so sure of. And the process of election to the chief power is a mystery. Certain provinces have in their gift certain high titles, or *names* as they are called. These can only be attributed to the descendants of particular lines. Once granted, each *name* conveys at once the principality (whatever that be worth) of the province which bestows it, and counts as one suffrage towards the general sovereignty of Samoa. To be indubitable king, they say—or some of them say, I find few in perfect harmony—a man should resume five of these names in his own person. But the case is purely hypothetical; local jealousy forbids its occurrence. There are rival provinces, far more concerned in the prosecution of their rivalry than in the choice of a right man for king. If one of these shall have bestowed its name on competitor A, it will be the signal and the sufficient reason for the other to bestow its name on competitor B or C. The majority of Savaii and that of Aana are thus in perennial opposition. Nor is this all. In 1881, Laupepa, the present king, held the three names of Malietoa, Natoaitele, and Tamasoalii; Tamasese held that of Tuiaana; and Mataafa that of Tuiatua. Laupepa had thus a majority of suffrages; he held perhaps as high a proportion as can be hoped in these distracted islands; and he counted among the number the preponderant name of Malietoa. Here, if ever, was an election. Here, if a king were at all possible, was the king. And yet the natives were not satisfied. Laupepa was crowned, March 19th; and next month, the provinces of Aana and Atua met in joint parliament, and elected their own two princes, Tamasese and Mataafa, to an alternate monarchy, Tamasese taking the first trick of two years. War was imminent when the consuls interfered, and any war were preferable to the terms of the peace which they procured...

If I am in the least right in my presentation of this obscure matter, no one need be surprised to hear that the land is full of war and rumours of war. Scarce a year goes by but what some province is in arms, or sits sulky and menacing, holding parliaments, disregarding the king's proclamations and planting food in the bush, the first step of military preparation. The religious sentiment of the people is indeed for peace at any price; no pastor can bear arms; and even the layman who does so is denied the sacraments. In the last war the college of Mālua, where the picked youth are prepared for the ministry, lost but a single student; the rest, in the bosom of a bleeding country and deaf to the voices of vanity and honour, peacefully pursued their studies. But if the church looks askance on war, the warrior in no extremity of need or passion forgets his consideration for the church. The houses and gardens of her ministers stand safe in the midst of armies; a way is reserved for themselves along the beach, where they may be seen in their white kilts and jackets openly passing the lines, while not a hundred yards behind the skirmishers will be exchanging the useless volleys of barbaric warfare. Women are also respected; they are not fired upon; and they are suffered to pass between the hostile camps, exchanging gossip, spreading rumour, and divulging to either army the secret councils of the other. This is plainly no savage war; it has all the punctilio of the barbarian, and all his parade; feasts precede battles, fine dresses and songs decorate and enliven the field; and the young soldier comes to camp burning (on the one hand) to distinguish himself by acts of valour,

(Above) **"Let us try... to conceive that etiquette and morals differ in one country and another."** **Sketch by Belle Strong of a head being formally presented at Vailima during the civil war.**

and (on the other) to display his acquaintance with field etiquette. Thus after Mataafa became involved in hostilities against the Germans, and had another code to observe besides his own, he was always asking his white advisers if "things were done correctly." Let us try to be as wise as Mataafa, and to conceive that etiquette and morals differ in one country and another. We shall be the less surprised to find Samoan war defaced with some unpalatable customs. The childish destruction of fruit trees in an enemy's country cripples the resources of Samoa; and the habit of head hunting not only revolts foreigners, but has begun to exercise the minds of the natives themselves. Soon after the German heads were taken, Mr. Carne, Wesleyan missionary, had occasion to visit Mataafa's camp, and spoke of the practice with abhorrence. "Misi Kāne," said one chief, "we have just been puzzling ourselves to guess where that custom came from. But, Misi, is it not so that when David killed Goliath, he cut off his head and carried it before the king?"

With the civil life of the inhabitants we have far less to do; and yet even here a word of preparation is inevitable. They are easy, merry, and pleasure loving; the gayest, though by far from either the most capable or the most beautiful of Polynesians. Fine dress is a passion, and makes a Samoan festival a thing of beauty. Song is almost ceaseless. The boatman sings at the oar, the family at evening worship, the girls at night in the guest house, sometimes the workman at his toil. No occasion is too small for the poets and musicians; a death, a visit, the day's news, the day's pleasantry, will be set to rhyme and harmony. Even half-grown girls, the occasion arising, fashion words and train choruses of children for its celebration. Song, as with all Pacific islanders, goes hand in hand with the dance, and both shade into the drama. Some of the performances are indecent and ugly, some only dull; others are pretty, funny, and attractive. Games are popular. Cricket matches, where a hundred played upon a side, endured at times for weeks, and ate up the country like the presence of an army. Fishing, the daily bath, flirtation; courtship, which is gone upon by proxy; conversation, which is largely political; and the delights of public oratory; fill in the long hours.

But the special delight of the Samoan is the *malanga*. When people form a party and go from village to village, junketing and gossiping, they are said to go on a *malanga*. Their songs have announced their approach ere they arrive; the guest house is prepared for their reception; the virgins of the village attend to prepare the kava bowl and entertain them with the dance; time flies in the enjoyment of every pleasure which an islander conceives; and when the *malanga* sets forth, the same welcome and the same joys expect them beyond the next cape, where the nearest village nestles in its grove of palms. To the visitors it is all golden; for the hosts, it has another side. In one or two words of the language the fact peeps slyly out. The same word *(afemoeima)* expresses "a long call" and "to come as a calamity"; the same word *(lesolosolou)* signifies "to have no intermission of pain" and "to have no cessation, as in the arrival of visitors" and *soua*, used of epidemics, bears the sense of being overcome as with "fire, flood, or visitors." But the gem of the dictionary is the verb *alovao*, which illustrates its pages like a humorous wood-cut. It is used in the sense of "to avoid visitors," but it means literally "hide in the wood." So, by the sure hand of popular speech, we have the picture of the house deserted, the *malanga* disappointed, and the host that should have been, quaking in the bush.

CONTEMPORARY HISTORY

18

THE BATTLE ON THE BEACH:

FANGALII, SAMOA

Stevenson told his New York publisher that half of any royalties for A Footnote to History *should be given to the Samoan people. (At first he intended to give all profits, but thought again about "the pinch of writing" for "the artisan", and changed his mind.) The book has always been discussed, on the rare occasions when it is noticed at all, as an expression of his commitment to Samoa. This is fair but inadequate. It is much more than a biographical footnote. The first time he mentions it in a letter, in February 1890, he writes of "interesting and picturesque details", and as he got into it he began to enthuse (in December 1891) about its purely literary potential and originality: "...the tale is so strange and mixed... Here is, for the first time, a tale of Greeks – Homeric Greeks – mingled with moderns, and all true; Odysseus alongside of Rajah Brooke... Here is for the first time since the Greeks (that I remember) the history of a handful of men, where all know each other in the eyes, and live close in a few acres, narrated at length, and with the seriousness of history. Talk of the modern novel; here is modern history."*

A writer in 1891 must be taking a book very seriously in literary terms to claim an epic-heroic quality comparable to Homer, combined with truth, topicality, strangeness, scale, intensity and the cutting edge of modern history.

From our 21st century perspective, we could now add (if it were ever read carefully enough) that A Footnote to History *is also a landmark in modern journalism, breaking down the barriers between reporting and history to produce something close to an "instant book" (published four years after the event). It is a precursor of Orwell's* Homage to Catalonia. *It is also, on the quality of its narrative reportage, a pioneering example of what is now called "creative non-fiction". Many of our own essays and literary reportage pieces, in what might be called the School of* Granta *and the* New Yorker*, as well as several major contemporary writers of documentary fiction, tread in the footsteps of* A Footnote.

Two extracts are offered to test these suggestions of a new way of reading the book. The first makes compelling and credible narrative out of the messy confusions of battle, as Stevenson of the Fight for the Stockade *in* Treasure Island *and the* Siege of the Round-House *in* Kidnapped *turns his hand to report an actual conflict on a Pacific shore. A German naval landing party plans to disarm Mata'afa's supporters as the first step to ending the civil war, but the Mata'afas suspect the Germans of complicity with the Tamaseses.*

December 16, 1888

MATAAFA sympathisers about Apia were on the alert. Knappe had informed the consuls that the ships were to put to sea next day for the protection of German property; but the Tamaseses had been less discreet. "To-morrow at the hour of seven," they had cried to their adversaries, "you will know of a difficulty, and our guns shall be made good in broken bones." An accident had pointed expectation towards Apia. The wife of Le Māmea washed for the German ships—a perquisite, I suppose, for her husband's unwilling fidelity. She sent a man with linen on board the *Adler*, where he was surprised to see Le Māmea in person, and to be himself ordered instantly on shore. The news spread. If Māmea were brought down from Lotonauu, others might have come at the same time. Tamasese himself and half his army might perhaps lie concealed on board the German ships. And a watch was accordingly set and warriors collected along the line of the shore.

One detachment lay in some rifle-pits by the mouth of the Fuisá. They were commanded by Seumanu; and with this party, probably as the most contiguous to Apia, was the war-correspondent, John Klein. Of English birth, but naturalised American, this gentleman had been for some time representing the *New York World* in a very effective manner, always in the front, living in the field with the Samoans, and in all vicissitudes of weather, toiling to and fro with his despatches. His wisdom was perhaps not equal to his energy. He made himself conspicuous, going about armed to the teeth in a boat under the stars and stripes; and on one occasion, when he supposed himself fired upon by the Tamaseses, had the petulance to empty his revolver in the direction of their camp. By the light of the moon, which was then nearly down, this party observed the *Olga's* two boats and the praam, which they describe as "almost sinking with men," the boats keeping well out towards the reef, the praam at the moment apparently heading for the shore.

An extreme agitation seems to have reigned in the rifle-pits. What were the newcomers? What was their errand? Were they Germans or Tamaseses? Had they a mind to attack? The praam was hailed in Samoan and did not answer. It was proposed to fire upon her ere she drew near. And at last, whether on his own suggestion or that of Seumanu, Klein hailed her in English and in terms of unnecessary melodrama. "Do not try to land here," he cried. "If you do your blood will be upon your head." Spengler, who had never the least intention to touch at the Fuisá, put up the head of the praam to her true course and continued to move up the lagoon with an offing of some seventy or eighty yards. Along all the irregularities and obstructions of the beach, across the mouth of the Vaivasa, and through the startled village of Matafangatele, Seumanu, Klein, and seven or eight others raced to keep up, spreading the alarm and rousing re-enforcements as they went. Presently a man on horseback made his appearance on the opposite beach of Fangalii. Klein and the natives distinctly saw him signal with a lantern; which is the more strange, as the horseman (Captain Hufnagel, plantation manager of Vailele) had never a lantern to signal with.

The praam kept in. Many men in white were seen to stand up, step overboard, and wade to shore. At the same time the eye of panic descried a breastwork of "foreign stones" (brick) upon the beach. Samoans are prepared to-day to swear to its existence, I believe conscientiously, although no such thing was ever made or ever intended in that place. The hour is doubtful. "It was the hour when the streak of dawn is seen, the hour known in the warfare of heathen times as the hour of the night attack," says the Mataafa official account. A native whom I met on the field declared it was at cockcrow. Captain Hufnagel, on the other hand, is sure it was long before the day. It was dark at least, and the moon down. Darkness made the Samoans bold; uncertainty as to the composition and purpose of the landing party made them desperate. Fire was opened on the Germans, one of whom was here killed. The Germans returned it and effected a lodgement on the beach; and the skirmish died again to silence. It was at this time, if not earlier, that Klein returned to Apia.

(Above) **"When the drums of war reverberate in the land." Samoan fort, 1888.**

Here, then, were Spengler and the ninety men of the praam, landed on the beach in no very enviable posture, the woods in front filled with unnumbered enemies, but for the time successful. Meanwhile, Jaeckel and the boats had gone outside the reef, and were to land on the other side of the Vailele promontory, at Sunga, by the buildings of the plantation. It was Hufnagel's part to go and meet them. His way led straight into the woods and through the midst of the Samoans, who had but now ceased firing. He went in the saddle and at a foot's pace, feeling speed and concealment to be equally helpless, and that if he were to fall at all, he had best fall with dignity. Not a shot was fired at him; no effort made to arrest him on his errand. As he went, he spoke and even jested with the Samoans, and they answered in good part. One fellow was leaping, yelling, and tossing his axe in the air, after the way of an excited islander. *"Faimalosi!* go it!" said Hufnagel, and the fellow laughed and redoubled his exertions.

As soon as the boats entered the lagoon, fire was again opened from the woods. The fifty blue-jackets jumped overboard, hove down the boats to be a shield, and dragged them towards the landing place. In this way, their rations, and (what was more unfortunate) some of their miserable provision of forty

THE BATTLE ON THE BEACH

rounds got wetted; but the men came to shore and garrisoned the plantation house without a casualty. Meanwhile the sound of the firing from Sunga immediately renewed the hostilities at Fangalii. The civilians on shore decided that Spengler must be at once guided to the house, and Haideln, the surveyor, accepted the dangerous errand. Like Hufnagel, he was suffered to pass without question through the midst of these platonic enemies. He found Spengler some way inland on a knoll, disastrously engaged, the woods around him filled with Samoans, who were continuously re-enforced. In three successive charges, cheering as they ran, the blue-jackets burst through their scattered opponents, and made good their junction with Jaeckel. Four men only remained upon the field, the other wounded being helped by their comrades or dragging themselves painfully along.

The force was now concentrated in the house and its immediate patch of garden. Their rear, to the seaward, was unmolested; but on three sides they were beleaguered. On the left, the Samoans occupied and fired from some of the plantation offices. In front, a long rising crest of land in the horse-pasture commanded the house and was lined with the assailants. And on the right, the hedge of the same paddock afforded them a dangerous cover. It was in this place that a Samoan sharp-shooter was knocked over by Jaeckel with his own hand. The fire was maintained by the Samoans in the usual wasteful style. The roof was made a sieve; the balls passed clean through the house; Lieutenant Sieger, as he lay, already dying, on Hufnagel's bed, was despatched with a fresh wound. The Samoans showed themselves extremely enterprising: pushed their lines forward, ventured beyond cover, and continually threatened to envelop the garden. Thrice, at least, it was necessary to repel them by a sally. The men were brought into the house from the rear, the front doors were thrown suddenly open, and the gallant blue-jackets issued cheering: necessary, successful, but extremely costly sorties. Neither could these be pushed far. The foes were undaunted; so soon as the sailors advanced at all deep in the horse-pasture, the Samoans began to close in upon both flanks; and the sally had to be recalled. To add to the dangers of the German situation, ammunition began to run low; and the cartridge-boxes of the wounded and the dead had been already brought in use before, at about eight o'clock, the *Eber* steamed into the bay. Her commander, Wallis, threw some shells into Letongo, one of which killed five men about their cooking-pot. The Samoans began immediately to withdraw; their movements were hastened by a sortie, and the remains of the landing party brought on board. This was an unfortunate movement; it gave an irremediable air of defeat to what might have been else claimed for a moderate success. The blue-jackets numbered a hundred and forty all told; they were engaged separately and fought under the worst conditions, in the dark, and among woods; their position in the house was scarce tenable; they lost in killed and wounded fifty-six—forty per cent; and their spirit to the end was above question. Whether we think of the poor sailor lads, always so pleasantly behaved in times of peace, or whether we call to mind the behaviour of the two civilians, Haideln and Hufnagel, we can only regret that brave men should stand to be exposed upon so poor a quarrel or lives cast away upon an enterprise so hopeless.

News of the affair reached Apia early, and Moors, always curious of these spectacles of war, was immediately in the saddle. Near Matafangatele, he met a Manono chief, whom he asked if there were any German dead. "I think there are about thirty of them knocked over," said he.—"Have you taken their heads?" asked Moors.—"Yes," said the chief. "Some foolish people did it, but I have stopped them. We ought not to cut off their heads when they do not cut off ours." He was asked what had been done with the heads. "Two have gone to Mataafa," he replied, "and one is buried right under where your horse is standing, in a basket wrapped in tapa." This was afterwards dug up, and I am told on native authority that, besides the three heads, two ears were taken. Moors next asked the Manono man how he came to be going away. "The man-of-war is throwing shells," said he. "When they stopped firing out of the house, we stopped firing also; so it was as well to scatter when the shells began. We could have killed all the white men. I wish they had been Tamaseses." This is an *ex parte* statement, and I give it for such; but the course of the affair, and in particular the adventures of Haideln and Hufnagel, testify to a surprising lack of animosity against the Germans.

About the same time or but a little earlier than this conversation, the same spirit was being displayed. Hufnagel, with a party of labourers, had gone out to bring in the German dead, when he was surprised to be suddenly fired on from the wood. The boys he had with him were not negritos, but Polynesians from the Gilbert Islands; and he suddenly remembered that these might be easily mistaken for a detachment of Tamaseses. Bidding his boys conceal themselves in a thicket, this brave man walked into the open. So soon as he was recognised, the firing ceased, and the labourers followed him in safety. This is

THE BATTLE ON THE BEACH

chivalrous war; but there was a side to it less chivalrous. As Moors drew near to Vailele, he began to meet Samoans with hats, guns, and even shirts taken from the German sailors. With one of these who had a hat and a gun, he stopped and spoke. The hat was handed up for him to look at; it had the late owner's name on the inside. "Where is he?" asked Moors—"He is dead; I cut his head off."—"You shot him?"—"No, somebody else shot him in the hip. When I came, he put up his hands, and cried: 'Don't kill me; I am a Malietoa man.' I did not believe him, and I cut his head off."—"Have you any ammunition to fit that gun?"—"I do not know."—"What has become of the cartridge belt?"—"Another fellow grabbed that and the cartridges, and he won't give them to me." A dreadful and silly picture of barbaric war. The words of the German sailor must be regarded as imaginary: how was the poor lad to speak native, or the Samoan to understand German?

When Moors came as far as Sunga, the *Eber* was yet in the bay, the smoke of battle still lingered among the trees, which were themselves marked with a thousand bullet-wounds. But the affair was over, the combatants, German and Samoan, were all gone, and only a couple of negrito labour boys lurked on the scene. The village of Letongo beyond was equally silent; part of it was wrecked by the shells of the *Eber*, and still smoked; the inhabitants had fled. On the beach were the native boats, perhaps five thousand dollars' worth, deserted by the Mataafas and overlooked by the Germans, in their common hurry to escape. Still Moors held eastward by the sea-paths. It was his hope to get a view from the other side of the promontory, towards Laulii. In the way he found a house hidden in the wood and among rocks, where an aged and sick woman was being tended by her elderly daughter. Last lingerers in that deserted piece of coast, they seemed indifferent to the events which had thus left them solitary, and, as the daughter said, did not know where Mataafa was, nor where Tamasese.

It is the official Samoan pretension that the Germans fired first at Fangalii. In view of all German and some native testimony, the text of Fritze's orders, and the probabilities of the case, no honest mind will believe it for a moment. Certainly the Samoans fired first. As certainly they were betrayed into the engagement in the agitation of the moment, and it was not till afterwards that they understood what they had done. Then, indeed, all Samoa drew a breath of wonder and delight. The invincible had fallen; the men of the vaunted warships had been met in the field by the braves of Mataafa: a superstition was no more. Conceive this people steadily as schoolboys; and, conceive the elation in any school if the head boy should suddenly arise and drive the rector from the schoolhouse. I have received one instance of the feeling instantly aroused. There lay at the time in the consular hospital an old chief who was a pet of the colonel's. News reached him of the glorious event; he was sick, he thought himself sinking, sent for the colonel, and gave him his gun. "Don't let the Germans get it," said the old gentleman, and having received a promise, was at peace.

19

THE HURRICANE:

APIA, SAMOA

The first thing Stevenson aboard the Equator *saw in Apia Harbour was "the warships still piled [on the reef] from last year's hurricane, some under water, one high and dry upon her side, the strangest figure of a ship was ever witnessed." To get the emotional force of that sight to a passenger by sea in 1889, you need to imagine six crashed aircraft piled alongside the runway as you land.*

He was soon pursuing the details of the disaster, and the war that was its context. "The truth often very hard to come at", he said, but worked up his German, "mugging with a dictionary from five to six hours a day", and took trouble "to call upon, keep sweet, and judiciously interview all sorts of persons – English, American, German, and Samoan. It makes a hard life."

*Compiled from those interviews is the chapter "The Hurricane", a piece of vivid reportage and an important piece of writing about a climactic Pacific event. In the context of "contemporary history", he ends by reflecting on the disaster's significance. By breaking "the sword-arm of each of the two angry powers", Germany and USA, the storm propelled them, along with Britain, to the conference table, and to sign the Treaty of Berlin on 14 July 1889. Although the freedom granted to the Samoans to appoint their own leaders proved only nominal, Bismarck was chastened, the next chapter says, to seek "a peaceable solution" and leave Fangalii (see **18**) unavenged. More epoch-making, its loss of three ships impelled America to the nationalistic decision to build a modern navy. If Stevenson is right (A Footnote was published 1892), the wrecking of the* Trenton, Nipsic *and* Vandalia *in Apia Harbour was prologue to the even more symbolically potent sinking of the Battleship* Maine *in Havana Harbour in 1898; and thus to the* *whole subsequent programme of naval-backed expansion by the United States. The navy that Stevenson says was conceived in the Apia hurricane became a central fact of Pacific and world history.*

Whatever the merits of these ideas, the hurricane chapter is unquestionably powerful as narrative, catching the hurl and fury and "sickening peril" in prose of surging urgency. Stevenson's telling makes it a fully human drama, with the decisions and indecisions of the captains and consuls, the helpless tragedy of so many seamen, the survivors on the doomed American flagship cheering the British vessel escaping out to sea, the officer dying "from agony of mind" in his capsized cabin, the captain swept from his deck, the brave perplexity of the German consul, the generous courage of the Samoan rescuers. Yet its dynamic comes always from the storm itself, and sometimes the prose almost gasps to find words for the enormity of what occurred: "...there she lies high and dry, the spray scarce touching her — the hugest structure of man's hands within a circuit of a thousand miles — tossed up there like a schoolboy's cap on a shelf; broken like an egg; a thing to dream of." As an image of humiliated hubris, that might almost have been an epitaph for the Titanic *two decades later.*

One letter to his publisher speaks of making the book attractive by "the high note of the hurricane and the warships". He struck it with resonance. It is a mark of his craft that he makes us so vividly witness to an event he had not actually seen, any more than Daniel Defoe had walked the streets of London in the Plague Year.

THE HURRICANE

March, 1889

THE so-called harbour of Apia is formed in part by a recess of the coast-line at Matautu, in part by the slim peninsula of Mulinuu, and in part by the fresh waters of the Mulivai and Vaisingano. The barrier reef—that singular break-water that makes so much of the circuit of Pacific islands—is carried far to sea at Matautu and Mulinuu; inside of these two horns it runs sharply landward, and between them it is burst or dissolved by the fresh water. The shape of the inclosed anchorage may be compared to a high-shouldered jar or bottle with a funnel mouth. Its sides are almost everywhere of coral; for the reef not only bounds it to seaward and forms the neck and mouth, but skirting about the beach, it forms the bottom also. As in the bottle of commerce, the bottom is re-entrant, and the shore-reef runs prominently forth into the basin and makes a dangerous cape opposite the fairway of the entrance. Danger is, therefore, on all hands. The entrance gapes three cables wide at the narrowest, and the formidable surf of the Pacific thunders both outside and in. There are days when speech is difficult in the chambers of shoreside houses; days when no boat can land, and when men are broken by stroke of sea against the wharves. As I write these words, three miles in the mountains, and with the land breeze still blowing from the island summit, the sound of that vexed harbour hums in my ears. Such a creek in my native coast of Scotland would scarce be dignified with the mark of an anchor in the chart; but in the favoured climate of Samoa, and with the mechanical regularity of the winds in the Pacific, it forms, for ten or eleven months out of the twelve, a safe if hardly a commodious port. The ill-found island traders ride there with their insufficient moorings the year through, and discharge, and are loaded, without apprehension. Of danger, when it comes, the glass gives timely warning; and that any modern war-ship, furnished with the power of steam, should have been lost in Apia, belongs not so much to nautical as to political history.

The weather throughout all that winter (the turbulent summer of the islands) was unusually fine, and the circumstance had been commented on as providential, when so many Samoans were lying on their weapons in the bush. By February it began to break in occasional gales. On February 10th, a German brigantine was driven ashore. On the 14th, the same misfortune befell an American brigantine and a schooner. On both these days, and again on the 7th March, the men-of-war must steam to their anchors. And it was in this last month, the most dangerous of the twelve, that man's animosities crowded that indentation of the reef with costly, populous, and vulnerable ships.

I have shown, perhaps already at too great a length, how violently passion ran upon the spot; how high this series of blunders and mishaps had heated the resentment of the Germans against all other nationalities and of all other nationalities against the Germans. But there was one country beyond the borders of Samoa where the question had aroused a scarce less angry sentiment. The breach of the Washington Congress, the evidence of Sewall before a sub-committee on foreign relations, the proposal to try Klein before a military court, and the rags of Captain Hamilton's flag, had combined to stir the people of the States to an unwonted fervour. Germany was for the time the abhorred of nations. Germans in America publicly disowned the country of their birth. In Honolulu, so near the scene of action, German and American young men fell to blows in the street. In the same city, from no traceable source and upon no possible authority, there arose tragic news to arrive by the next occasion, that the *Nipsic* had opened fire on the *Adler*, and the *Adler* had sunk her on the first reply. Punctually on the day appointed, the news came; and the two nations, instead of being plunged in war, could only mingle tears over the loss of heroes.

By the second week in March, three American ships were in Apia bay— the *Nipsic*, the *Vandalia*, and the *Trenton*, carrying the flag of Rear-Admiral Kimberley; three German—the *Adler*, the *Eber*, and the *Olga*; and one British—the *Calliope*, Captain Kane. Six merchantmen, ranging from twenty-five up to five hundred tons, and a number of small craft, further encumbered the anchorage. Its capacity is estimated by Captain Kane at four large ships; and the latest arrivals, the *Vandalia*, and *Trenton*, were in consequence excluded, and lay without in the passage. Of the seven warships, the sea-worthiness of two was questionable: the *Trenton's*, from an original defect in her construction, often reported, never remedied—her hawse-pipes leading in on the berth-deck; the *Eber's*, from an injury to her screw in the blow of February 14th. In this over-crowding of ships in an open entry of the reef, even the eye of a landsman could spy danger; and Captain-Lieutenant Wallis of the *Eber* openly blamed and lamented, not many hours before the catastrophe, their helpless posture. Temper once more triumphed. The army of Mataafa still hung imminent behind the town; the German quarter was still daily garrisoned with fifty sailors from the squadron; what was yet more influential, Germany and the States, at least in Apia bay, were on the brink of war, viewed each other with looks of hatred, and scarce observed the letter of civility. On the day of the admiral's arrival, Knappe failed to call on him, and on the morrow called on him while he was on shore. The slight was remarked and resented, and the two squadrons clung the more obstinately to their dangerous station.

On the 15th, the barometer fell to 29.11 in. by 2 P.M. This was the moment when every sail in port should have escaped. Kimberley, who flew the only broad pennant, should certainly have led the way: he clung, instead, to his moorings, and the Germans doggedly followed his example: semi-belligerents, daring each other and the violence of heaven. Kane, less immediately involved, was led in error by the report of residents and a fallacious rise in the glass; he stayed with the others, a misjudgment that was like to cost him dear. All were moored, as is the custom in Apia, with two anchors practically east and west, clear hawse to the north, and a kedge astern. Topmasts were struck, and the ships made snug. The night closed black, with sheets of rain. By midnight it blew a gale; and by the morning watch, a tempest. Through what remained of darkness the captains impatiently expected day, doubtful if they were dragging, steaming gingerly to their moorings, and afraid to steam too much.

Day came about six, and presented to those on shore a seizing and terrific spectacle. In the pressure of the squalls, the bay was obscured as if by midnight, but between them a great part of it was clearly if darkly visible amid driving mist and rain. The wind blew into the harbour mouth. Naval authorities describe it as of hurricane force. It had, however, few or none of the effects on shore suggested by that ominous word, and was successfully withstood by trees and buildings. The agitation of the sea, on the other hand, surpassed experience and description. Seas that might have awakened surprise and terror in the midst of the Atlantic, ranged bodily and (it seemed to observers) almost without diminution into the belly of that flask-shaped harbour; and the war-ships were alternately buried from view in the trough, or seen standing on end against the breast of billows.

The *Trenton* at daylight still maintained her position in the neck of the bottle. But five of the remaining ships tossed, already close to the bottom, in a perilous and helpless crowd; threatening ruin to each other as they tossed; threatened with a common and imminent destruction on the reefs. Three had been already in collision: the *Olga* was injured in the quarter, the *Adler* had lost her bowsprit; the *Nipsic* had lost her smoke-stack, and was making steam with difficulty, maintaining her fire with barrels of pork, and the smoke and sparks pouring along the level of the deck. For the seventh war-ship, the day had come too late; the *Eber* had finished her last cruise; she was to be seen no more save by the eyes of divers. A coral reef is not only an instrument of destruction, but a place of sepulture; the submarine cliff is profoundly undercut, and presents the mouth of a huge antre, in which the bodies of men and the hulls of ships are alike hurled down and buried. The *Eber* had dragged anchors with the rest; her injured screw disabled her from steaming vigorously up; and a little before day, she had struck the front of the coral, come off, struck again, and gone down stern foremost, oversetting as she went, into the gaping hollow of the reef. Of her whole complement of nearly eighty, four souls were cast alive on the beach; and the bodies of the remainder were, by the voluminous outpouring of the flooded streams, scoured at last from the harbour, and strewed naked on the seaboard of the island.

Five ships were immediately menaced with the same destruction. The *Eber* vanished—the four poor survivors on shore read a dreadful commentary on their danger; which was swelled out of all proportion by the violence of their own movements as they leaped and fell among the billows. By seven, the *Nipsic* was so fortunate as to avoid the reef and beach upon a space of sand; where she was immediately deserted by her crew, with the assistance of Samoans, not without loss of life. By about eight, it was the turn of the *Adler*. She was close down upon the reef; doomed herself, it might yet be possible to save a portion of her crew; and for this end, Captain Fritze placed his reliance on the very hugeness of the seas that threatened him. The moment was watched for with the anxiety of despair, but the coolness of disciplined courage. As she rose on the fatal wave, her moorings were simultaneously slipped; she broached to in rising; and the sea heaved her bodily upward and cast her down with a concussion on the summit of the reef, where she lay on her beam ends, her back broken, buried in breaching seas, but safe. Conceive a table: the *Eber* in the darkness had been smashed against the rim and flung below; the *Adler*, cast free in the nick of opportunity, had been thrown upon the top. Many were injured in the concussion; many tossed into the water; twenty perished. The survivors crept again on board their ship, as it now lay, and as it still remains, keel to the waves, a monument of the sea's potency. In still weather, under a cloudless sky, in those seasons when that ill-named ocean, the Pacific, suffers its vexed shores to rest, she lies high and dry, the spray scarce touching her—the hugest structure of man's hands within a circuit of a thousand miles—tossed up there like a schoolboy's cap upon a shelf; broken like an egg: a thing to dream of.

The unfriendly consuls of Germany and Britain were both that morning in Matautu, and both displayed their nobler qualities. De Coetlogon, the grim old soldier, collected his family and kneeled with them in an agony of prayer for those exposed. Knappe, more fortunate in that he was called to a more active service, must, upon the striking of the *Adler*, pass to his own consulate. From this he was divided by the Vaisingano, now a raging torrent, impetuously charioting the trunks of trees. A kelpie might have dreaded to attempt

(Above) **"The hugest structure of man's hands within a circuit of a thousand miles – tossed up there like a schoolboy's cap upon a shelf; broken like an egg."** Wrecked ships in Apia Harbour after hurricane.

the passage; we may conceive this brave but unfortunate and now ruined man to have found a natural joy in the exposure of his life; and twice that day, coming and going, he braved the fury of the river. It was possible, in spite of the darkness of the hurricane and the continual breaching of the seas, to remark human movements on the *Adler*; and by the help of Samoans, always nobly forward in the work, whether for friend or enemy, Knappe sought long to get a line conveyed from shore, and was for long defeated. The shore guard of fifty men stood to their arms the while upon the beach, useless themselves, and a great deterrent of Samoan usefulness. It was perhaps impossible that this mistake should be avoided. What more natural, to the mind of a European, than that the Mataafas should fall upon the Germans in this hour of their disadvantage? But they had no other thought than to assist; and those who now rallied beside Knappe braved (as they supposed) in doing so a double danger, from the fury of the sea and the weapons of their enemies. About nine, a quartermaster swam ashore, and reported all the officers and some sixty men alive, but in pitiable case; some with broken limbs, others insensible from the drenching of the breakers. Later in the forenoon, certain valorous Samoans succeeded in reaching the wreck and returning with a line; but it was speedily broken; and all subsequent attempts proved unavailing, the strongest adventurers being cast back again by the bursting seas. Thenceforth, all through that day and night, the deafened survivors must continue to endure their martyrdom; and one officer died, it was supposed from agony of mind, in his inverted cabin.

Three ships still hung on the next margin of destruction, steaming desperately to their moorings, dashed helplessly together. The *Calliope* was the nearest in; she had the *Vandalia* close on her port side and a little ahead, the *Olga* close a-starboard, the reef under her heel; and steaming and veering on her cables, the unhappy ship fenced with her three dangers. About a quarter to nine she carried away the *Vandalia's* quarter gallery with her jib-boom; a moment later, the *Olga* had near rammed her from the other side. By nine the *Vandalia* dropped down on her too fast to be avoided, and clapped her stern under the bowsprit of the English ship, the fastenings of which were burst asunder as she rose. To avoid cutting her down, it was necessary for the *Calliope* to stop and even to reverse her engines; and her rudder was at the moment—or it seemed so to the eyes of those on board—within ten feet of the reef. "Between the *Vandalia* and the reef" (writes Kane, in his excellent report) "it was destruction." To repeat Fritze's manoeuvre with the *Adler* was impossible; the *Calliope* was too heavy. The one possibility of escape was to go out. If the engines should stand, if they should have power to drive the ship against wind and sea, if she should answer the helm, if the wheel, rudder, and gear should hold out, and if they were favoured with a clear blink of weather in which to see and avoid the outer reef—there, and there only, were safety. Upon this catalogue of "ifs" Kane staked his all. He signalled to the engineer for every pound of steam—and at that moment (I am told) much of the machinery was already red hot. The ship was sheered well to starboard of the *Vandalia*, the last remaining cable slipped. For a time—and there was no on-looker so cold-blooded as to offer a guess at its duration—the *Calliope* lay stationary; then gradually drew ahead. The highest speed claimed for her that day is of one sea-mile an hour. The question of times and seasons, throughout all this roaring business, is obscured by a dozen contradictions; I have but chosen what appeared to be the most consistent; but if I am to pay any attention to the time named by Admiral Kimberley, the *Calliope*, in this first stage of her escape, must have taken more than two hours to cover less than four cables. As she thus crept seaward, she buried bow and stern alternately under the billows.

In the fairway of the entrance, the flagship *Trenton* still held on. Her rudder was broken, her wheel carried away; within she was flooded with water from the peccant hawse-pipes; she had just made the signal "fires extinguished," and lay helpless, awaiting the inevitable end. Between this melancholy hulk and the external reef, Kane must find a path. Steering within fifty yards of the reef (for which she was actually headed) and her foreyard passing on the other hand over the *Trenton's* quarter as she rolled, the *Calliope* sheered between the rival dangers, came to the wind triumphantly, and was once more pointed for the sea and safety. Not often in naval history was there a moment of more sickening peril, and it was dignified by one of those incidents that reconcile the chronicler with his otherwise abhorrent task. From the doomed flagship, the Americans hailed the success of the English with a cheer. It was led by the old admiral in person, rang out over the storm with holiday vigour, and was answered by the Calliopes with an emotion easily conceived. This ship of their kinsfolk was almost the last external object seen from the *Calliope* for hours; immediately after, the mists closed about her till the morrow. She was safe at sea again—*una de multis*—with a damaged foreyard, and a loss of all the ornamental work about her bow and stern, three anchors, one kedge anchor, fourteen lengths of chain, four boats, the jib-boom, bobstay, and bands and fastenings of the bowsprit.

Shortly after Kane had slipped his cable, Captain Schoonmaker, despairing of the *Vandalia*, succeeded in passing astern of the *Olga*, in the hope to beach his ship beside the *Nipsic*. At a quarter to eleven her stern took the reef, her head swung to starboard, and she began to fill and settle. Many lives of brave men were sacrificed in the attempt to get a line ashore; the captain, exhausted by his exertions, was swept from deck by a sea; and the rail being soon awash, the survivors took refuge in the tops.

Out of thirteen that had lain there the day before, there were now but two ships afloat in Apia harbour, and one of these was doomed to be the bane of the other. About 3 P.M. the *Trenton* parted one cable, and shortly after second. It was sought to keep her head to wind with storm sails and by the ingenious expedient of filling the rigging with seamen; but in the fury of the gale, and in that sea perturbed alike by the gigantic billows and the volleying discharges of the rivers, the rudderless ship drove down stern foremost into the inner basin; ranging, plunging, and striking like a frightened horse; drifting on destruction for herself and bringing it to others. Twice the *Olga* (still well under command) avoided her impact by the skilful use of helm and engines. But about four the vigilance of the Germans was deceived, and the ships collided; the *Olga* cutting into the *Trenton's* quarters, first from one side, then from the other, and losing at the same time two of her own cables. Captain von Ehrhardt instantly slipped the remainder of his moorings, and setting fore and aft canvas and going full steam ahead, succeeded in beaching his ship in Matautu; whither Knappe, recalled by this new disaster, had returned. The berth was perhaps the best in the harbour, and von Ehrhardt signalled that ship and crew were in security.

The *Trenton*, guided apparently by an undertow or eddy from the discharge of the Vaisingano, followed in the course of the *Nipsic* and *Vandalia*, and skirted south-eastward along the front of the shore reef, which her keel was at times almost touching. Hitherto she had brought disaster to her foes; now she was bringing it to friends. She had already proved the ruin of the *Olga*, the one ship that had rid out the hurricane in safety; now she beheld across her course the submerged *Vandalia*, the tops filled with exhausted seamen. Happily the approach of the *Trenton* was gradual, and the time employed to advantage. Rockets and lines were thrown into the tops of the friendly wreck; the approach of danger was transformed into a means of safety; and before the ships struck, the men from the *Vandalia's* main and mizzen masts, which went immediately by the board in the collision, were already mustered on the *Trenton's* decks. Those from the foremast were next rescued; and the flagship settled gradually into a position alongside her neighbour, against which she beat all night with violence. Out of the crew of the *Vandalia* forty-three had perished; of the four hundred and fifty on board the *Trenton*, only one.

The night of the 16th was still notable for a howling tempest and extraordinary floods of rain. It was feared the wrecks could scarce continue to endure the breaching of the seas; among the Germans, the fate of those on board the *Adler* awoke keen anxiety; and Knappe, on the beach of Matautu, and the other officers of his consulate on that of Matafele, watched all night. The morning of the 17th displayed a scene of devastation rarely equalled: the *Adler* high and dry, the *Olga* and *Nipsic* beached, the *Trenton* partly piled on the *Vandalia* and herself sunk to the gundeck; no sail afloat; and the beach heaped high with the débris of ships and the wreck of mountain forests. Already, before the day, Seumanu, the chief of Apia, had gallantly ventured forth by boat through the subsiding fury of the seas, and had succeeded in communicating with the admiral; already, or as soon after as the dawn permitted, rescue lines were rigged, and the survivors were with difficulty and danger begun to be brought to shore. And soon the cheerful spirit of the admiral added a new feature to the scene. Surrounded as he was by the crews of two wrecked ships, he paraded the band of the *Trenton*, and the bay was suddenly enlivened with the strains of "Hail Columbia."

During a great part of the day, the work of rescue was continued, with many instances of courage and devotion; and for a long time succeeding, the almost inexhaustible harvest of the beach was to be reaped. In the first employment, the Samoans earned the gratitude of friend and foe; in the second, they surprised all by an unexpected virtue, that of honesty. The greatness of the disaster, and the magnitude of the treasure now rolling at their feet, may perhaps have roused in their bosoms an emotion too serious for the rule of greed, or perhaps that greed was for the moment satiated. Sails that twelve strong Samoans could scarce drag from the water, great guns (one of which was rolled by the sea on the body of a man, the only native slain in all the hurricane), an infinite wealth of rope and wood, of tools and weapons, tossed upon the beach. Yet I have never heard that much was stolen; and beyond question, much was very honestly returned. On both accounts, for the saving of life and the restoration of property, the government of the United States showed themselves generous in reward. A fine boat was fitly presented to Seumanu; and rings, watches, and money were lavished on all who had assisted. The Germans also gave money at the rate (as I receive the tale) of three dollars a head for every German saved. The obligation was in this instance incommensurably deep; those with whom they were at war had saved the German blue-jackets at the venture of their lives; Knappe was, besides, far from ungenerous; and I can only explain the niggard figure, by supposing it was paid from his own pocket. In one case, at least, it was refused. "I have saved three Germans," said the rescuer; "I will make you a present of the three."

The crews of the American and German squadrons were now cast, still in a bellicose temper, together on the beach. The discipline of the Americans was notoriously loose; the crew of the *Nipsic* had earned a character for lawlessness in other ports; and recourse was had to stringent and indeed extraordinary measures. The town was divided in two camps, to which the different nationalities were confined. Kimberley had his quarter sentinelled and patrolled. Any seaman disregarding a challenge was to be shot dead; any tavern-keeper who sold spirits to an American sailor was to have his tavern broken and his stock destroyed. Many of the publicans were German; and Knappe, having narrated these rigorous but necessary dispositions, wonders (grinning to himself over his despatch) how far these Americans will go in their assumption of jurisdiction over Germans? Such as they were, the measures were successful. The incongruous mass of castaways was kept in peace, and at last shipped in peace out of the islands.

Kane returned to Apia on the 19th, to find the *Calliope* the sole survivor of thirteen sail. He thanked his men, and in particular the engineers, in a speech of unusual feeling and beauty, of which one who was present remarked to another, as they left the ship, "This has been a means of grace." Nor did he forget to thank and compliment the admiral; and I cannot deny myself the pleasure of transcribing from Kimberley's reply some generous and engaging words. "My dear captain," he wrote, "your kind note received. You went out splendidly, and we all felt from our hearts for you, and our cheers came with sincerity and admiration for the able manner in which you handled your ship. We could not have been gladder if it had been one of our ships, for in a time like that I can say truly with old Admiral Josiah Tatnall, 'that blood *is* thicker than water.'" One more trait will serve to build up the image of this typical sea-officer. A tiny schooner, the *Equator*, Captain Edwin Reid, dear to myself from the memories of a six months' cruise, lived out upon the high seas the fury of that tempest which had piled with wrecks the harbour of Apia, found a refuge in Pango-pango, and arrived at last in the desolated port with a welcome and lucrative cargo of pigs. The admiral was glad to have the pigs; but what most delighted the man's noble and childish soul was to see once more afloat the colours of his country.

Thus, in what seemed the very article of war, and within the duration of a single day, the sword-arm of each of the two angry powers was broken; their formidable ships reduced to junk; their disciplined hundreds to a horde of castaways, fed with difficulty, and the fear of whose misconduct marred the sleep of their commanders. Both paused aghast; both had time to recognise that not the whole Samoan Archipelago was worth the loss in men and costly ships already suffered. The so-called hurricane of March 16th made thus a marking epoch in world-history; directly, and at once, it brought about the congress and treaty of Berlin; indirectly, and by a process still continuing, it founded the modern navy of the States. Coming years and other historians will declare the influence of that.

20

THE ROAD OF GRATITUDE:
VAILIMA, SAMOA

A Footnote to History *is strongly supportive of the chief Mata'afa, and critical of Germany's imperiousness in appointing his rival, Malieto Laupepa, as nominal king against majority wishes. Stevenson pursued the matter in a series of vigorous letters to the* Times *of London and other journals, from October 1891 to May 1894, making outspoken attacks on the deviousness and incompetence of two officials appointed under the Berlin Treaty, a German President of Council and a Swedish Chief Justice. He was blazing with indignation about them and their secret and unauthorized deportation of Mata'afa: "...our two officials preferred a policy of irritating dissimulation"; "...these gentlemen were trafficking in a merchandise which they did not possess"; "What must be done immediately, is to give us a new Chief Justice... who shall not have the appearance of trying to coin money at every joint of our affairs." In* A Footnote *he identified the German plantation company as "the head of the boil" of Samoa's sickness.*

Unsurprisingly, he was threatened with action for defamation and with deportation. The German translation of A Footnote *had the distinction of being impounded and burnt.*

The political situation, as is customary in Samoa, was complicated, local rivalries intersecting with a tenuous colonial balance, as America and Britain shufflingly sought to discourage German dominance. Yet for all that, and the intemperance of some of his attacks, and the clumsy histrionics of some of his actions, Stevenson's position remained consistent from the moment he first took interest in King Kalakaua's pan-Pacific vision in Hawaii in 1889 – he believed the Pacific nations should have the greatest possible freedom to run their own

affairs, however differently from European ways. Foreigners, he says in A Foot-note, *"know little of the course of native intrigue. Partly the Samoans cannot explain, partly they will not tell."*

He was willing to act on his opinions, as was Fanny, a feisty partisan for Mata'afa. From their arrival in Apia, they exchanged visits with Mata'afa in his semi-royal, semi-rebel village court, on one occasion creating a celebrity P.R. event by taking Lady Jersey, wife of the Governor of New South Wales. Stevenson gave provocative speeches, presented chiefs with seed to help them become independent, and lobbied the British Consul.

Mata'afa was defeated in the brief hostilities of 1893, and imprisoned with his 23 supporting chiefs in "a wretched little building" in Apia. In November 1893, just back from a visit to Honolulu, Stevenson with his family "drove in great style" to take gifts and drink ceremonial kava with the political prisoners. As a gesture of respect for the chiefs' mana in their humiliating situation, this showed sensitivity to Samoan protocol, as well as being a calculated insult to colonial officialdom. On Boxing Day, the chiefs reciprocated by inviting the Stevensons to a formal feast in the prison courtyard, and loading them with gifts as significant as precious ula (seed necklaces). All this was done with the collaboration of the gaol commander, a courteous Austrian. These were complicated times.

Life at Vailima continued to be full, and often stressful. During the war, the fighting came almost to the door, and Belle Strong was able to send eye-witness reports illustrated with her own sketches to the San Francisco Examiner *(see also* Poem 10 in 27).

In 1893 Fanny, in what may have been a menopausal phase, lapsed into a form of psychosis, with fits of hyperactivity, irritability, delusion, and depression. Seeking tonic, they visited Sydney in February 1893, and in September Stevenson went to Honolulu, where he caught pneumonia and had to be rescued by the recuperating Fanny. They worked on the estate and the house, entertained house guests, nursed the sick during a measles epidemic, battened down during hurricanes, quarrelled with Lloyd Osbourne over a local love affair, and looked after Austin Strong on his vacations from Wellington College (he became a landscape architect and planned Cornwall Park in Auckland, before making a career as a successful Broadway and West End playwright). They held parties and dances, and

(Left) "I love the land, I have chosen it to be my home while I live, and my grave after I am dead." Tusitala in front of a new fale (house) at Vailima.

a famous November 1894 American Thanksgiving Dinner that was Stevenson's last big event. He lived always under the shadow of death; "fiddling under Vesuvius" was his own phrase.

When Mata'afa was exiled and his supporters released, they made an extraordinary gesture of gratitude for Stevenson's support during their imprisonment. They constructed a new access road to Vailima, enabling wheeled vehicles to reach the estate for the first time. It was a conscious expression of alofa, an act unique in its significance. The chiefs worked by hand alongside their village men, clearing bush and digging, using Vailima tools but declining food. They named it 'O le ala o le loto alofa', the Road of Loving Hearts, or Road of Gratitude, and an inscribed sign records in Samoan "the great love of Tusitala in his loving care of us in our distress in the prison... It shall never be muddy, it shall endure for ever, this road that we have dug." It is still the road that carries all visitors to Vailima.

Stevenson acknowledged the gift with a feast in the new Samoan ceremonial house he had had built at Vailima. His speech is a courteous and considered expression of his commitment to Samoa. It gives recognition to those who nurture the land, not those who exploit it, or fight over its ownership. It returns to his great tragic theme of cultural and racial decline. It makes some sharp political points. Delivered also in Samoan (by Lloyd Osbourne), it affirms his audience's own culture (few whites accepted the invitation), by adopting some of their oratorical protocol, speaking in metaphors, proverbs and analogies, acknowledging ancestors, land, the continuing authority of Mata'afa, and the long-term future of the place and the people.

STEVENSON'S SPEECH TO THE CHIEFS

October 1894

WE are met together to-day to celebrate an event and to do honour to certain chiefs, my friends—Lelei, Mataafa, Salevao, Poè Teleso, Tupuola Lotofaga, Tupuola Amaile, Muliaiga, Ifopo, and Fatialofa. You are all aware in some degree of what has happened. You know these chiefs to have been prisoners; you perhaps know that during the term of their confinement I had it in my power to do them certain favours. One thing some of you cannot know, that they were immediately repaid by answering attentions. They were liberated by the new administration; by the King, and the Chief

Justice, and the Ta'its'ifono, who are here amongst us to-day, and to whom we all desire to tender our renewed and perpetual gratitude for that favour. As soon as they were free men—owing no man anything—instead of going home, to their own places and families, they came to me; they offered to do this work for me as a free gift, without hire, without supplies, and I was tempted at first to refuse their offer. I knew the country to be poor, I knew famine threatening; I knew their families long disorganised for want of supervision. Yet I accepted, because I thought the lesson of that road might be more useful to Samoa than a thousand breadfruit trees; and because to myself it was an exquisite pleasure to receive that which was so handsomely offered. It is now done; you have trod it to-day in coming hither. It has been made for me by chiefs; some of them old, some sick, all newly delivered from a harassing confinement, and in spite of weather unusually hot and insalubrious. I have seen these chiefs labour valiantly with their own hands upon the work, and I have set up over it, now that it is finished, the name of "The Road of Gratitude" (the road of loving hearts) and the names of those that built it. "In perpetuam memoriam," we say, and speak idly. At least so long as my own life shall be spared, it shall be here perpetuated; partly for my pleasure and in my gratitude; partly for others; to continually publish the lesson of this road.

I will tell you, Chiefs, that, when I saw you working on that road, my heart grew warm; not with gratitude only, but with hope. It seemed to me that I read the promise of something good for Samoa: it seemed to me, as I looked at you, that you were a company of warriors in a battle, fighting for the defence of our common country against all aggression. For there is a time to fight, and a time to dig. You Samoans may fight, you may conquer twenty times, and thirty times, and all will be in vain. There is but one way to defend Samoa. Hear it before it is too late. It is to make roads, and gardens, and care for your trees, and sell their produce wisely, and, in one word, to occupy and use your country. If you do not, others will...

God has both sown and strawed for you here in Samoa; He has given you a rich soil, a splendid sun, copious rain; all is ready to your hand, half done. And I repeat to you that thing which is sure: if you do not occupy and use your country, others will. It will not continue to be yours or your children's, if you occupy it for nothing. You and your children will in that case be cast out into outer darkness, where shall be weeping and gnashing of teeth; for that is the law of God which passeth not away. I who speak to you have seen these things.

I have seen them with my eyes—these judgments of God. I have seen them in Ireland, and I have seen them in the mountains of my own country—Scotland—and my heart was sad. These were a fine people in the past—brave, gay, faithful, and very much like Samoans, except in one particular, that they were much wiser and better at that business of fighting of which you think so much. But the time came to them as it now comes to you, and it did not find them ready. The messenger came into their villages, and they did not know him; they were told, as you are told, to use and occupy their country, and they would not hear. And now you may go through great tracts of the land and scarce meet a man or a smoking house, and see nothing but sheep feeding. The other people that I tell you of have come upon them like a foe in the night, and these are the other people's sheep who browse upon the foundation of their houses. To come nearer; and I have seen this judgment in Oahu also. I have ridden there the whole day along the coast of an island. Hour after hour went by and I saw the face of no living man except that of the guide who rode with me. All along that desolate coast, in one bay after another, we saw, still standing, the churches that have been built by the Hawaiians of old. There must have been many hundreds, many thousands, dwelling there in old times, and worshipping God in these now empty churches. For to-day they were empty; the doors were closed, the villages had disappeared, the people were dead and gone; only the church stood on like a tombstone over a grave, in the midst of the white men's sugar fields. The other people had come and used that country, and the Hawaiians who occupied it for nothing had been swept away, "where is weeping and gnashing of teeth."

I do not speak of this lightly, because I love Samoa and her people. I love the land, I have chosen it to be my home while I live, and my grave after I am dead; and I love the people, and have chosen them to be my people to live and die with. And I see that the day is come now of the great battle; of the great and the last opportunity by which it shall be decided, whether you are to pass away like these other races of which I have been speaking, or to stand fast, and have your children living on and honouring your memory in the land you received of your fathers.

The Land Commission and the Chief Justice will soon have ended their labours. Much of your land will be restored to you, to do what you can with. Now is the time the messenger is come into your villages to summon you; the man is come with the measuring rod; the fire is lighted in which you shall be

(Above) "The Romans were the bravest and greatest of people! mighty men of their hands." Most photographs of RLS show him in repose, static, often withdrawn. This vivid sketch by Belle Strong shows him giving her son Austin a lesson in history, and catches an animated mobility that may have been part of his extraordinary charm. It has never before been reproduced.

tried; whether you are gold or dross. Now is the time for the true champions of Samoa to stand forth. And who is the true champion of Samoa? It is not the man who blackens his face, and cuts down trees, and kills pigs and wounded men. It is the man who makes roads, who plants food trees, who gathers harvests, and is a profitable servant before the Lord, using and improving that great talent that has been given him in trust. That is the brave soldier; that is the true champion; because all things in a country hang together like the links of the anchor cable, one by another: but the anchor itself is industry.

There is a friend of most of us, who is far away; not to be forgotten where I am, where Tupuola is, where Poè, Lelei, Mataafa, Salevao, Poè Teleso, Tupuola Lotofaga, Tupuola Amaile, Muliaiga, Ifopo, Fatialofa, Lemusu are. He knew what I am telling you; no man better. He saw the day was come when Samoa had to walk in a new path, and to be defended, not only with guns and blackened faces, and the noise of men shouting, but by digging and planting, reaping and sowing. When he was still here amongst us, he busied himself planting cacao; he was anxious and eager about agriculture and

THE ROAD OF GRATITUDE

commerce, and spoke and wrote continually; so that when we turn our minds to the same matters, we may tell ourselves that we are still obeying Mataafa. Ua tautala mai pea o ia ua mamao.

I know that I do not speak to idle or foolish hearers. I speak to those who are not too proud to work for gratitude. Chiefs! You have worked for Tusitala, and he thanks you from his heart. In this, I could wish you could be an example to all Samoa—I wish every chief in these islands would turn to, and work, and build roads, and sow fields, and plant food trees, and educate his children and improve his talents—not for love of Tusitala, but for the love of his brothers, and his children, and the whole body of generations yet unborn.

Chiefs! On this road that you have made many feet shall follow. The Romans were the bravest and greatest of people! mighty men of their hands, glorious fighters and conquerors. To this day in Europe you may go through parts of the country where all is marsh and bush, and perhaps after struggling through a thicket, you shall come forth upon an ancient road, solid and useful as the day it was made. You shall see men and women bearing their burdens along that even way, and you may tell yourself that it was built for them perhaps fifteen hundred years before—perhaps before the coming of Christ, —by the Romans. And the people still remember and bless them for that convenience, and say to one another, that as the Romans were the bravest men to fight, so they were the best at building roads.

Chiefs! Our road is not built to last a thousand years, yet in a sense it is. When a road is once built, it is a strange thing how it collects traffic, how every year as it goes on, more and more people are found to walk thereon, and others are raised up to repair and perpetuate it, and keep it alive; so that perhaps even this road of ours may, from reparation to reparation, continue to exist and be useful hundreds and hundreds of years after we are mingled in the dust. And it is my hope that our far-away descendants may remember and bless those who laboured for them to-day.

21

FABLES

Few receive a tribute such as the Road of Gratitude during their lifetime. It was just in time. When Stevenson gave his speech of acknowledgement (20), he had only a month to live. To the end, he wrote as assiduously as ever, now with Belle as amanuensis. Letters about war, head-taking and Fanny's health also report on the progress of Catriona, The Ebb-Tide *and* Weir of Hermiston. *He read and corresponded with George Meredith, Henry James, Conan Doyle, W.B. Yeats, J.M. Barrie, and Edmund Gosse, still a tingling website of literary interchange. He planned ambitious Pacific literary projects, including stories of cross-cultural encounter (only 'The Beach of Falesá' was written), a volume of supernatural tales (starting with 'The Bottle Imp' and 'The Isle of Voices'), and a collection and translation of Samoan poetry. By late 1894, he had published* In The South Seas, Ballads, The Wrecker, A Footnote to History, Island Nights' Entertainments *and* The Ebb-Tide. *Together they form a contribution to the literature in English of the Pacific, in five genres, that still stands unmatched. And add letters often of very high literary quality.*

In yet another genre, Stevenson wrote about a dozen short "fables" at different times, though none were published until after his death. They were included in a new 1896 edition of Jekyll and Hyde, *and are found in that volume (v 5) of his collected works. Two have Pacific themes and settings.*

'The Cart-Horses and the Saddle-Horse' satirizes the condescending attitudes of "colonials" (Australians and New Zealanders, mostly) towards "Kanakas", and the undue deference the local people showed them. A poem written at the same time for Austin Strong, on holiday from Wellington College, New Zealand, says the boy's

task was to "two enormous, dapple grey/ New Zealand pack-horses array", and to take them into Apia. The fable may therefore have been for him, a cautionary tale against bringing any attitudes of superiority home from school.

'Something In It' reflects Stevenson's interest in indigenous beliefs, and distrust of the missionaries who sought to supplant them. He was not credulous, but he understood the cultural and psychological importance of the Pacific's supernatural traditions, and relished their affinity to Scottish ones. His irritation with those who take it for granted that European or Christian beliefs are intrinsically superior, or unquestionably right, is often evident in his Pacific writings, in the non-fiction above (for instance, in 4, 7, 17), or when Keola in 'The Isle of Voices', taken aboard the schooner, "knew that white men are like children and only believe their own stories; so about himself he told them what he pleased."

He was far from condemning all missionaries. The naïve one at the end of 'The Isle of Voices', who reproves Keola about sex, and tips off the police about coining, has hilariously missed the point by being so oblivious to the magic of the story he has heard, but Tarleton in 'The Beach of Falesá' is flexible, humane, and intelligently committed in his beliefs.

The missionary in 'Something In It' is a quite complex mix of arrogance, integrity and heroism. The fable opens, like A Footnote to History, by insisting that non-Samoan readers do some work to understand Samoan matters, as well as scaring them with necrophagia. The story dramatises some of the beliefs described in 'Graveyard Stories' (7). The missionary is satirized for his ignorance of local beliefs, and complacent insistence that "my stories are the true ones", until by exposure to the dread place of the dead he is obliged to acknowledge other systems. Yet he also shows strength. He holds to his belief in temperance ("I am a blue-ribbon man myself"), and more significantly in the existence of "right and wrong... your ovens cannot alter that." And so he survives, and learns. "Sanctions and tales dislimn like mist", the Moral says, but the simple essence of morality stands unshaken, whatever narratives surround and express it.

THE CART-HORSES AND THE SADDLE-HORSE

TWO cart-horses, a gelding and a mare, were brought to Samoa, and put in the same field with a saddlehorse to run free on the island. They were rather afraid to go near him, for they saw he was a saddle-horse, and supposed he

(Above) "'Lady and gentleman,' said the saddle-horse, 'I understand you are from the colonies. I offer you my affectionate compliments.'" Lloyd, RLS, Joe Strong, two staff members and two of the horses, laden for the journey between Apia and Vailima.

would not speak to them. Now the saddle-horse had never seen creatures so big. "These must be great chiefs," thought he, and he approached them civilly. "Lady and gentleman," said he, "I understand you are from the colonies. I offer you my affectionate compliments, and make you heartily welcome to the islands."

The colonials looked at him askance, and consulted with each other.

"Who can he be?" said the gelding.

"He seems suspiciously civil," said the mare.

"I do not think he can be much account," said the gelding.

"Depend upon it he is only a Kanaka," said the mare.

Then they turned to him.

"Go to the devil!" said the gelding.

"I wonder at your impudence, speaking to persons of our quality!" cried the mare.

FABLES

The saddle-horse went away by himself. "I was right," said he, "they are great chiefs."

SOMETHING IN IT

THE natives told him many tales. In particular, they warned him of the house of yellow reeds tied with black sinnet, how any one who touched it became instantly the prey of Akaānga, and was handed on to him by Miru the ruddy, and hocussed with the kava of the dead, and baked in the ovens and eaten by the eaters of the dead.

"There is nothing in it," said the missionary.

There was a bay upon that island, a very fair bay to look upon; but, by the native saying, it was death to bathe there. "There is nothing in that," said the missionary; and he came to the bay, and went swimming. Presently an eddy took him and bore him towards the reef. "Oho!" thought the missionary, "it seems there is something in it after all." And he swam the harder, but the eddy carried him away. "I do not care about this eddy," said the missionary; and even as he said it, he was aware of a house raised on piles above the sea; it was built of yellow reeds, one reed joined with another, and the whole bound with black sinnet; a ladder led to the door, and all about the house hung calabashes. He had never seen such a house, nor yet such calabashes; and the eddy set for the ladder. "This is singular," said the missionary, "but there can be nothing in it." And he laid hold of the ladder and went up. It was a fine house; but there was no man there; and when the missionary looked back he saw no island, only the heaving of the sea. "It is strange about the island," said the missionary, "but who's afraid? my stories are the true ones." And he laid hold of a calabash, for he was one that loved curiosities. Now he had no sooner laid hand upon the calabash than that which he handled, and that which he saw and stood on, burst like a bubble and was gone; and night closed upon him, and the waters, and the meshes of the net; and he wallowed there like a fish.

"A body would think there was something in this," said the missionary. "But if these tales are true, I wonder what about my tales!"

Now the flaming of Akaānga's torch drew near in the night; and the misshapen hands groped in the meshes of the net; and they took the missionary between the finger and the thumb, and bore him dripping in the night and silence to the place of the ovens of Miru. And there was Miru, ruddy in the glow of the ovens; and there sat her four daughters, and made the kava of the dead; and there sat the comers out of the islands of the living, dripping and lamenting.

This was a dread place to reach for any of the sons of men. But of all who ever came there, the missionary was the most concerned; and, to make things worse, the person next him was a convert of his own.

"Aha," said the convert, "so you are here like your neighbours? And how about all your stories?"

"It seems," said the missionary, with bursting tears, "that there was nothing in them."

By this the kava of the dead was ready, and the daughters of Miru began to intone in the old manner of singing. "Gone are the green islands and the bright sea, the sun and the moon and the forty million stars, and life and love and hope. Henceforth is no more, only to sit in the night and silence, and see your friends devoured; for life is a deceit, and the bandage is taken from your eyes."

Now when the singing was done, one of the daughters came with the bowl. Desire of that kava rose in the missionary's bosom; he lusted for it like a swimmer for the land, or a bridegroom for his bride; and he reached out his hand, and took the bowl, and would have drunk. And then he remembered, and put it back.

"Drink!" sang the daughter of Miru. "There is no kava like the kava of the dead, and to drink of it once is the reward of living."

"I thank you. It smells excellent," said the missionary. "But I am a blue-ribbon man myself; and though I am aware there is a difference of opinion even in our own confession, I have always held kava to be excluded."

"What!" cried the convert. "Are you going to respect a taboo at a time like this? And you were always so opposed to taboos when you were alive!"

"To other people's," said the missionary. "Never to my own."

"But yours have all proved wrong," said the convert.

"It looks like it," said the missionary, "and I can't help that. No reason why I should break my word."

"I never heard the like of this!" cried the daughter of Miru. "Pray, what do you expect to gain?"

"That is not the point," said the missionary. "I took this pledge for others, I am not going to break it for myself."

The daughter of Miru was puzzled; she came and told her mother, and Miru was vexed; and they went and told Akaānga.

"I don't know what to do about this," said Akaānga; and he came and reasoned with the missionary.

"But there *is* such a thing as right and wrong," said the missionary; "and your ovens cannot alter that."

"Give the kava to the rest," said Akaānga to the daughters of Miru. "I must get rid of this sea-lawyer instantly, or worse will come of it."

The next moment the missionary came up in the midst of the sea, and there before him were the palm trees of the island. He swam to the shore gladly, and landed. Much matter of thought was in that missionary's mind.

"I seem to have been misinformed upon some points," said he. "Perhaps there is not much in it, as I supposed; but there is something in it after all. Let me be glad of that."

And he rang the bell for service.

MORAL

The sticks break, the stones crumble,
The eternal altars tilt and tumble,
Sanctions and tales dislimn like mist
About the amazed evangelist.
He stands unshook from age to youth
Upon one pin-point of the truth.

22

THE BOTTLE IMP

[With illustrations from the First Edition.]

'The Bottle Imp' was the first of Stevenson's Pacific stories to be completed, written during his busy first stay in Samoa in December 1889-January 1890, according to Colvin, the editor of the Letters. *It was serialized in American and British magazines in the first half of 1891, and then appeared in Samoan in the London Missionary Society's newspaper* O Le Sulu Samoa, *May-December 1891, under the title* O Le Fagu Aitu, *with the author shown as Tusitala. Having moved into Vailima, Stevenson spent a rainy evening in March 1891 "going over the Samoan translation with Claxton the missionary." He also said, in the note he appended to the story, that it was "designed and written for a Polynesian audience." Another Samoa missionary, Rev. W.E. Clarke (who was to conduct Stevenson's funeral; see* **28**), *said it was "the first serial tale... in their own language, and was read with wonder and delight in many a thatched Samoan hut."*

Clearly Stevenson also had readers in English in mind, and the story thus has a significant claim to be regarded as a bilingual work of Samoan and Pacific literature, as well as British literature. This is much more than a matter of setting – no one would propose Treasure Island *as a work of Caribbean literature – or even style. For all the story's origins in German folklore and British melodrama, Stevenson's version is imbued with the Pacific's traditional culture and contemporary society. Its whole texture of reference is to a Pacific way of life, to Pacific beliefs and values. Its metaphors, as much as its locations, are specifically of the Pacific. It begins, as he did, in San Francisco, moves to Honolulu, where some recognisable locations are evoked, then (by the same ferry he* used, the W.G. Hall) *to the Big Island of Hawaii, which he visited in early* *1889, climaxes in Papeete, and ends happily in Hawaii. As a journey of* *discovery and enlightenment, and a search for married peace threatened by fear* *of sickness, it might be read as an imaginary equivalent of his own.*

As moral allegory, it contrasts the honesty and self-sacrificial love shown by *Keawe and Kokua with the devious American who brings the bottle into the* *story, the spineless embezzler who sells it back to Keawe, and the brutal drunken* *boatswain who carries it out at the end. Deeper than race, it sets worldly* *aspirations against care for the soul, though remaining perfectly realistic about* *the contribution of material wealth and sexual fulfillment to human happiness.* *It offers that unusual thing for 1891, a young female character who by her* *intelligence, knowledge, generosity and judgment initiates many key develop-* *ments in the action.*

Stevenson described in a letter how some of his Samoan friends, visiting *Vailima, used to spend the evening looking uneasily about for the actual demonic* *bottle. Like them, the story enjoys being not quite sure about the division* *between reality and the darker world of the human imagination. It provides* *with some relish a set of credible narrative evidence for the unbelievable. The* *imp is a fantasy, but the things it deals in – human love, desire for happiness,* *greed, mortality – are real. Such ambiguity is not unique to the Pacific, nor to* *be dismissed as mere superstition. After all, the friend Stevenson was writing to* *was Arthur Conan Doyle, whose fictitious detective's non-existent Baker Street* *flat is still visited by sophisticated readers, with the same uneasy excitement as* *those Samoans looking round Vailima for the imaginary bottle.*

THE BOTTLE IMP

THERE was a man of the Island of Hawaii, whom I shall call Keawe; for the truth is, he still lives, and his name must be kept secret; but the place of his birth was not far from Honaunau, where the bones of Keawe the Great lie hidden in a cave. This man was poor, brave, and active; he could read and write like a schoolmaster; he was a first-rate mariner besides, sailed for some

Note—Any student of that very unliterary product, the English drama of the early part of the century, will here recognise the name and the root idea of a piece once rendered popular by the redoubtable O. Smith. The root idea is there and identical, and yet I hope I have made it a new thing. And the fact that the tale has been designed and written for a Polynesian audience may lend it some extraneous interest nearer home.—R.L.S.

time in the island steamers, and steered a whaleboat on the Hamakua coast. At length it came in Keawe's mind to have a sight of the great world and foreign cities, and he shipped on a vessel bound to San Francisco.

This is a fine town, with a fine harbour, and rich people uncountable; and, in particular, there is one hill which is covered with palaces. Upon this hill Keawe was one day taking a walk with his pocket full of money, viewing the great houses upon either hand with pleasure. "What fine houses these are!" he was thinking, "and how happy must those people be who dwell in them, and take no care for the morrow!" The thought was in his mind when he came abreast of a house that was smaller than some others, but all finished and beautified like a toy; the steps of that house shone like silver, and the borders of the garden bloomed like garlands, and the windows were bright like diamonds; and Keawe stopped and wondered at the excellence of all he saw. So stopping, he was aware of a man that looked forth upon him through a window so clear that Keawe could see him as you see a fish in a pool upon the reef. The man was elderly, with a bald head and a black beard; and his face was heavy with sorrow, and he bitterly sighed. And the truth of it is, that as Keawe looked in upon the man, and the man looked out upon Keawe, each envied the other.

All of a sudden, the man smiled and nodded, and beckoned Keawe to enter, and met him at the door of the house.

"This is a fine house of mine," said the man, and bitterly sighed. "Would you not care to view the chambers?"

So he led Keawe all over it, from the cellar to the roof, and there was nothing there that was not perfect of its kind, and Keawe was astonished.

"Truly," said Keawe, "this is a beautiful house; if I lived in the like of it, I should be laughing all day long. How comes it, then, that you should be sighing?"

"There is no reason," said the man, "why you should not have a house in all points similar to this, and finer, if you wish. You have some money, I suppose?"

"I have fifty dollars," said Keawe; "but a house like this will cost more than fifty dollars."

The man made a computation. "I am sorry you have no more," said he, "for it may raise you trouble in the future; but it shall be yours at fifty dollars."

"'THIS IS THE BOTTLE,' SAID THE MAN."

"The house?" asked Keawe.

"No, not the house," replied the man; "but the bottle. For, I must tell you, although I appear to you so rich and fortunate, all my fortune, and this house itself and its garden, came out of a bottle not much bigger than a pint. This is it."

And he opened a lockfast place, and took out a round-bellied bottle with a long neck; the glass of it was white like milk, with changing rainbow colours in the grain. Withinsides something obscurely moved, like a shadow and a fire.

"This is the bottle," said the man; and, when Keawe laughed, "You do not believe me?" he added. "Try, then, for yourself. See if you can break it."

So Keawe took the bottle up and dashed it on the floor till he was weary; but it jumped on the floor like a child's ball, and was not injured.

"This is a strange thing," said Keawe. "For by the touch of it, as well as by the look, the bottle should be of glass."

"Of glass it is," replied the man, sighing more heavily than ever; "but the glass of it was tempered in the flames of hell. An imp lives in it, and that is the shadow we behold there moving: or so I suppose. If any man buy this bottle the imp is at his command; all that he desires—love, fame, money, houses like this house, ay, or a city like this city—all are his at the word uttered. Napoleon had this bottle, and by it he grew to be the king of the world; but he sold it at the last, and fell. Captain Cook had this bottle, and by it he found his way to so many islands; but he, too, sold it, and was slain upon Hawaii. For, once it is sold, the power goes and the protection; and unless a man remain content with what he has, ill will befall him."

"And yet you talk of selling it yourself?" Keawe said.

"I have all I wish, and I am growing elderly," replied the man. "There is one thing the imp cannot do—he cannot prolong life; and, it would not be fair to conceal from you, there is a drawback to the bottle; for if a man die before he sells it, he must burn in hell forever."

"To be sure, that is a drawback and no mistake," cried Keawe. "I would not meddle with the thing. I can do without a house, thank God; but there is one thing I could not be doing with one particle, and that is to be damned."

"Dear me, you must not run away with things," returned the man. "All you have to do is to use the power of the imp in moderation, and then sell it to someone else, as I do to you, and finish your life in comfort."

"Well, I observe two things," said Keawe. "All the time you keep sighing like a maid in love, that is one; and, for the other, you sell this bottle very cheap."

"I have told you already why I sigh," said the man. "It is because I fear my health is breaking up; and, as you said yourself, to die and go to the devil is a pity for anyone. As for why I sell so cheap, I must explain to you there is a peculiarity about the bottle. Long ago, when the devil brought it first upon earth, it was extremely expensive, and was sold first of all to Prester John for many millions of dollars; but it cannot be sold at all, unless sold at a loss. If you sell it for as much as you paid for it, back it comes to you again like a homing pigeon. It follows that the price has kept falling in these centuries, and the bottle is now remarkably cheap. I bought it myself from one of my great neighbours on this hill, and the price I paid was only ninety dollars. I could sell it for as high as eighty-nine dollars and ninety-nine cents, but not a penny dearer, or back the thing must come to me. Now, about this there are two bothers. First, when you offer a bottle so singular for eighty odd dollars, people suppose you to be jesting. And second—but there is no hurry about that—and I need not go into it. Only remember it must be coined money that you sell it for."

"How am I to know that this is all true?" asked Keawe.

"Some of it you can try at once," replied the man. "Give me your fifty dollars, take the bottle, and wish your fifty dollars back into your pocket. If that does not happen, I pledge you my honour I will cry off the bargain and restore your money."

"You are not deceiving me?" said Keawe.

The man bound himself with a great oath.

"Well, I will risk that much," said Keawe, "for that can do no harm." And he paid over his money to the man, and the man handed him the bottle.

"Imp of the bottle," said Keawe, "I want my fifty dollars back." And sure enough he had scarce said the word before his pocket was as heavy as ever.

"To be sure this is a wonderful bottle," said Keawe.

"And now good-morning to you, my fine fellow, and the devil go with you for me!" said the man.

"Hold on," said Keawe, "I don't want any more of this fun. Here, take your bottle back."

"You have bought it for less than I paid for it," replied the man, rubbing his hands. "It is yours now; and, for my part, I am only concerned to see the back of you." And with that he rang for his Chinese servant, and had Keawe shown out of the house.

Now, when Keawe was in the street, with the bottle under his arm, he began to think. "If all is true about this bottle, I may have made a losing bargain," thinks he. "But perhaps the man was only fooling me." The first thing he did was to count his money; the sum was exact—forty-nine dollars American money, and one Chili piece. "That looks like the truth," said Keawe. "Now I will try another part."

The streets in that part of the city were as clean as a ship's decks, and though it was noon, there were no passengers. Keawe set the bottle in the gutter and walked away. Twice he looked back, and there was the milky, round-bellied bottle where he left it. A third time he looked back, and turned a corner; but he had scarce done so, when something knocked upon his elbow, and behold! it was the long neck sticking up, and as for the round belly, it was jammed into the pocket of his pilot-coat.

"And that looks like the truth," said Keawe.

The next thing he did was to buy a corkscrew in a shop, and go apart into a secret place in the fields. And there he tried to draw the cork, but as often as he put the screw in, out it came again, and the cork as whole as ever.

"This is some new sort of cork," said Keawe, and all at once he began to shake and sweat, for he was afraid of that bottle.

On his way back to the port-side, he saw a shop where a man sold shells and clubs from the wild islands, old heathen deities, old coined money, pictures from China and Japan; and all manner of things that sailors bring in their sea-chests. And here he had an idea. So he went in and offered the bottle for a hundred dollars. The man of the shop laughed at him at the first, and offered him five; but, indeed, it was a curious bottle—such glass was never blown in any human glassworks, so prettily the colours shone under the milky white, and so strangely the shadow hovered in the midst; so, after he had disputed awhile after the manner of his kind, the shop-man gave Keawe sixty silver dollars for the thing, and set it on a shelf in the midst of his window.

"Now," said Keawe, "I have sold that for sixty which I bought fifty—or, to say truth, a little less, because one of my dollars was from Chili. Now I shall know the truth upon another point."

He went back on board his ship, and, when he opened his chest, there was the bottle, and had come more quickly than himself. Now Keawe had a mate on board whose name was Lopaka.

"What ails you?" said Lopaka, "that you stare in your chest?"

They were alone in the ship's forecastle, and Keawe bound him to secrecy, and told all.

"This is is a very strange affair," said Lopaka; "and I fear you will be in trouble about this bottle. But there is one point very clear—that you are sure of the trouble, and you had better have the profit in the bargain. Make up your mind what you want with it; give the order, and if it is done as you desire, I will buy, the bottle myself; for I have an idea of my own, to get a schooner, and go trading through the islands."

"That is not my idea," said Keawe; "but to have a beautiful house and garden on the Kona Coast, where I was born, the sun shining in at the door, flowers in the garden, glass in the windows, pictures on the walls, and toys and fine carpets on the tables, for all the world like the house I was in this day—only a storey higher, and with balconies all about like the King's palace; and to live there without care and make merry with my friends and relatives."

"Well," said Lopaka, "let us carry it back with us to Hawaii; and if all comes true, as you suppose, I will buy the bottle, as I said, and ask a schooner."

Upon that they were agreed, and it was not long before the ship returned to Honolulu, carrying Keawe and Lopaka, and the bottle. They were scarce come ashore when they met a friend upon the beach, who began at once to condole with Keawe.

"I do not know what I am to be condoled about," said Keawe.

"Is it possible you have not heard," said the friend, "your uncle—that good old man—is dead, and your cousin—that beautiful boy—was drowned at sea?"

Keawe was filled with sorrow, and, beginning to weep and to lament, he forgot about the bottle. But Lopaka was thinking to himself, and presently, when Keawe's grief was a little abated, "I have been thinking," said Lopaka. "Had not your uncle lands in Hawaii, in the district of Kaü?"

"No," said Keawe, "not in Kaü; they are on the mountain side—a little way south of Hookena."

"These lands will now be yours?" asked Lopaka.

"And so they will," says Keawe, and began again to lament for his relatives.

"No," said Lopaka, "do not lament at present. I have a thought in my mind. How if this should be the doing of the bottle? For here is the place ready for your house."

"If this be so," cried Keawe, "it is a very ill way to serve me by killing my relatives. But it may be, indeed, for it was in just such a station that I saw the house with my mind's eye."

"The house, however, is not yet built," said Lopaka.

"No, nor like to be!" said Keawe; "for though my uncle has some coffee and ava and bananas, it will not be more than will keep me in comfort; and the rest of that land is the black lava."

"Let us go to the lawyer," said Lopaka; "I have still this idea in my mind."

Now, when they came to the lawyer's, it appeared Keawe's uncle had grown monstrous rich in the last days, and there was a fund of money.

"And here is the money for the house!" cried Lopaka.

"If you are thinking of a new house," said the lawyer, "here is the card of a new architect, of whom they tell me great things."

"Better and better!" cried Lopaka. "Here is all made plain for us. Let us continue to obey orders."

So they went to the architect, and he had drawings of houses on his table.

"You want something out of the way," said the architect. "How do you like this?" and he handed a drawing to Keawe.

Now, when Keawe set eyes on the drawing, he cried out aloud, for it was the picture of his thought exactly drawn.

"I am in for this house," thought he. "Little as I like the way it comes to me, I am in for it now, and I may as well take the good along with the evil."

So he told the architect all that he wished, and how he would have that house furnished, and about the pictures on the wall and the knick-knacks on the tables; and he asked the man plainly for how much he would undertake the whole affair.

The architect put many questions, and took his pen and made a computation; and when he had done he named the very sum that Keawe had inherited.

Lopaka and Keawe looked at one another and nodded.

"It is quite clear," thought Keawe, "that I am to have this house, whether or no. It comes from the devil, and I fear I will get little good by that; and of one thing I am sure, I will make no more wishes as long as I have this bottle. But with the house I am saddled, and I may as well take the good along with the evil."

So he made his terms with the architect, and they signed a paper; and Keawe and Lopaka took ship again and sailed to Australia; for it was concluded between them they should not interfere at all, but leave the architect and the bottle imp to build and to adorn that house at their own pleasure.

The voyage was a good voyage, only all the time Keawe was holding in his breath, for he had sworn he would utter no more wishes, and take no more favours from the devil. The time was up when they got back. The architect told them that the house was ready, and Keawe and Lopaka took a passage in the *Hall*, and went down Kona way to view the house, and see if all had been done fitly according to the thought that was in Keawe's mind.

Now, the house stood on the mountain side, visible to ships. Above, the forest ran up into the clouds of rain; below the black lava fell in cliffs, where the kings of old lay buried. A garden bloomed about that house with every hue of flowers; and there was an orchard of papaia on the one hand and an orchard of breadfruit on the other, and right in front, toward the sea, a ship's mast had been rigged up and bore a flag. As for the house, it was three storeys high, with great chambers and broad balconies on each. The windows were of glass, so excellent that it was as clear as water and as bright as day. All manner of furniture adorned the chambers. Pictures hung upon the wall in golden frames: pictures of ships, and men fighting, and of the most beautiful women, and of singular places; nowhere in the world are there pictures of so bright a colour as those Keawe found hanging in his house. As for the knick-knacks, they were extraordinary fine; chiming clocks and musical boxes, little men with nodding heads, books filled with pictures, weapons of price from all quarters of the world, and the most elegant puzzles to entertain the leisure of a solitary man. And as no one would care to live in such chambers, only to walk through and view them, the balconies were made so broad that a whole town might have lived upon them in delight; and Keawe knew not which to prefer, whether the back porch, where you got the land breeze, and looked upon the orchards and the flowers, or the front balcony, where you could drink the wind of the sea, and look down the steep wall of the mountain and see the *Hall* going by once a week or so between Hookena and the hills of Pele, or the schooners plying up the coast for wood and ava and bananas.

When they had viewed all, Keawe and Lopaka sat on the porch.

"Well," asked Lopaka, "is it all as you designed?"

"Words cannot utter it," said Keawe. "It is better than I dreamed, and I am sick with satisfaction."

"There is but one thing to consider," said Lopaka; "all this may be quite natural, and the bottle imp have nothing whatever to say to it. If I were to buy the bottle, and got no schooner after all, I should have put my hand in the fire for nothing. I gave you my word, I know; but yet I think you would not grudge me one more proof."

"I have sworn I would take no more favours," said Keawe. "I have gone already deep enough."

"This is no favour I am thinking of," replied Lopaka. "It is only to see the imp himself. There is nothing to be gained by that, and so nothing to be ashamed of; and yet, if I once saw him, I should be sure of the whole matter. So indulge me so far, and let me see the imp; and, after that, here is the money in my hand, and I will buy it."

"There is only one thing I am afraid of," said Keawe. "The imp may be very ugly to view; and if you once set eyes upon him you might be very undesirous of the bottle."

"I am a man of my word," said Lopaka. "And here is the money betwixt us."

"Very well," replied Keawe. "I have a curiosity myself. So come, let us have one look at you, Mr Imp."

Now as soon as that was said, the imp looked out of the bottle, and in again, swift as a lizard; and there sat Keawe and Lopaka turned to stone. The night had quite come, before either found a thought to say or voice to say it with; and then Lopaka pushed the money over and took the bottle.

"I am a man of my word," said he, "and had need to be so, or I would not touch this bottle with my foot. Well, I shall get my schooner and a dollar or two for my pocket; and then I will be rid of this devil as fast as I can. For to tell you the plain truth, the look of him has cast me down."

"Lopaka," said Keawe, "do not you think any worse of me than you can help; I know it is night, and the roads bad, and the pass by the tombs an ill place to go by so late, but I declare since I have seen that little face, I cannot eat or sleep or pray till it is gone from me. I will give you a lantern, and a basket to put the bottle in, and any picture or fine thing in all my house that takes your fancy—and be gone at once, and go sleep at Hookena with Nahinu."

"Keawe," said Lopaka, "many a man would take this ill; above all, when I am doing you a turn so friendly, as to keep my word and buy the bottle; and for that matter, the night and the dark, and the way by the tombs, must be all tenfold more dangerous to a man with such a sin upon his conscience, and such a bottle under his arm. But for my part, I am so extremely terrified myself, I have not the heart to blame you. Here I go then; and I pray God you may be happy in your house, and I fortunate with my schooner, and both get to heaven in the end in spite of the devil and his bottle."

So Lopaka went down the mountain; and Keawe stood in his front balcony and listened to the clink of the horse's shoes, and watched the lantern go shining down the path, and along the cliff of caves where the old dead are buried; and all the time he trembled and clasped his hands, and prayed for his friend, and gave glory to God that he himself was escaped out of that trouble.

But the next day came very brightly, and that new house of his was so delightful to behold that he forgot his terrors. One day followed another, and Keawe dwelt there in perpetual joy. He had his place on the back porch; it was there he ate and lived, and read the stories in the Honolulu newspapers; but when anyone came by they would go in and view the chambers

"'I THOUGHT I KNEW EVERYONE IN THIS COUNTRY'"

and the pictures. And the fame of the house went far and wide; it was called *Ka-Hale Nui*—the Great House—in all Kona; and sometimes the Bright

House, for Keawe kept a Chinaman, who was all day dusting and furbishing; and the glass, and the gilt, and the fine stuffs, and the pictures, shone as bright as the morning. As for Keawe himself, he could not walk in the chambers without singing, his heart was so enlarged; and when ships sailed by upon the sea, he would fly his colours on the mast.

So time went by, until one day Keawe went upon a visit as far as Kailua to certain of his friends. There he was well feasted; and left as soon as he could the next morning, and rode hard, for he was impatient to behold his beautiful house; and, besides, the night then coming on was the night in which the dead of old days go abroad in the sides of Kona; and having already meddled with the devil, he was the more chary of meeting with the dead. A little beyond Honaunau, looking far ahead, he was aware of a woman bathing in the edge of the sea; and she seemed a well-grown girl, but he thought no more of it. Then he saw her white shift flutter as she put it on, and then her red holoku; and by the time he came abreast of her she was done with her toilet, and had come up from the sea, and stood by the track-side in her red holoku, and she was all freshened with the bath, and her eyes shone and were kind. Now Keawe no sooner beheld her than he drew rein.

"I thought I knew everyone in this country," said he. "How comes it that I do not know you?"

"I am Kokua, daughter of Kiano," said the girl, "and I have just returned from Oahu. Who are you?"

"I will tell you who I am in a little," said Keawe, dismounting from his horse, "but not now. For I have a thought in my mind, and if you knew who I was, you might have heard of me, and would not give me a true answer. But tell me, first of all, one thing: Are you married?"

At this Kokua laughed out aloud. "It is you who ask questions," she said. "Are you married yourself?"

"Indeed, Kokua, I am not," replied Keawe, "and never thought to be until this hour. But here is the plain truth. I have met you here at the road-side, and I saw your eyes, which are like the stars, and my heart went to you as swift as a bird. And so now, if you want none of me, say so, and I will go on to my own place; but if you think me no worse than any other young man, say so, too, and I will turn aside to your father's for the night, and tomorrow I will talk with the good man."

Kokua said never a word, but she looked at the sea and laughed.

"Kokua," said Keawe, "if you say nothing, I will take that for the good answer; so let us be stepping to your father's door."

She went on ahead of him, still without speech; only sometimes she glanced back and glanced away again, and she kept the strings of her hat in her mouth.

Now, when they had come to the door, Kiano came out on his verandah, and cried out and welcomed Keawe by name. At that the girl looked over, for the fame of the great house had come to her ears; and, to be sure, it was a great temptation. All that evening they were very merry together; and the girl was as bold as brass under the eyes of her parents, and made a mock of Keawe, for she had a quick wit. The next day he had a word with Kiano, and found the girl alone.

"Kokua," said he, "you made a mock of me all the evening; and it is still time to bid me go. I would not tell you who I was, because I have so fine a house, and I feared you would think too much of that house and too little of the man that loves you. Now you know all, and if you wish to have seen the last of me, say so at once."

"No," said Kokua; but this time she did not laugh, nor did Keawe ask for more.

This was the wooing of Keawe; things had gone quickly; but so an arrow goes, and the ball of a rifle swifter still, and yet both may strike the target. Things had gone fast, but they had gone far also, and the thought of Keawe rang in the maiden's head; she heard his voice in the breach of the surf upon the lava, and for this young man that she had seen but twice she would have left father and mother and her native islands. As for Keawe himself, his horse flew up the path of the mountain under the cliff of tombs, and the sound of the hoofs, and the sound of Keawe singing to himself for pleasure, echoed in the caverns of the dead. He came to the Bright House, and still he was singing. He sat and ate in the broad balcony, and the Chinaman wondered at his master, to hear how he sang between the mouthfuls. The sun went down into the sea, and the night came; and Keawe walked the balconies by lamplight, high on the mountains, and the voice of his singing startled men on ships.

"Here am I now upon my high place," he said to himself. "Life may be no better; this is the mountain top; and all shelves about me toward the worse. For the first time I will light up the chambers, and bathe in my fine bath with the hot water and the cold, and sleep alone in the bed of my bridal chamber."

So the Chinaman had word, and he must rise from sleep and light the furnaces; and as he wrought below, beside the boilers, he heard his master singing and rejoicing above him in the lighted chambers. When the water began to be hot the Chinaman cried to his master; and Keawe went into the bath room; and the Chinaman heard him sing as he filled the marble basin; and heard him sing, and the singing broken, as he undressed; until of a sudden, the song ceased. The Chinaman listened, and listened; he called up the house to Keawe to ask if all were well, and Keawe answered him "Yes," and bade him go to bed; but there was no more singing in the Bright House; and all night long, the Chinaman heard his master's feet go round and round the balconies without repose.

Now the truth of it was this: as Keawe undressed for his bath, he spied upon his flesh a patch like a patch of lichen on a rock, and it was then that he stopped singing. For he knew the likeness of that patch, and knew that he was fallen in the Chinese Evil.

Now, it is a sad thing for any man to fall into this sickness. And it would be a sad thing for anyone to leave a house so beautiful and so commodious, and depart from all his friends to the north coast of Molokai between the mighty cliff and the sea-breakers. But what was that to the case of the man Keawe, he who had met his love but yesterday, and won her but that morning, and now saw all his hopes break, in a moment, like a piece of glass?

Awhile he sat upon the edge of the bath; then sprang, with a cry, and ran outside; and to and fro, to and fro, along the balcony, like one despairing.

"Very willingly could I leave Hawaii, the home of my fathers," Keawe was thinking. "Very lightly could I leave my house, the high-placed, the many-windowed, here upon the mountains. Very bravely could I go to Molokai, to Kalaupapa by the cliffs, to live with the smitten and to sleep there, far from my fathers. But what wrong have I done, what sin lies upon my soul, that I should have encountered Kokua coming cool from the sea-water in the evening? Kokua, the soul ensnarer! Kokua, the light of my life! Her may I never wed, her may I look upon no longer, her may I no more handle with my loving hand; and it is for this, it is for you, O Kokua! that I pour my lamentations!"

Now you are to observe what sort of a man Keawe was, for he might

"Keawe of the Bright House is out of spirits"

have dwelt there in the Bright House for years, and no one been the wiser of his sickness; but he reckoned nothing of that, if he must lose Kokua. And again, he might have wed Kokua even as he was; and so many would have done, because they have the souls of pigs; but Keawe loved the maid manfully, and he would do her no hurt and bring her in no danger.

A little beyond the midst of the night, there came in his mind the recollection of that bottle. He went round to the back porch, and called to memory the day when the devil had looked forth; and at the thought ice ran in his veins.

"A dreadful thing is the bottle," thought Keawe, "and dreadful is the imp, and it is a dreadful thing to risk the flames of hell. But what other hope have I to cure my sickness or to wed Kokua? What!" he thought, "would I beard the devil once, only to get me a house, and not face him again to win Kokua?"

Thereupon he called to mind it was the next day the *Hall* went by on her return to Honolulu. "There must I go first," he thought, "and see Lopaka. For the best hope that I have now is to find that same bottle I was so pleased to be rid of."

Never a wink could he sleep; the food stuck in his throat; but he sent a letter to Kiano, and about the time when the steamer would be coming, rode down beside the cliff of the tombs. It rained; his horse went heavily, he looked up at the black mouths of the caves, and he envied the dead that slept there and were done with trouble; and called to mind how he had galloped by the day before, and was astonished. So he came down to Hookena, and there was all the country gathered for the steamer as usual. In the shed before the store they sat and jested and passed the news; but there was no matter of speech in Keawe's bosom, and he sat in their midst and looked without on the rain falling on the houses, and the surf beating among the rocks, and the sighs arose in his throat.

"Keawe of the Bright House is out of spirits," said one to another. Indeed, and so he was, and little wonder.

Then the *Hall* came, and the whaleboat carried him on board. The after-part of the ship was full of Haoles who had been to visit the volcano, as their custom is; and the midst was crowded with Kanakas, and the fore-part with wild bulls from Hilo and horses from Kaü; but Keawe sat apart from all in his sorrow, and watched for the house of Kiano. There it sat, low upon the shore in the black rocks, and shaded by the cocoa palms, and there by the door was a red holoku, no greater than a fly, and going to and fro with a fly's busyness. "Ah, queen of my heart," he cried, "I'll venture my dear soul to win you!"

Soon after, darkness fell, and the cabins were lit up, and the Haoles sat and played at the cards and drank whiskey as their custom is; but Keawe walked the deck all night; and all the next day, as they steamed under the lee of Maui or of Molokai, he was still pacing to and fro like a wild animal in a menagerie.

Towards evening they passed Diamond Head, and came to the pier of Honolulu. Keawe stepped out among the crowd and began to ask for Lopaka. It seemed he had become the owner of a schooner—none better in the islands—and was gone upon an adventure as far as Pola-Pola or Kahiki; so there was no help to be looked for from Lopaka. Keawe called to mind a friend of his, a lawyer in the town (I must not tell his name), and inquired of him. They said he was grown suddenly rich, and had a fine new house upon Waikiki shore; and this put a thought in Keawe's head, and he called a hack and drove to the lawyer's house.

The house was all brand new, and the trees in the garden no greater than walking-sticks, and the lawyer, when he came, had the air of a man well pleased.

"What can I do to serve you?" said the lawyer.

"You are a friend of Lopaka's," replied Keawe, "and Lopaka purchased from me a certain piece of goods that I thought you might enable me to trace."

The lawyer's face became very dark. "I do not profess to misunderstand you, Mr Keawe," said he, "though this is an ugly business to be stirring in. You may be sure I know nothing, but yet I have a guess, and if you would apply in a certain quarter I think you might have news."

And he named the name of a man, which, again, I had better not repeat. So it was for days, and Keawe went from one to another, finding everywhere new clothes and carriages, and fine new houses and men everywhere in great contentment, although, to be sure, when he hinted at his business their faces would cloud over.

"No doubt I am upon the track," thought Keawe. "These new clothes and carriages are all the gifts of the little imp, and these glad faces are the faces of men who have taken their profit and got rid of the accursed thing in safety. When I see pale cheeks and hear sighing, I shall know that I am near the bottle."

So it befell at last that he was recommended to a Haole in Beritania Street. When he came to the door, about the hour of the evening meal, there were the usual marks of the new house, and the young garden, and the electric light shining in the windows; but when the owner came, a shock of hope and fear ran through Keawe; for here was a young man, white as a corpse, and black about the eyes, the hair shedding from his head, and such a look in his countenance as a man may have when he is waiting for the gallows.

"Here it is, to be sure," thought Keawe, and so with this man he noways veiled his errand. "I am come to buy the bottle," said he.

At the word, the young Haole of Beritania Street reeled against the wall.

"The bottle!" he gasped. "To buy the bottle!" Then he seemed to choke, and seizing Keawe by the arm carried him into a room and poured out wine in two glasses.

"Here is my respects," said Keawe, who had been much about with Haoles in his time. "Yes," he added, "I am come to buy the bottle. What is the price by now?"

At that word the young man let his glass slip through his fingers, and looked upon Keawe like a ghost.

"The price," says he; "the price! You do not know the price?"

"THE YOUNG MAN FELL UPON HIS KNEES.
'FOR GOD'S SAKE BUY IT!' HE CRIED"

"It is for that I am asking you," returned Keawe. "But why are you so much concerned? Is there anything wrong about the price?"

"It has dropped a great deal in value since your time, Mr Keawe," said the young man, stammering.

"Well, well, I shall have the less to pay for it," says Keawe. "How much did it cost you?"

The young man was as white as a sheet. "Two cents," said he.

"What?" cried Keawe, "two cents? Why, then, you can only sell it for one. And he who buys it—" The words died upon Keawe's tongue; he who bought it could never sell it again, the bottle and the bottle imp must abide with him until he died, and when he died must carry him to the red end of hell.

The young man of Beritania Street fell upon his knees. "For God's sake buy it!" he cried. "You can have all my fortune in the bargain. I was mad when I bought it at that price. I had embezzled money at my store; I was lost else; I must have gone to jail."

"Poor creature," said Keawe, "you would risk your soul upon so desperate an adventure, and to avoid the proper punishment of your own disgrace;

and you think I could hesitate with love in front of me. Give me the bottle, and the change which I make sure you have all ready. Here is a five-cent piece."

It was as Keawe supposed; the young man had the change ready in a drawer; the bottle changed hands, and Keawe's fingers were no sooner clasped upon the stalk than he had breathed his wish to be a clean man. And, sure enough, when he got home to his room, and stripped himself before a glass, his flesh was whole like an infant's. And here was the strange thing: he had no sooner seen this miracle, than his mind was changed within him, and he cared naught for the Chinese Evil, and little enough for Kokua; and had but the one thought, that here he was bound to the bottle imp for time and for eternity, and had no better hope but to be a cinder for ever in the flames of hell. Away ahead of him he saw them blaze with his mind's eye, and his soul shrank, and darkness fell upon the light.

When Keawe came to himself a little, he was aware it was the night when the band played at the hotel. Thither he went, because he feared to be alone; and there, among happy faces, walked to and fro, and heard the tunes go up and down, and saw Berger beat the measure, and all the while he heard the flames crackle, and saw the red fire burning in the bottomless pit. Of a sudden the band played *Hiki-ao-ao*; that was a song that he had sung with Kokua, and at the strain courage returned to him.

"It is done now," he thought, "and once more let me take the good along with the evil."

So it befell that he returned to Hawaii by the first steamer, and as soon as it could be managed he was wedded to Kokua, and carried her up the mountain side to the Bright House.

Now it was so with these two, that when they were together, Keawe's heart was stilled; but so soon as he was alone he fell into a brooding horror, and heard the flames crackle, and saw the red fire burn in the bottomless pit. The girl, indeed, had come to him wholly; her heart leapt in her side at sight of him, her hand clung to his; and she was so fashioned from the hair upon her head to the nails upon her toes that none could see her without joy. She was pleasant in her nature. She had the good word always. Full of song she was, and went to and fro in the Bright House, the brightest thing in its three storeys, carolling like the birds. And Keawe beheld and heard her with delight, and then must shrink upon one side, and weep and groan to think upon the price that he had paid for her; and then he must dry his eyes, and wash his face, and go and sit with her on the broad balconies, joining in her songs, and, with a sick spirit, answering her smiles.

There came a day when her feet began to be heavy and her songs more rare; and now it was not Keawe only that would weep apart, but each would sunder from the other and sit in opposite balconies with the whole width of the Bright House betwixt. Keawe was so sunk in his despair, he scarce observed the change, and was only glad he had more hours to sit alone and brood upon his destiny, and was not so frequently condemned to pull a smiling face on a sick heart. But one day, coming softly through the house, he heard the sound of a child sobbing, and there was Kokua rolling her face upon the balcony floor, and weeping like the lost.

"You do well to weep in this house, Kokua," he said. "And yet I would give the head off my body that you (at least) might have been happy."

"Happy!" she cried. "Keawe, when you lived alone in your Bright House, you were the word of the island for a happy man; laughter and song were in your mouth, and your face was as bright as the sunrise. Then you wedded poor Kokua; and the good God knows what is amiss in her—but from that day you have not smiled. Oh!" she cried, "what ails me? I thought I was pretty, and I knew I loved him. What ails me that I throw this cloud upon my husband?"

"Poor Kokua," said Keawe. He sat down by her side, and sought to take her hand; but that she plucked away. "Poor Kokua," he said, again. "My poor child—my pretty. And I had thought all this while to spare you! Well, you shall know all. Then, at least, you will pity poor Keawe; then you will understand how much he loved you in the past—that he dared hell for your possession—and how much he loves you still (the poor condemned one), that he can yet call up a smile when he beholds you."

With that, he told her all, even from the beginning.

"You have done this for me?" she cried. "Ah, well, then what do I care!"—and she clasped and wept upon him.

"Ah, child!" said Keawe, "and yet, when I consider of the fire of hell, I care a good deal!"

"Never tell me," said she; "no man can be lost because he loved Kokua, and no other fault. I tell you, Keawe, I shall save you with these hands, or perish in your company. What! you loved me, and gave your soul, and you think I will not die to save you in return?"

"Ah, my dear! you might die a hundred times, and what difference would that make?" he cried, "except to leave me lonely till the time comes of my damnation?"

"You know nothing," said she. "I was educated in a school in Honolulu; I am no common girl. And I tell you, I shall save my lover. What is this you say about a cent? But all the world is not American. In England they have a piece they call a farthing, which is about half a cent. Ah! sorrow!" she cried, "that makes it scarcely better, for the buyer must be lost, and we shall find none so brave as my Keawe! But, then, there is France; they have a small coin there which they call a centime, and these go five to the cent or thereabout. We could not do better. Come, Keawe, let us go to the French islands; let us go to Tahiti, as fast as ships can bear us. There we have four centimes, three centimes, two centimes, one centime; four possible sales to come and go on; and two of us to push the bargain. Come, my Keawe! kiss me, and banish care. Kokua will defend you."

"Gift of God!" he cried. "I cannot think that God will punish me for desiring aught so good! Be it as you will, then; take me where you please: I put my life and my salvation in your hands."

Early the next day Kokua was about her preparations. She took Keawe's chest that he went with sailoring; and first she put the bottle in a corner; and then packed it with the richest of their clothes and the bravest of the knick-knacks in the house. "For," said she, "we must seem to be rich folks, or who will believe in the bottle?" All the time of her preparation she was as gay as a bird; only when she looked upon Keawe, the tears would spring in her eye, and she must run and kiss him. As for Keawe, a weight was off his soul; now that he had his secret shared, and some hope in front of him, he seemed like a new man, his feet went lightly on the earth, and his breath was good to him again. Yet was terror still at his elbow; and ever and again, as the wind blows out a taper, hope died in him, and he saw the flames toss and the red fire burn in hell.

It was given out in the country they were gone pleasuring to the States, which was thought a strange thing, and yet not so strange as the truth, if any could have guessed it. So they went to Honolulu in the *Hall*, and thence in the *Umatilla* to San Francisco with a crowd of Haoles, and at San Francisco took their passage by the mail brigantine, the *Tropic Bird*, for Papeete, the chief place of the French in the south islands. Thither they came, after a pleasant voyage, on a fair day of the Trade Wind, and saw the reef with the surf breaking, and Motuiti with its palms, and the schooner riding within-side, and the white houses of the town low down along the shore among green trees, and overhead the mountains and the clouds of Tahiti, the wise island.

It was judged the most wise to hire a house, which they did accordingly, opposite the British Consul's, to make a great parade of money, and them-selves conspicuous with carriages and horses. This it was very easy to do, so long as they had the bottle in their possession; for Kokua was more bold than Keawe, and, whenever she had a mind, called on the imp for twenty or a hundred dollars. At this rate they soon grew to be remarked in the town; and the strangers from Hawaii, their riding and their driving, the fine holokus and the rich lace of Kokua, became the matter of much talk.

They got on well after the first with the Tahitian language, which is indeed like to the Hawaiian, with a change of certain letters, and as soon as they had any freedom of speech, began to push the bottle. You are to consider it was not an easy subject to introduce; it was not easy to persuade people you were in earnest, when you offered to sell them for four centimes the spring of health and riches inexhaustible. It was necessary besides to explain the dangers of the bottle; and either people disbelieved the whole thing and laughed, or they thought the more of the darker part, became overcast with gravity, and drew away from Keawe and Kokua, as from persons who had dealings with the devil. So far from gaining ground, these two began to find they were avoided in the town; the children ran away from them screaming, a thing intolerable to Kokua; Catholics crossed themselves as they went by; and all persons began with one accord to disengage them-selves from their advances.

Depression fell upon their spirits. They would sit at night in their new house, after a day's weariness, and not exchange one word, or the silence would be broken by Kokua bursting suddenly into sobs. Sometimes they would pray together; sometimes they would have the bottle out upon the floor, and sit all evening watching how the shadow hovered in the midst. At such times they would be afraid to go to rest. It was long ere slumber came to them, and, if either dozed off, it would be to wake and find the other silently weeping in the dark, or, perhaps, to wake alone, the other having

"THERE, UNDER THE BANANAS, LAY KEAWE, HIS MOUTH
IN THE DUST, AND AS HE LAY HE MOANED"

fled from the house and the neighbourhood of that bottle, to pace under the bananas in the little garden, or to wander on the beach by moonlight.

One night it was so when Kokua awoke. Keawe was gone. She felt in the bed and his place was cold. Then fear fell upon her, and she sat up in bed.

THE BOTTLE IMP

A little moonshine filtered through the shutters. The room was bright, and she could spy the bottle on the floor. Outside it blew high, the great trees of the avenue cried aloud, and the fallen leaves rattled in the verandah. In the midst of this Kokua was aware of another sound; whether of a beast or of a man she could scarce tell, but it was as sad as death, and cut her to the soul. Softly she arose, set the door ajar, and looked forth into the moonlit yard. There, under the bananas, lay Keawe, his mouth in the dust, and as he lay he moaned.

It was Kokua's first thought to run forward and console him; her second potently withheld her. Keawe had borne himself before his wife like a brave man; it became her little in the hour of weakness to intrude upon his shame. With the thought she drew back into the house.

"Heaven!" she thought, "how careless have I been—how weak! It is he, not I, that stands in this eternal peril; it was he, not I, that took the curse upon his soul. It is for my sake, and for the love of a creature of so little worth and such poor help, that he now beholds so close to him the flames of hell—ay, and smells the smoke of it, lying without there in the wind and moonlight. Am I so dull of spirit that never till now I have surmised my duty, or have I seen it before and turned aside? But now, at least, I take up my soul in both the hands of my affection; now I say farewell to the white steps of heaven and the waiting faces of my friends. A love for a love, and let mine be equalled with Keawe's! A soul for a soul, and be it mine to perish!"

She was a deft woman with her hands, and was soon apparelled. She took in her hands the change—the precious centimes they kept ever at their side; for this coin is little used, and they had made provision at a Government office. When she was forth in the avenue clouds came on the wind, and the moon was blackened. The town slept, and she knew not whither to turn till she heard one coughing in the shadow of the trees.

"Old man," said Kokua, "what do you here abroad in the cold night?"

The old man could scarce express himself for coughing, but she made out that he was old and poor, and a stranger in the island.

"Will you do me a service?" said Kokua. "As one stranger to another, and as an old man to a young woman, will you help a daughter of Hawaii?"

"Ah," said the old man. "So you are the witch from the eight islands, and even my old soul you seek to entangle. But I have heard of you, and defy your wickedness."

"Sit down here," said Kokua, "and let me tell you a tale." And she told him the story of Keawe from the beginning to the end.

"And now," said she, "I am his wife, whom he bought with his soul's welfare. And what should I do? If I went to him myself and offered to buy it, he would refuse. But if you go, he will sell it eagerly; I will await you here; you will buy it for four centimes, and I will buy it again for three. And the Lord strengthen a poor girl!"

"If you meant falsely," said the old man, "I think God would strike you dead."

"He would!" cried Kokua. "Be sure he would. I could not be so treacherous—God would not suffer it."

"Give me the four centimes and await me here," said the old man.

Now, when Kokua stood alone in the street, her spirit died. The wind roared in the trees, and it seemed to her the rushing of the flames of hell; the shadows tossed in the light of the street lamp, and they seemed to her the snatching hands of evil ones. If she had had the strength, she must have run away, and if she had had the breath she must have screamed aloud; but, in truth, she could do neither; and stood and trembled in the avenue, like an affrighted child.

Then she saw the old man returning, and he had the bottle in his hand.

"I have done your bidding," said he. "I left your husband weeping like a child; tonight he will sleep easy." And he held the bottle forth.

"Before you give it me," Kokua panted, "take the good with the evil—ask to be delivered from your cough."

"I am an old man," replied the other, "and too near the gate of the grave to take a favour from the devil. But what is this? Why do you not take the bottle? Do you hesitate?"

"Not hesitate!" cried Kokua. "I am only weak. Give me a moment. It is my hand resists, my flesh shrinks back from the accursed thing. One moment only!"

The old man looked upon Kokua kindly. "Poor child!" said he, "you fear; your soul misgives you. Well, let me keep it. I am old, and can never more be happy in this world, and as for the next—"

"Give it me!" gasped Kokua. "There is your money. Do you think I am so base as that? Give me the bottle."

"God bless you, child," said the old man.

THE BOTTLE IMP

Kokua concealed the bottle under her holoku, said farewell to the old man, and walked off along the avenue, she cared not whither. For all roads were now the same to her, and led equally to hell. Sometimes she walked, and sometimes ran; sometimes she screamed out loud in the night, and sometimes lay by the wayside in the dust and wept. All that she had heard of hell came back to her; she saw the flames blaze, and she smelt the smoke, and her flesh withered on the coals.

Near day she came to her mind again, and returned to the house. It was even as the old man said—Keawe slumbered like a child. Kokua stood and gazed upon his face.

"Now, my husband," said she, "it is your turn to sleep. When you wake it will be your turn to sing and laugh. But for poor Kokua, alas! that meant no evil—for poor Kokua no more sleep, no more singing, no more delight, whether in earth or heaven."

With that she lay down in the bed by his side, and her misery was so extreme that she fell in a deep slumber instantly.

Late in the morning her husband woke her and gave her the good news. It seemed he was silly with delight, for he paid no heed to her distress, ill though she dissembled it. The words stuck in her mouth, it mattered not; Keawe did the speaking. She ate not a bite, but who was to observe it? for Keawe cleared the dish. Kokua saw and heard him, like some strange thing in a dream; there were times when she forgot, or doubted, and put her hands to her brow; to know herself doomed and hear her husband babble, seemed so monstrous.

All the while Keawe was eating and talking, and planning the time of their return, and thanking her for saving him, and fondling her, and calling her the true helper after all. He laughed at the old man that was fool enough to buy that bottle.

"A worthy old man he seemed," Keawe said. "But no one can judge by appearances. For why did the old reprobate require the bottle?"

"My husband," said Kokua, humbly, "his purpose may have been good."

Keawe laughed like an angry man.

"Fiddle-de-dee!" cried Keawe. "An old rogue, I tell you; and an old ass to boot. For the bottle was hard enough to sell at four centimes; and at three it will be quite impossible. The margin is not broad enough, the thing begins to smell of scorching—brrr!" said he, and shuddered. "It is true I bought it

myself at a cent, when I knew not there were smaller coins. I was a fool for my pains; there will never be found another, and whoever has that bottle now will carry it to the pit."

"O my husband!" said Kokua. "Is it not a terrible thing to save oneself by the eternal ruin of another? It seems to me I could not laugh. I would be humbled. I would be filled with melancholy. I would pray for the poor holder."

Then Keawe, because he felt the truth of what she said, grew the more angry. "Heighty-teighty!" cried he. "You may be filled with melancholy if you please. It is not the mind of a good wife. If you thought at all of me, you would sit shamed."

Thereupon he went out, and Kokua was alone.

What chance had she to sell that bottle at two centimes? None, she perceived. And if she had any, here was her husband hurrying her away to a country where there was nothing lower than a cent. And here—on the morrow of her sacrifice—was her husband leaving her and blaming her.

She would not even try to profit by what time she had, but sat in the house, and now had the bottle out and viewed it with unutterable fear, and now, with loathing, hid it out of sight.

By-and-by, Keawe came back, and would have her take a drive.

"My husband, I am ill," she said. "I am out of heart. Excuse me, I can take no pleasure."

Then was Keawe more wroth than ever. With her, because he thought she was brooding over the case of the old man; and with himself, because he thought she was right, and was ashamed to be so happy.

"This is your truth," cried he, "and this your affection! Your husband is just saved from eternal ruin, which he encountered for the love of you—and you can take no pleasure! Kokua, you have a disloyal heart."

He went forth again furious, and wandered in the town all day. He met friends, and drank with them; they hired a carriage and drove into the country, and there drank again. All the time Keawe was ill at ease, because he was taking this pastime while his wife was sad, and because he knew in his heart that she was more right than he; and the knowledge made him drink the deeper.

Now there was an old brutal Haole drinking with him, one that had been a boatswain of a whaler, a runaway, a digger in gold mines, a convict

"THERE WAS KOKUA ON THE FLOOR, THE LAMP AT HER SIDE; BEFORE HER
WAS A MILK-WHITE BOTTLE, WITH A ROUND BELLY AND A LONG NECK"

in prisons. He had a low mind and a foul mouth; he loved to drink and
to see others drunken; and he pressed the glass upon Keawe. Soon there was
no more money in the company.

"Here, you!" says the boatswain, "you are rich, you have been always saying. You have a bottle or some foolishness."

"Yes," says Keawe, "I am rich; I will go back and get some money from my wife, who keeps it."

"That's a bad idea, mate," said the boatswain. "Never you trust a petticoat with dollars. They're all as false as water; you keep an eye on her."

Now, this word struck in Keawe's mind; for he was muddled with what he had been drinking.

"I should not wonder but she was false, indeed," thought he. "Why else should she be so cast down at my release? But I will show her I am not the man to be fooled. I will catch her in the act."

Accordingly, when they were back in town, Keawe bade the boatswain wait for him at the corner, by the old calaboose, and went forward up the avenue alone to the door of his house. The night had come again; there was a light within, but never a sound; and Keawe crept about the corner, opened the back door softly, and looked in.

There was Kokua on the floor, the lamp at her side; before her was a milk-white bottle, with a round belly and a long neck; and as she viewed it, Kokua wrung her hands.

A long time Keawe stood and looked in the doorway. At first he was struck stupid; and then fear fell upon him that the bargain had been made amiss, and the bottle had come back to him as it came at San Francisco; and at that his knees were loosened, and the fumes of the wine departed from his head like mists off a river in the morning. And then he had another thought; and it was a strange one, that made his cheeks to burn.

"I must make sure of this," thought he.

So he closed the door, and went softly round the corner again, and then came noisily in, as though he were but now returned. And, lo! by the time he opened the front door no bottle was to be seen; and Kokua sat in a chair and started up like one awakened out of sleep.

"I have been drinking all day and making merry," said Keawe. "I have been with good companions, and now I only come back for money, and return to drink and carouse with them again."

Both his face and voice were as stern as judgment, but Kokua was too troubled to observe.

"You do well to use your own, my husband," said she, and her words trembled.

"O, I do well in all things," said Keawe, and he went straight to the chest and took out money. But he looked besides in the corner where they kept the bottle, and there was no bottle there.

At that the chest heaved upon the floor like a sea-billow, and the house span about him like a wreath of smoke, for he saw he was lost now, and there was no escape. "It is what I feared," he thought. "It is she who has bought it."

And then he came to himself a little and rose up; but the sweat streamed on his face as thick as the rain and as cold as the well-water.

"Kokua," said he, "I said to you today what ill became me. Now I return to carouse with my jolly companions," and at that he laughed a little quietly. "I will take more pleasure in the cup if you forgive me."

She clasped his knees in a moment; she kissed his knees with flowing tears.

"O," she cried, "I asked but a kind word!"

"Let us never one think hardly of the other," said Keawe, and was gone out of the house.

Now, the money that Keawe had taken was only some of that store of centime pieces they had laid in at their arrival. It was very sure he had no mind to be drinking. His wife had given her soul for him, now he must give his for hers; no other thought was in the world with him.

At the corner, by the old calaboose, there was the boatswain waiting.

"My wife has the bottle," said Keawe, "and, unless you help me to recover it, there can be no more money and no more liquor tonight."

"You do not mean to say you are serious about that bottle?" cried the boatswain.

"There is the lamp," said Keawe. "Do I look as if I was jesting?"

"That is so," said the boatswain. "You look as serious as a ghost."

"Well, then," said Keawe, "here are two centimes; you must go to my wife in the house, and offer her these for the bottle, which (if I am not much mistaken) she will give you instantly. Bring it to me here, and I will buy it back from you for one; for that is the law with this bottle, that it still must be sold for a less sum. But whatever you do, never breathe a word to her that you have come from me."

"Mate, I wonder are you making a fool of me?" asked the boatswain.

"It will do you no harm if I am," returned Keawe.

"That is so, mate," said the boatswain.

"And if you doubt me," added Keawe, "you can try. As soon as you are clear of the house, wish to have your pocket full of money, or a bottle of the best rum, or what you please, and you will see the virtue of the thing."

"Very well, Kanaka," says the boatswain. "I will try; but if you are having your fun out of me, I will take my fun out of you with a belaying pin."

So the whaler-man went off up the avenue; and Keawe stood and waited. It was near the same spot where Kokua had waited the night before; but Keawe was more resolved, and never faltered in his purpose; only his soul was bitter with despair.

It seemed a long time he had to wait before he heard a voice singing in the darkness of the avenue. He knew the voice to be the boatswain's; but it was strange how drunken it appeared upon a sudden.

Next, the man himself came stumbling into the light of the lamp. He had the devil's bottle buttoned in his coat; another bottle was in his hand; and even as he came in view he raised it to his mouth and drank.

"You have it," said Keawe. "I see that."

"Hands off!" cried the boatswain, jumping back. "Take a step near me, and I'll smash your mouth. You thought you could make a cat's-paw of me, did you?"

"What do you mean?" cried Keawe.

"Mean?" cried the boatswain. "This is a pretty good bottle, this is; that's what I mean. How I got it for two centimes I can't make out; but I'm sure you shan't have it for one."

"You mean you won't sell?" gasped Keawe.

"No, *sir!*" cried the boatswain. "But I'll give you a drink of the rum, if you like."

"I tell you," said Keawe, "the man who has that bottle goes to hell."

"I reckon I'm going anyway," returned the sailor; "and this bottle's the best thing to go with I've struck yet. No, sir!" he cried again, "this is my bottle now, and you can go and fish for another."

"Can this be true?" Keawe cried. "For your own sake, I beseech you, sell it me!"

"I don't value any of your talk," replied the boatswain. "You thought I was a flat; now you see I'm not; and there's an end. If you won't have a swallow of the rum, I'll have one myself. Here's your health, and good-night to you!"

So off he went down the avenue towards town, and there goes the bottle out of the story.

But Keawe ran to Kokua light as the wind; and great was their joy that night; and great, since then, has been the peace of all their days in the Bright House.

23

THE BEACH OF FALESÁ

[With complete illustrations from the First Edition.]

Readers of Island Nights' Entertainments *in Cassell's first edition found a handsome book bound in Pacific blue, with a gilt front-cover picture and frontispiece of a beauteous, bare-breasted, pale-dusky damsel, her face more like an Anglicized teenage Cleopatra than a Polynesian, holding a giant leaf. The subsequent illustrations to 'The Beach of Falesá' (done by two different artists, without control by Stevenson) sustain the impression of a conventional exotic romance. Europeans converse, or perform tricks, or have fisticuffs, with native figures in the background, the pale-dusky beauty in one picture serving tea. On her last appearance, getting shot in white Grecian lingerie and flying necklace, she has become totally white-skinned.*

This packaging presented the story as a Rider Haggard or G.A. Henty adventure with some "south seas" fantasy grafted on. And for most of the last 110 years, that is how it has been read, as a settler romance that doesn't quite come off. A rewritten version by Dylan Thomas in 1959, intended as story for a film, is typical, in its sanitised-lyrical enfeeblement of the original, and in missing its irony, viciousness and satiric sub-text.

Most reviewers recommended Stevenson to stick to Scottish history, and Henry James judged that "Samoa was susceptible of no 'style'". In fact, Stevenson's Pacific adventure was a progress to that style, and 'The Beach of Falesá' incorporates the expectations of colonial romance in order to subvert them. The idea for the story "just shot through me... in one of my moments of awe, alone in that tragic jungle", the bush behind Vailima. He worked hard on the story for two years (from 1890), striving to make it "real" as a rendering of the Pacific:

"UMA"

"Everybody else... got carried away by the romance, and ended in a kind of sugar candy sham epic", he wrote. "Now I have got the smell and the look of the thing." From the seedy settlers to the awesome strangeness of the bush, the result is surprizing and complex.

The illustrations conceal more of the text than they reveal. When Uma is submissively serving tea, what is happening is that her trader "husband" Wiltshire, whose narration makes evident his many shortcomings, has become so convinced of her worth and their shared love that he has just asked the missionary – unthinkably, courageously – to legalize their marriage. She does not die gracefully and conveniently in the gun-fight, but lives on to become "the old lady... a powerful big woman now, and could throw a London bobby over her shoulder". This was not chosen for illustration. Nor was the marriage night scene. In the serialized magazine and first book publication, the story was much censored. The rough edge of Wiltshire's language was smoothed off, and the false marriage certificate made less sexually exploitative. In fact, it was based closely on an actual certificate Stevenson recorded in Butaritari (12) where he refers to another false marriage with the vows made "on a work of mine in a pirated edition", like the "odd volume of a novel" used in the story. The text below, though based on the first edition, restores the publisher's excisions from the manuscript.

At one stage the story was called 'Uma'. Like Kokua in 'The Bottle Imp', she proves intelligent, honest, loving, strongly sexual, and, as her husband at his most eloquent puts it, "a trump". In Wiltshire, Stevenson uses his genius with spoken idiom to create one of his most complex characters, and a masterpiece of "limited narration". Every sentence (including the last) embodies the struggle of a flawed but decent man torn between his experience of "Kanakas", especially his adored wife, and his conditioned, inescapable racism. Narrative information also comes through the captain, Case, Uma and Tarleton, a texture of voices that dramatises the complex mix of cultures and values trying to co-exist on the small island.

Though Wiltshire never knows it, his narration also poignantly shows how the islanders see the alien, dangerous Europeans. Uma's first glance at him is "like a child dodging a blow". As he narrates his campaign against Case, we perceive that neither has any right there, and that a rich social and metaphysical life proceeds around them. When Wiltshire earns his place, it is not with superior technology (his final fight with Case is pure animal) or language (to which he is obtuse) or religion (in which he is worse than ignorant) or culture, but because he was honest enough to admit that he was "clean gone" for a woman who couldn't boil an egg. In that, 'The Beach of Falesá', which its author called both "queer" and "real", and which even opens in ambiguity ("neither night nor morning"), is after all, a romance. It is also a powerful, perceptive interpretation of contemporary Pacific life, and one of the most finely crafted works of narratorial art in English fiction.

Chapter I
A SOUTH SEA BRIDAL

I SAW that island first when it was neither night nor morning. The moon was to the west, setting but still broad and bright. To the east, and right amidships of the dawn, which was all pink, the daystar sparkled like a diamond. The land breeze blew in our faces and smelt strong of wild lime and vanilla: other things besides, but these were the most plain; and the chill of it set me sneezing. I should say I had been for years on a low island near the line, living for the most part solitary among natives. Here was a fresh experience; even the tongue would be quite strange to me; and the look of these woods and mountains, and the rare smell of them, renewed my blood.

The captain blew out the binnacle lamp.

"There," said he, "there goes a bit of smoke, Mr Wiltshire, behind the break of the reef. That's Falesá where your station is, the last village to the east; nobody lives to windward, I don't know why. Take my glass, and you can make the houses out."

I took the glass; and the shores leaped nearer, and I saw the tangle of the woods and the breach of the surf, and the brown roofs and the black insides of houses peeped among the trees.

"Do you catch a bit of white there to the east'ard?" the captain continued. "That's your house. Coral built, stands high, verandah you could walk on three abreast: best station in the South Pacific. When old Adams saw it, he took and shook me by the hand.—'I've dropped into a soft thing here,' says he.—'So you have,' says I, 'and time too!' Poor Johnny! I never saw him again but the once, and then he had changed his tune—couldn't get on with the natives, or the whites, or something; and the next time we came round, there he was dead and buried. I took and put up a bit of stick to him: 'John Adams, *obit* eighteen and sixty eight. Go thou and do likewise.' I missed that man; I never could see much harm in Johnny."

"What did he die of?" I inquired.

"Some kind of a sickness," says the captain. "It appears it took him sudden. Seems he got up in the night, and filled up on Pain-Killer and Kennedy's Discovery: no go—he was booked beyond Kennedy. Then he had tried to open a case of gin; no go again: not strong enough. Then he must have turned to and run out on the verandah, and capsized over the rail. When they found him the next day, he was clean crazy—carried on all the time about somebody watering his copra. Poor John!"

"Was it thought to be the island?" I asked.

"Well, it was thought to be the island, or the trouble, or something," he replied. "I never could hear but what it was a healthy place. Our last man,

Vigours, never turned a hair. He left because of the beach; said he was afraid of Black Jack and Case and Whistling Jimmie, who was still alive at the time but got drowned soon afterward when drunk. As for old Captain Randall, he's been here any time since eighteen forty, forty five. I never could see much harm in Billy, nor much change. Seems as if he might live to be old Kafoozleum. No, I guess it's healthy."

"There's a boat coming now," said I. "She's right in the pass; looks to be a sixteen foot whale; two white men in the stern sheets."

"That's the boat that drowned Whistling Jimmie!" cried the captain. "Let's see the glass. Yes: that's Case, sure enough, and the darkie. They've got a gallows bad reputation, but you know what a place the beach is for talking. My belief, that Whistling Jimmie was the worst of the trouble; and he's gone to glory, you see. What'll you bet they ain't after gin? Lay you five to two they take six cases."

When these two traders came aboard I was pleased with the looks of them at once; or rather, with the looks of both, and the speech of one. I was sick for white neighbours after my four years at the line, which I always counted years of prison; getting tabooed, and going down to the Speak House to see and get it taken off; buying gin, and going on a break, and then repenting; sitting in my house at night with the lamp for company; or walking on the beach and wondering what kind of a fool to call myself for being where I was. There were no other whites upon my island; and when I sailed to the next, rough customers made the most of the society. Now to see these two when they came aboard, was a pleasure. One was a negro to be sure; but they were both rigged out smart in striped pyjamas and straw hats, and Case would have passed muster in a city. He was yellow and smallish; had a hawk's nose to his face, pale eyes, and his beard trimmed with scissors. No man knew his country, beyond he was of English speech; and it was clear he came of a good family and was splendidly educated. He was accomplished too; played the accordion first rate; and give him a piece of string or a cork or a pack of cards, and he could show you tricks equal to any professional. He could speak when he chose fit for a drawing room; and when he chose he could blaspheme worse than a Yankee boatswain and talk smut to sicken a kanaka. The way he thought would pay best at the moment, that was Case's way; and it always seemed to come natural and like as if he was born to it. He had the courage of a lion and the cunning of a rat; and if he's not in Hell today, there's no such place. I know but one good point to the man; that he was fond of his wife and kind to her. She was a Sāmoa woman, and dyed her hair red, Sāmoa style; and when he came to die (as I have to tell of) they found one strange thing, that he had made a will like a Christian and the widow got the lot. All his, they said, and all Black Jack's, and the most of Billy Randall's in the bargain; for it was Case that kept the books. So she went off home in the schooner *Manu'a*, and does the lady to this day in her own place.

But of all this, on that first morning, I knew no more than a fly. Case used me like a gentleman and like a friend, made me welcome to Falesá, and put his services at my disposal, which was the more helpful from my ignorance of the native. All the early part of the day, we sat drinking better acquaintance in the cabin, and I never heard a man talk more to the point. There was no smarter trader, and none dodgier, in the islands. I remember one bit of advice he gave that morning, and one yarn he told. The bit of advice was this. "Whenever you get hold of any money," says he—"any Christian money, I mean—the first thing to do is to fire it up to Sydney to the bank. It's only a temptation to a copra merchant; some day, he'll be in a row with the other traders, and he'll get his shirt out and buy copra with it. And the name of the man that buys copra with gold is Damfool," says he. That was the advice; and this was the yarn, which might have opened my eyes to the danger of that man for a neighbour, if I had been anyway suspicious. It seems Case was trading somewhere in the Ellices. There was a man Miller a Dutchman there, who had a strong hold with the natives and handled the bulk of what there was. Well one fine day a schooner got wrecked in the lagoon, and Miller bought her (the way these things are usually managed) for an old song, which was the ruin of him. For having a lot of trade on hand that had cost him practically nothing, what does he do but begin cutting rates? Case went round to the other traders. "Wants to lower prices?" says Case. "All right, then. He has five times the turn-over of any one of us; if buying at a loss is the game, he stands to lose five times more. Let's give him the bed rock; let's bilge the ——!" And so they did, and five months after, Miller had to sell out his boat and station, and begin again somewhere in the Carolines.

All this talk suited me, and my new companion suited me, and I thought Falesá seemed to be the right kind of a place; and the more I drank, the lighter my heart. Our last trader had fled the place at half an hour's notice, taking a chance passage in a labour ship from up west; the captain, when he came, had found the station closed, the keys left with the native pastor, and a letter from the runaway confessing he was fairly frightened of his life. Since then the firm had not been represented and of course there was no cargo; the wind besides was fair, the captain hoped he could make his next island by dawn, with a good tide; and the business of landing my trade was gone about lively. There was no call for me to fool with it, Case said; nobody would touch my things, everyone was honest in Falesá, only about chickens or an odd knife or an odd stick of tobacco; and the best I could do was to sit quiet till the vessel left, then come straight to his house, see old Captain Randall, the father of the Beach, take pot luck, and go home to sleep when it got dark. So it was high noon, and the schooner was under way, before I set my foot on shore at Falesá.

I had a glass or two on board, I was just off a long cruise and the ground heaved under me like a ship's deck. The world was like all new painted; my foot went along to music; Falesá might have been Fiddler's Green, if there is such a place, and more's the pity if there isn't! It was good to foot the grass, to look aloft at the green mountains, to see the men with their green wreaths and the women in their bright dresses, red and blue. On we went, in the strong sun and the cool shadow, liking both; and all the children in the town came trotting after with their shaven heads and their brown bodies, and raising a thin kind of a cheer in our wake, like crowing poultry.

"By the by," says Case, "we must get you a wife."

"That's so," said I, "I had forgotten."

There was a crowd of girls about us, and I pulled myself up and looked among them like a Bashaw. They were all dressed out for the sake of the ship being in; and the women of Falesá are a handsome lot to see. If they have a fault, they are a trifle broad in the beam; and I was just thinking so when Case touched me.

"That's pretty," says he.

I saw one coming on the other side alone. She had been fishing; all she wore was a chemise, and it was wetted through, and a cutty sark at that. She was young and very slender for an island maid, with a long face, a high forehead, and a sly, strange, blindish look between a cat's and a baby's.

"Who's she?" said I. "She'll do."

"That's Uma," said Case, and he called her up and spoke to her in the native. I didn't know what he said; but when he was in the midst, she looked up at me quick and timid like a child dodging a blow; then down again; and presently smiled. She had a wide mouth, the lips and the chin cut like any statue's; and the smile came out for a moment and was gone. There she stood with her head bent and heard Case to an end; spoke back in the pretty Polynesian voice, looking him full in the face; heard him again in answer; and then with an obeisance started off. I had just a share of the bow, but never another shot of her eye; and there was no more word of smiling.

"I guess it's all right," said Case. "I guess you can have her. I'll make it square with the old lady. You can have your pick of the lot for a plug of tobacco," he added, sneering.

I suppose it was the smile stuck in my memory, for I spoke back sharp. "She doesn't look that sort," I cried.

"I don't know that she is," said Case. "I believe she's as right as the mail. Keeps to herself, don't go round with the gang, and that. O, no, don't you misunderstand me—Uma's on the square." He spoke eager I thought, and that surprised and pleased me. "Indeed," he went on, "I shouldn't make so sure of getting her, only she cottoned to the cut of your jib. All you have to do is to keep dark and let me work the mother my own way; and I'll bring the girl round to the captain's for the marriage."

I didn't care for the word marriage, and I said so.

"O, there's nothing to hurt in the marriage," says he. "Black Jack's the chaplain."

By this time we had come in view of the house of these three white men; for a negro is counted a white man—and so is Chinese! a strange idea, but common in the islands. It was a board house with a strip of rickety verandah. The store was to the front, with a counter, scales and the poorest possible display of trade: a case or two of tinned meats; a barrel of hard bread; a few bolts of cotton stuff, not to be compared with mine; the only thing well represented being the contraband—firearms and liquor. "If these are my only rivals," thinks I, "I should do well in Falesá." Indeed there was only the one way they could touch me, and that was with the guns and drink.

In the back room was old Captain Randall, squatting on the floor native fashion, fat and pale, naked to the waist, grey as a badger and his eyes set with drink. His body was covered with grey hair and crawled over by flies;

one was in the corner of his eye—he never heeded; and the mosquitoes hummed about the man like bees. Any clean-minded man would have had the creature out at once and buried him; and to see him, and think he was seventy, and remember he had once commanded a ship, and come ashore in his smart togs, and talked big in bars and consulates, and sat in club verandahs, turned me sick and sober.

He tried to get up when I came in, but that was hopeless; so he reached me a hand instead and stumbled out some salutation.

"Papa's pretty full this morning," observed Case. "We've had an epidemic here; and Captain Randall takes gin for a prophylactic—don't you, papa?"

"Never took such thing my life!" cried the captain, indignantly. "Take gin for my health's sake, Mr Wha's-ever-your-name. 'S a precaution'ry measure."

"That's all right, papa," said Case. "But you'll have to brace up. There's going to be a marriage—Mr Wiltshire here is going to get spliced."

The old man asked to whom.

"To Uma," said Case.

"Uma?" cried the captain. "Wha's he want Uma for? 'S he come here for his health, anyway? Wha' 'n hell's he want Uma for?"

"Dry up papa," said Case. "'Tain't you that's to marry her. I guess you're not her godfather and godmother. I guess Mr Wiltshire's going to please himself."

With that he made an excuse to me that he must move about the marriage, and left me alone with the poor wretch that was his partner and (to speak truth) his gull. Trade and station belonged both to Randall; Case and the negro were parasites; they crawled and fed upon him like the flies, he none the wiser. Indeed I have no harm to say of Billy Randall, beyond the fact that my gorge rose at him, and the time I now passed in his company was like a nightmare.

The room was stifling hot and full of flies; for the house was dirty and low and small, and stood in a bad place, behind the village, in the borders of the bush, and sheltered from the trade. The three men's beds were on the floor, and a litter of pans and dishes. There was no standing furniture, Randall, when he was violent, tearing it to laths. There I sat, and had a meal which was served us by Case's wife; and there I was entertained all day by

THE BEACH OF FALESÁ

that remains of man, his tongue stumbling among low old jokes and long old stories, and his own wheezy laughter always ready, so that he had no sense of my depression. He was nipping gin all the while; sometimes he fell asleep and awoke again whimpering and shivering; and every now and again he would ask me why in Hell I wanted to marry Uma. "My friend," I was telling myself all day, "you must not be an old gentleman like this."

It might be four in the afternoon perhaps, when the backdoor was thrust slowly open, and a strange old native woman crawled into the house almost on her belly. She was swathed in black stuff to her heels; her hair was gray in swatches; her face was tattooed, which was not the practice in that island; her eyes big and bright and crazy. These she fixed upon me with a wrapt expression that I saw to be part acting; she said no plain word, but smacked and mumbled with her lips, and hummed aloud, like a child over its Christmas pudding. She came straight across the house heading for me, and as soon as she was alongside, caught up my hand and purred and crooned over it like a great cat. From this she slipped into a kind of song.

"Who the devil's this?" cried I, for the thing startled me.

"It's Faavao," says Randall, and I saw he had hitched along the floor into the farthest corner.

"You ain't afraid of her?" I cried.

"Me 'fraid!" cried the captain. "My dear friend, I defy her! I don't let her put her foot in here. Only I suppose 's diff'ent today for the marriage. 'S Uma's mother."

"Well, suppose it is, what's she carrying on about?" I asked, more irritated, perhaps more frightened, than I cared to show; and the captain told me she was making up a quantity of poetry in my praise because I was to marry Uma. "All right, old lady," says I, with rather a failure of a laugh, "anything to oblige. But when you're done with my hand, you might let me know."

She did as though she understood; the song rose into a cry and stopped; the woman crouched out of the house the same way that she came in, and must have plunged straight into the bush, for when I followed her to the door she had already vanished.

"These are rum manners," said I.

"'S a rum crowd," said the captain, and to my surprise, he made the sign of the cross on his bare bosom.

"Hillo!" says I, "are you a Papist?"

He repudiated the idea with contempt. "Hard-shell Baptis'," said he. "But, my dear friend, the Papists got some good ideas too; and tha' 's one of 'em. You take my advice, and whenever you come across Uma or Faavao or Vigours or any of that crowd, you take a leaf out o' the priests, and do what I do. Savvy?" says he, repeated the sign, and winked his dim eye at me. "No, sir!" he broke out again, "no Papists here!" and for a long time entertained me with his religious opinions.

I must have been taken with Uma from the first, or I should certainly have fled from that house and got into the clean air, and the clean sea or some convenient river. Though it's true I was committed to Case; and besides I could never have held my head up in that island, if I had run from a girl upon my wedding night.

The sun was down, the sky all on fire, and the lamp had been some time lighted, when Case came back with Uma and the negro. She was dressed and scented; her kilt was of fine tapa, looking richer in the folds than any silk; her bust, which was of the colour of dark honey, she wore bare only for some half a dozen necklaces of seeds and flowers; and behind her ears and in her hair, she had the scarlet flowers of the hybiscus. She showed the best bearing for a bride conceivable, serious and still; and I thought shame to stand up with her in that mean house and before that grinning negro. I thought shame I say; for the mountebank was dressed with a big paper collar, the book he made believe to read from was an odd volume of a novel, and the words of his service not fit to be set down. My conscience smote me when we joined hands; and when she got her certificate, I was tempted to throw up the bargain and confess. Here is the document: it was Case that wrote it, signatures and all, in a leaf out of the ledger.

This is to certify that _Uma_ daughter of _Faavao_ of Falesá island of ——, is illegally married to _Mr John Wiltshire_ for one night, and Mr John Wiltshire is at liberty to send her to hell next morning.

JOHN BLACKAMOOR

Chaplain to the Hulks.

Extracted from the register
by William T Randall
Master Mariner.

THE BEACH OF FALESÁ

"Uma showed the best bearing for a bride conceivable"

A nice paper to put in a girl's hand and see her hide away like gold. A man might easily feel cheap for less. But it was the practice in these parts, and (as I told myself) not the least fault of us white men but of the missionaries. If they had let natives be, I had never needed this deception, but taken all the wives I wished, and left them when I pleased, with a clear conscience.

The more ashamed I was, the more hurry I was in to be gone; and our desires thus jumping together, I made the less remark of a change in the traders. Case had been all eagerness to keep me; now, as though he had attained a purpose, he seemed all eagerness to have me go. Uma, he said, could show me to my house, and the three bade us farewell indoors.

The night was nearly come; the village smelt of trees, and flowers and the sea, and breadfruit cooking; there came a fine roll of sea from the reef, and from a distance, among the woods and houses, many pretty sounds of men and children. It did me good to breathe free air; it did me good to be done with the captain and see, instead, the creature at my side. I felt for all the world as though she were some girl at home in the Old Country, and forgetting myself for the minute, took her hand to walk with. Her fingers nestled into mine; I heard her breathe deep and quick; and all at once she caught my hand to her face and pressed it there. "You good!" she cried, and ran ahead of me, and stopped and looked back and smiled, and ran ahead of me again; thus guiding me through the edge of the bush and by a quiet way to my own house.

The truth is Case had done the courting for me in style—told her I was mad to have her, and cared nothing for the consequence; and the poor soul, knowing that which I was still ignorant of, believed it, every word, and had her head nigh turned with vanity and gratitude. Now, of all this I had no guess; I was one of those most opposed to any nonsense about native women, having seen so many whites eaten up by their wives' relatives and made fools of in the bargain; and I told myself I must make a stand at once, and bring her to her bearings. But she looked so quaint and pretty as she ran away and then awaited me, and the thing was done so like a child or a kind dog, that the best I could do was just to follow her whenever she went on, to listen for the fall of her bare feet, and to watch in the dusk for the shining of her body. And there was another thought came in my head. She played kitten with me now when we were alone; but in the house she had carried it the way a countess might, so proud and humble. And what with her dress—for all there was so little of it, and that native enough—what with her fine tapa and fine scents, and her red flowers and seeds, that were quite as bright as jewels, only larger—it came over me she was a kind of a countess really, dressed to hear great singers at a concert, and no even mate for a poor trader like myself.

She was the first in the house; and while I was still without, I saw a match flash and the lamplight kindle in the windows. The station was a wonderful fine place, coral built, with quite a wide verandah, and the main room high and wide. My chests and cases had been piled in, and made rather of a mess; and there, in the thick of the confusion, stood Uma by the table, awaiting me. Her shadow went all the way up behind her into the hollow of the iron roof; she stood against it bright, the lamplight shining on her skin. I stopped in the door, and she looked at me, not speaking, with eyes that were eager and yet daunted. Then she touched herself on the bosom.

"Me—your wifie," she said. It had never taken me like that before; but the want of her took and shook all through me, like the wind in the luff of a sail.

I could not speak if I had wanted; and if I could, I would not. I was ashamed to be so much moved about a native; ashamed of the marriage too, and the certificate she had treasured in her kilt; and I turned aside and made believe to rummage among my cases. The first thing I lighted on was a case of gin, the only one that I had brought; and partly for the girl's sake, and partly for horror of the recollection of old Randall, took a sudden resolve. I prized the lid off. One by one, I drew the bottles with a pocket corkscrew, and sent Uma out to pour the stuff from the verandah.

She came back after the last, and looked at me puzzled like.

"Why you do that?" she asked.

"No good," said I, for I was now a little better master of my tongue. "Man he drink, he no good."

She agreed with this, but kept considering. "Why you bring him?" she asked presently. "Suppose you no want drink, you no bring him, I think."

"That's all right," said I. "One time I want drink too much; now no want. You see I no savvy I get one little wifie. Suppose I drink gin, my little wifie he 'fraid."

To speak to her kindly was about more than I was fit for; I had made my vow I would never let on to weakness with a native; and I had nothing for it but to stop.

She stood looking gravely down at me where I sat by the open case. "I think you good man," she said. And suddenly she had fallen before me on the floor. "I belong you all-e-same pig!" she cried.

Chapter II

THE BAN

I came on the verandah just before the sun rose on the morrow. My house was the last on the east; there was a cape of woods and cliffs behind that hid the sunrise. To the west, a swift cold river ran down, and beyond was the green of the village, dotted with cocoa-palms and breadfruits and houses. The shutters were some of them down and some open; I saw the mosquito bars still stretched, with shadows of people new wakened sitting up inside; and all over the green others were stalking silent, wrapped in their many-coloured sleeping clothes like Bedouins in Bible pictures. It was mortal still and solemn and chilly, and the light of the dawn on the lagoon was like the shining of a fire.

But the thing that troubled me was nearer hand. Some dozen young men and children made a piece of a half-circle, flanking my house; the river divided them, some were on the near side, some on the far, and one on a boulder in the midst; and they all sat silent, wrapped in their sheets, and stared at me and my house as straight as pointer dogs. I thought it strange as I went out. When I had bathed and come back again, and found them all there, and two or three more along with them, I thought it stranger still. What could they see to gaze at in my house? I wondered, and went in.

But the thought of these starers stuck in my mind, and presently I came out again. The sun was now up, but it was still behind the cape of woods. Say quarter of an hour had come and gone. The crowd was greatly increased, the far bank of the river was lined for quite a way—perhaps thirty grown folk, and of children twice as many, some standing, some squatted on the ground, and all staring at my house. I have seen a house in a South Sea village thus surrounded, but then a trader was thrashing his wife inside, and she singing out. Here was nothing: the stove was alight, the smoke going up in a Christian manner; all was shipshape and Bristol fashion. To be sure, there was a stranger come, but they had a chance to see that stranger yester-day, and took it quiet enough. What ailed them now? I leaned my arms on the rail and stared back. Devil a wink they had in them! Now and then I could see the children chatter, but they spoke so low not even the hum of their speaking came my length. The rest were like graven images; they stared at me, dumb and sorrowful, with their bright eyes; and it came upon me things would look not much different, if I were on the platform of the gallows, and these good folk had come to see me hanged.

I felt I was getting daunted, and began to be afraid I looked it, which would never do. Up I stood, made believe to stretch myself, came down the verandah stair, and strolled towards the river. There went a short buzz from one to the other, like what you hear in theatres when the curtain goes up; and some of the nearest gave back the matter of a pace. I saw a girl lay one hand on a young man and make a gesture upward with the other; at the same time she said something in the native with a gasping voice. Three little boys sat beside my path, where I must pass within three feet of them. Wrapped in their sheets, with their shaved heads and bits of topknots, and queer faces, they looked like figures on a chimney piece. Awhile they sat their ground, solemn as judges; I came up hand over fist, doing my five knots, like a man that meant business; and I thought I saw a sort of a wink and gulp in the three faces. Then one jumped up (he was the farthest off) and ran for his mammy. The other two, trying to follow suit, got foul, came to ground together bawling, wriggled right out of their sheets mother-naked and in a moment there were all three of them scampering for their lives and singing out like pigs. The natives, who would never let a joke slip even at a burial, laughed and let up, as short as a dog's bark.

They say it scares a man to be alone. No such thing. What scares him in the dark or the high bush, is that he can't make sure, and there might be an army at his elbow. What scares him worst is to be right in the midst of a crowd, and have no guess of what they're driving at. When that laugh stopped, I stopped too. The boys had not yet made their offing; they were still on the full stretch going the one way, when I had already gone about ship and was sheering off the other. Like a fool I had come out, doing my five knots; like a fool I went back again. It must have been the funniest thing to see, and what knocked me silly, this time no one laughed; only one old woman gave a kind of pious moan, the way you have heard Dissenters in their chapels at the sermon.

"I never saw such damfool Kanakas as your people here," I said once to Uma, glancing out of the window at the starers.

"Savvy nothing," says Uma, with a kind of a disgusted air that she was good at.

And that was all the talk we had upon the matter, for I was put out, and Uma took the thing so much as a matter of course that I was fairly ashamed.

All day, off and on, now fewer and now more, the fools sat about the west end of my house and across the river, waiting for the show, whatever that was—fire to come down from heaven, I suppose, and consume me, bones and baggage. But by evening, like real islanders, they had wearied of the business, and got away, and had a dance instead in the big house of the village, where I heard them singing and clapping hands till, maybe, ten at night, and the next day, it seemed they had forgotten I existed. If fire had come down from heaven or the earth opened and swallowed me, there would have been nobody to see the sport or take the lesson, or whatever you like to call it. But I was to find they hadn't forgot either, and kept an eye lifting for phenomena over my way.

I was hard at it both these days getting my trade in order, and taking stock of what Vigours had left. This was a job that made me pretty sick, and kept me from thinking on much else. Ben had taken stock the trip before—I knew I could trust Ben—but it was plain somebody had been making free in the meantime. I found I was out by what might easy cover six months' salary and profit, and I could have kicked myself all round the village to have been such a blamed ass, sitting boozing with that Case, instead of attending to my own affairs and taking stock.

However, there's no use crying over spilt milk. It was done now, and couldn't be undone. All I could do was to get what was left of it, and my new stuff (my own choice) in order, to go round and get after the rats and cock-roaches, and to fix up that store regular Sydney style. A fine show I made of it; and the third morning, when I had lit my pipe and stood in the doorway and looked in, and turned and looked far up the mountain, and saw the cocoanuts waving, and footed up the tons of copra, and over the village green and saw the island dandies, and reckoned up the yards of print they wanted for their kilts and dresses, I felt as if I was in the right place to make a fortune, and go home again, and start a public house. There was I sitting in that verandah, in as handsome a piece of scenery as you could find, a splendid sun, and a fine, fresh healthy trade that stirred up a man's blood like sea-bathing; and the whole thing was clean gone from me, and I was dream-ing England, which is after all a nasty, cold, muddy hole, with not enough light to see to read by; and dreaming the looks of my public, by a cant of a broad highroad like an avenue, and with the sign on a green tree.

So much for the morning, but the day passed and the devil any one looked near me, and from all I knew of natives in other islands, I thought this strange. People laughed a little at our firm and their fine stations, and at this station of Falesá in particular; all the copra in the district wouldn't

"'WHAT DOES FUSSY-OCKY MEAN?' I ASKED OF UMA"

pay for it (I had heard them say) in fifty years, which I supposed was an exaggeration. But when the day went, and no business came at all, I began to get downhearted; and about three in the afternoon, I went out for a stroll to cheer me up. On the green I saw a white man coming with a cassock on, by which and by the face of him, I knew he was a priest. He was a good natured old soul to look at, gone a little grizzled, and so dirty you could have written with him on a piece of paper.

"Good day, sir," says I.

He answered me eagerly in native.

"Don't you speak any English?" said I.

"Franch," says he.

"Well," said I, "I'm sorry, but I can't do anything there."

He tried me awhile in the French, and then again in native, which he seemed to think was the best chance. I made out he was after more than passing the time of day with me, but had something to communicate, and I listened the harder. I heard the names of Adams and Case and of Randall—Randall the oftenest—and the word "poison" or something like it, and a native word that he said very often. I went home repeating it to myself.

"What does *fussy-ocky* mean?" I asked of Uma, for that was as near as I could come to it.

"Make dead," said she.

"The devil it does!" says I. "Did ever you hear that Case had poisoned Johnny Adams?"

"Every man he savvy that," says Uma, scornful like. "Give him white sand—bad sand. He got the bottle still. Suppose he give you gin, you no take him."

Now I had heard much the same sort of story in other islands, and the same white powder always to the front, which made me think the less of it. For all that I went over to Randall's place to see what I could pick up, and found Case on the door step cleaning a gun.

"Good shooting here?" says I.

"A 1," says he. "The bush is full of all kinds of birds. I wish copra was as plenty," says he, I thought slyly, "but there don't seem anything doing."

I could see Black Jack in the store, serving a customer.

"That looks like business, though," said I.

"That's the first sale we've made in three weeks," said he.

"You don't tell me?" says I. "Three weeks? Well, well."

"If you don't believe me," he cries, a little hot, "you can go and look at the copra house. It's half empty to this blesséd hour."

"I shouldn't be much the better for that, you see," says I. "For all I can tell, it might have been whole empty yesterday."

"That's so," says he, with a bit of a laugh.

"By the bye," I said, "what sort of a party is that priest? Seems rather a friendly sort."

At this Case laughed right out loud. "Ah," says he, "I see what ails you now! Galuchet's been at you." *Father Galoshes* was the name he went by mostly, but Case always gave it the French quirk, which was another reason we had for thinking him above the common.

"Yes, I have seen him," I says. "I made out he didn't think much of your Captain Randall."

"That he don't!" says Case. "It was the trouble about poor Adams. The last day, when he lay dying, there was young Buncombe round. Ever met Buncombe?"

I told him no.

"He's a cure, is Buncombe!" laughs Case. "Well, Buncombe took it in his head that as there was no other clergyman about, bar Kanaka pastors, we ought to call in Father Galuchet, and have the old man administered and take the sacrament. It was all the same to me, you may suppose; but I said I thought Adams was the fellow to consult. He was jawing away about watered copra and a sight of foolery. 'Look here,' I said. 'You're pretty sick. Would you like to see Galoshes?' He sat right up on his elbow. 'Get the priest,' says he, 'get the priest, don't let me die here like a dog.' He spoke kind of fierce and eager, but sensible enough; there was nothing to say against that, so we sent and asked Galuchet if he would come. You bet he would! He jumped in his dirty linen at the thought of it. But we had reckoned without Papa. He's a hard-shell Baptist, is Papa; no Papists need apply; and he took and locked the door. Buncombe told him he was bigoted, and I thought he would have had a fit. 'Bigoted!' he says. 'Me bigoted? Have I lived to hear it from a jackanapes like you?' And he made for Buncombe, and I had to hold them apart—and there was Adams in the middle, gone luny again, and carrying on about copra like a born fool. It was good as the play, and I was about knocked out of time with laughing, when all of a sudden Adams sat up, clapped his hands to his chest, and went into the horrors. He died hard, did John Adams," says Case with a kind of a sudden sternness.

"And what became of the priest?" I asked.

"The priest?" says Case. "O, he was hammering on the door outside, and crying on the natives to come and beat it in, and singing out it was a soul he wished to save, and that. He was in a hell of a taking was the priest. But what would you have? Johnny had slipped his cable; no more Johnny in the market! and the administration racket clean played out. Next thing, word came to Randall the priest was praying upon Johnny's grave. Papa was pretty full, and got a club, and lit out straight for the place, and there was Galoshes on his knees, and a lot of natives looking on. You wouldn't think Papa cared that much about anything, unless it was liquor; but he and the priest stuck to it two hours, slanging each other in native; and every time Galoshes tried to kneel down, Papa went for him with the club. There never were such larks in Falesá. The end of it was that Captain Randall knocked over with some kind of a fit or stroke, and the priest got in his goods after all. But he was the angriest priest you ever heard of, and complained to the chiefs about the outrage, as he called it. That was no account, for our chiefs are Protestant here; and anyway he had been making trouble about the drum for morning school, and they were glad to give him a wipe. Now he swears old Randall gave Adams poison or something, and when the two meet they grin at each other like baboons."

He told this story as natural as could be, and like a man that enjoyed the fun; though now I come to think of it after so long, it seems rather a sickening yarn. However Case never set up to be soft, only to be square and hearty and a man all round; and to tell the truth, he puzzled me entirely.

I went home, and asked Uma if she were a *Popey*, which I had made out to be the native word for Catholics.

"*E le ai!*" says she—she always used the native when she meant "no" more than usually strong, and indeed there's more of it. "No good, Popey," she added.

Then I asked her about Adams and the priest, and she told me much the same yarn in her own way. So that I was left not much farther on, but inclined upon the whole, to think the bottom of the matter was the row about the sacrament, and the poisoning only talk.

The next day was a Sunday, when there was no business to be looked for. Uma asked me in the morning if I was going to "pray"; I told her she bet not; and she stopped home herself with no more words. I thought this seemed unlike a native, and a native woman, and a woman that had new clothes to show off; however, it suited me to the ground, and I made the less of it. The queer thing was that I came next door to going to church after all, a thing I'm little likely to forget. I had turned out for a stroll, and heard the hymn tune up. You know how it is. If you hear folk singing, it seems to draw you; and pretty soon I found myself alongside the church. It was a little long low place, coral built, rounded off at both ends like a whale-boat, a big native roof on the top of it, windows without sashes and doorways without doors. I stuck my head into one of the windows, and the sight was so new to me—for things went quite different in the islands I was acquainted with—that I stayed and looked on. The congregation sat on the floor on mats, the women on one side, the men on the other; all rigged out to kill, the women with dresses and trade hats, the men in white jackets and shirts. The hymn was over; the pastor, a big buck Kanaka, was in the pulpit preaching for his life; and by the way he wagged his hand, and worked his voice, and made his points, and seemed to argue with the folk, I made out he was a gun at the business. Well, he looked up suddenly and caught my eye; and I give you my word he staggered in the pulpit. His eyes bulged out of his head, his hand rose and pointed at me like as if against his will, and the sermon stopped right there.

It isn't a fine thing to say for yourself, but I ran away; and if the same kind of a shock was given me, I should run away again tomorrow. To see that palavering Kanaka struck all of a heap at the mere sight of me, gave me a feeling as if the bottom had dropped out of the world. I went right home, and stayed there, and said nothing. You might think I would tell Uma, but that was against my system. You might have thought I would have gone over and consulted Case; but the truth was I was ashamed to speak of such a thing, I thought everyone would blurt out laughing in my face. So I held my tongue, and thought all the more, and the more I thought, the less I liked the business.

By Monday night, I got it clearly in my head I must be tabooed. A new store to stand open two days in a village, and not a man or woman come to see the trade, was past believing.

"Uma," said I, "I think I'm tabooed."

"I think so," said she.

I thought awhile whether I should ask her more, but it's a bad idea to set natives up with any notion of consulting them, so I went to Case. It was dark, and he was sitting alone, as he did mostly, smoking on the stairs.

"Case," said I, "here's a queer thing. I'm tabooed."

"O, fudge!" says he. "'Tain't the practice in these islands."

"That may be, or it mayn't," said I. "It's the practice where I was before; you can bet I know what it's like; and I tell it you for a fact, I'm tabooed."

"Well," said he, "what have you been doing?"

"That's what I want to find out," said I.

"O, you can't be," said he; "it ain't possible. However, I'll tell you what I'll do. Just to put your mind at rest, I'll go round and find out for sure. Just you waltz in and talk to Papa."

"Thank you," I said, "I'd rather stay right out here on the verandah. Your house is so close."

"I'll call Papa out here, then," says he.

"My dear fellow," I says, "I wish you wouldn't. The fact is I don't take to

Mr Randall."

Case laughed, took a lantern from the store, and set out into the village. He was gone perhaps quarter of an hour; and he looked mighty serious when he came back.

"Well," said he, clapping down the lantern on the verandah steps, "I would never have believed it. I don't know where the impudence of these Kanakas 'll go next; they seem to have lost all idea of respect for whites. What we want is a man of war—a German, if we could—they know how to manage Kanakas."

"I *am* tabooed then?" I cried.

"Something of the sort," said he. "It's the worst thing of the kind I've heard of yet. But I'll stand by you, Wiltshire, man to man. You come round here tomorrow about nine and we'll have it out with the chiefs. They're afraid of me; or they used to be, but their heads are so big by now I don't know what to think. Understand me, Wiltshire, I don't count this your quarrel," he went on with a great deal of resolution; "I count it all of our quarrel, I count it the White Man's Quarrel, and I'll stand to it through thick and thin, and there's my hand on it."

"Have you found out what's the reason?" I asked.

"Not yet," said Case. "But we'll fix them down tomorrow."

Altogether I was pretty well pleased with his attitude, and almost more the next day when we met to go before the chiefs, to see him so stern and resolved. The chiefs awaited us in one of their big oval houses, which was marked out to us from a long way off by the crowd about the eaves, a hundred strong if there was one, men, women and children. Many of the men were on their way to work and wore green wreaths; and it put me in thoughts of the first of May at home. This crowd opened and buzzed about the pair of us as we went in, with a sudden angry animation. Five chiefs were there, four mighty stately men, the fifth old and puckered. They sat on mats in their white kilts and jackets; they had fans in their hands, like fine ladies; and two of the younger ones wore Catholic medals, which gave me matter of reflection. Our place was set and the mats laid for us over against these grandees on the near side of the house; the midst was empty; the crowd, close at our backs, murmured and craned and jostled to look on, and the shadows of them tossed in front of us on the clean pebbles of the floor. I was just a hair put out by the excitement of the commons, but the quiet, civil appearance of the chiefs reassured me, all the more when their spokesman began and made a long speech in a low tone of voice, sometimes waving his hand toward Case, sometimes toward me, and sometimes knocking with his knuckles on the mat. One thing was clear: there was no sign of anger in the chiefs.

"What's he been saying?" I asked, when he had done.

"O, just that they're glad to see you, and they understand by me you wish to make some kind of a complaint, and you're to fire away, and they'll do the square thing."

"It took a precious long time to say that," said I.

"O, the rest was sawder and *bonjour* and that," says Case—"you know what Kanakas are!"

"Well, they don't get much *bonjour* out of me," said I. "You tell them who I am. I'm a white man, and a British subject, and no end of a big chief at home; and I've come here to do them good, and bring them civilization; and no sooner have I got my trade sorted out, than they go and taboo me and no one dare come near my place! Tell them I don't mean to fly in the face of anything legal; and if what they want's a present, I'll do what's fair. I don't blame any man looking out for himself, tell them, for that's human nature; but if they think they're going to come any of their native ideas over me, they'll find themselves mistaken. And tell them plain, that I demand the reason of this treatment as a white man and a British subject."

That was my speech. I know how to deal with Kanakas; give them plain sense and fair dealing, and I'll do them that much justice, they knuckle under every time. They haven't any real government or any real law, that's what you've got to knock into their heads; and even if they had, it would be a good joke if it was to apply to a white man. It would be a strange thing if we came all this way and couldn't do what we pleased. The mere idea has always put my monkey up, and I rapped my speech out pretty big. Then Case translated it—or made believe to, rather—and the first chief replied, and then a second and a third, all in the same style, easy and genteel but solemn underneath. Once a question was put to Case, and he answered it, and all hands (both chiefs and commons) laughed out loud and looked at me. Last of all, the puckered old fellow and the big young chief that spoke first, started in to put Case through a kind of catechism. Sometimes I made out that Case was trying to fence, and they stuck to him like hounds, and the sweat ran down his face, which was no very pleasant sight to me; and at some of his answers, the crowd moaned and murmured, which was a worse hearing. It's a cruel shame I knew no native; for (as I now believe) they were asking Case about my marriage, and he must have had a tough job of it to clear his feet. But leave Case alone; he had the brains to run a parliament.

"Well, is that all?" I asked, when a pause came.

"Come along," says he, mopping his face. "I'll tell you outside."

"Do you mean they won't take the taboo off?" I cried.

"It's something queer," said he. "I'll tell you outside. Better come away."

"I won't take it at their hands," cried I. "I ain't that kind of a man. You don't find me turn my back on a parcel of Kanakas."

"You'd better," said Case.

He looked at me with a signal in his eye, and the five chiefs looked at me civilly enough but kind of pointed; and the people looked at me and craned and jostled. I remembered the folks that watched my house, and how the pastor had jumped in his pulpit at the bare sight of me; and the whole business seemed so out of the way that I rose and followed Case. The crowd opened again to let us through, but wider than before, the children on the skirts running and singing out; and as we two white men walked away, they all stood and watched us.

"And now," said I, "what is all this about?"

"The truth is I can't rightly make it out myself. They have a down on you," says Case.

"Taboo a man because they have a down on him!" I cried. "I never heard the like."

"It's worse than that, you see," said Case. "You ain't tabooed—I told you that couldn't be. The people won't go near you, Wiltshire; and there's where it is."

"They won't go near me? What do you mean by that? Why won't they go near me?" I cried.

Case hesitated. "Seems they're frightened," says he, in a low voice.

I stopped dead short. "Frightened?" I repeated. "Are you gone crazy, Case? What are they frightened of?"

"I wish I could make out," Case answered, shaking his head.

"Appears like one of their tomfool superstitions. That's what I don't cotton to," he said. "It's like the business about Vigours."

"I'd like to know what you mean by that, and I'll trouble you to tell me," says I.

"Well, you know, Vigours lit out and left all standing," said he. "It was some superstition business—I never got the hang of it—but it began to look bad before the end."

"I've heard a different story about that," said I, "and I had better tell you so. I heard he ran away because of you."

"O, well, I suppose he was ashamed to tell the truth," says Case; "I guess he thought it silly. And it's a fact that I packed him off. 'What would you do, old man?' says he—'Get,' says I, 'and not think twice about it.' I was the gladdest kind of man to see him clear away. It ain't my notion to turn my back on a mate when he's in a tight place, but there was that much trouble in the village that I couldn't see where it might likely end. I was a fool to be so much about with Vigours. They cast it up to me today. Didn't you hear Maea—that's the young chief, the big one—ripping out about 'Vika'? That was him they were after. They don't seem to forget it, somehow."

"This is all very well," said I, "but it don't tell me what's wrong; it don't tell me what they're afraid of—what their idea is."

"Well, I wish I knew," said Case. "I can't say fairer than that."

"You might have asked, I think," says I.

"And so I did," says he. "But you must have seen for yourself, unless you're blind, that the asking got the other way. I'll go as far as I dare for another white man; but when I find I'm in the scrape myself, I think first of my own bacon. The loss of me is I'm too good-natured. And I'll take the freedom of telling you, you show a queer kind of gratitude to a man who's got into all this mess along of your affairs."

"There's a thing I'm thinking of," said I. "You were a fool to be so much about with Vigours. One comfort, you haven't been much about with me. I notice you've never been inside my house. Own up, now: you had word of this before?"

"It's a fact I haven't been," said he. "It was an oversight, and I'm sorry for it, Wiltshire. But about coming now, I'll be quite plain."

"You mean you won't?" I asked.

"Awfully sorry, old man, but that's the size of it," says Case.

"In short, you're afraid?" says I.

"In short, I'm afraid," says he.

"And I'm still to be tabooed for nothing?" I asked.

"I tell you you're not tabooed," said he. "The Kanakas won't go near you, that's all. And who's to make 'em? We traders have a lot of gall, I must say; we make these poor Kanakas take back their laws, and take up their taboos, and that, whenever it happens to suit us. But you don't mean to say you expect a law obliging people to deal in your store whether they want to or not? You don't mean to tell me you've got the gall for that? And if you had, it would be a queer thing to propose to me. I would just like to point out to you, Wiltshire, that I'm a trader myself."

"I don't think I would talk of gall if I was you," said I. "Here's about what it comes to, as well as I can make out. None of the people are to trade with me, and they're all to trade with you. You're to have the copra, and I'm to go to the devil and shake myself. And I don't know any native, and you're the only man here worth mention that speaks English, and you have the gall to up and hint to me my life's in danger, and all you've got to tell me is, you don't know why!"

"Well, it *is* all I have to tell you," said he. "I don't know—I wish I did."

"And so you turn your back and leave me to myself! Is that the position?" says I.

"If you like to put it nasty," says he. "I don't put it so. I say merely I'm going to keep clear of you, or if I don't I'll get in danger for myself."

"Well," says I, " you're a nice kind of a white man!"

"O, I understand you're riled," said he. "I would be myself. I can make excuses."

"All right," I said, "go and make excuses somewhere else. Here's my way, there's yours."

With that we parted, and I went straight home, in a holy temper, and found Uma trying on a lot of trade goods like a baby.

"Here," I said, "you quit that foolery! Here's a pretty mess to have made—as if I wasn't bothered enough anyway! And I thought I told you to get dinner?"

And then I believe I gave her a bit of the rough side of my tongue, as she deserved. She stood up at once, like a sentry to his officer; for I must say she was always well brought up and had a great respect for whites.

"And now," says I, "you belong round here, you're bound to understand this. What am I tabooed for anyway? Or if I ain't tabooed, what makes the folks afraid of me?"

She stood and looked at me with eyes like saucers.

"You no savvy?" she gasps at last.

"No," said I. "How would you expect me to? We don't have any such craziness where I come from."

"Ese no tell you?" she asked again.

(*Ese* was the name the natives had for Case; it may mean foreign, or extraordinary; or it might mean a mummy apple; but most like it was only his own name misheard and put in a Kanaka spelling.)

"Not much!" said I.

"Damn Ese!" she cried.

You might think it was funny to hear this Kanaka girl come out with a big swear. No such thing. There was no swearing in her—no, nor anger; she was beyond anger, and meant the word simple and serious. She stood there straight as she said it. I cannot justly say that ever I saw a woman look like that before or after, and it struck me mum. Then she made a kind of an obeisance, but it was the proudest kind, and threw her hands out open.

"I 'shamed," she said. "I think you savvy. Ese he tell me you savvy, he tell me you no mind—tell me you love me too much. Taboo belong me," she said, touching herself on the bosom, as she had done upon our wedding night. "Now I go 'way, taboo he go 'way too. Then you get too much copra. You like more better, I think. Tofá, alii," says she in the native—"Farewell, chief!"

"Hold on," I cried. "Don't be in such a blamed hurry."

She looked at me sidelong with a smile. "You see, you get copra," says she, the same as you might offer candies to a child.

"Uma," said I, "hear reason. I didn't know, and that's a fact; and Case seems to have played it pretty mean upon the pair of us. But I do know now, and I don't mind: I love you too much. You no go 'way, you no leave me, I too much sorry."

"You no love me!" she cried, "You talk me bad words!" And she threw herself in a corner on the floor, and began to cry.

Well, I'm no scholar, but I wasn't born yesterday, and I thought the worst of that trouble was over. However, there she lay—her back turned, her face to the wall—and shook with sobbing like a little child, so that her feet jumped with it. It's strange how it hits a man when he's in love; for there's no use mincing things – Kanaka and all, I was in love with her, or just as good. I tried to take her hand, but she would none of that. "Uma," I said, "there's no sense in carrying on like this. I want you stop here, I want my little wifie, I tell you true."

"No tell me true!" she sobbed.

"All right," says I, "I'll wait till you're through with this." And I sat right down beside her on the floor, and set to smoothe her hair with my hand. At first she wriggled away when I touched her; then she seemed to notice me no more; then her sobs grew gradually less, and presently stopped; and the next thing I knew, she raised her face to mine.

"You tell me true? You like me stop?" she asked.

"Uma," I said, "I would rather have you than all the copra in the South Seas," which was a very big expression, and the strangest thing was that I meant it.

She threw her arms about me, sprang close up, and pressed her face to mine in the island way of kissing, so that I was all wetted with her tears and my heart went out to her wholly. I never had anything so near me as this little brown bit of a girl. Many things went together and all helped to turn my head. She was pretty enough to eat; it seemed she was my only friend in that queer place; I was ashamed that I had spoken rough to her; and she was a woman, and my wife, and a kind of a baby besides that I was sorry for; and the salt of her tears was in my mouth. And I forgot Case and the natives; and I forgot that I knew nothing of the story, or only remembered it to banish the remembrance; and I forgot that I was to get no copra and so could make no livelihood; and I forgot my employers, and the strange kind of service I was doing them, when I preferred my fancy to their business; and I forgot even that Uma was no true wife of mine, but just a maid beguiled, and that in a pretty shabby style. But that is to look too far on. I will come to that part of it next.

It was late before we thought of getting dinner. The stove was out, and gone stone-cold; but we fired up after awhile, and cooked each a dish, helping and hindering each other, and making a play of it like children. I was so greedy of her nearness that I sat down to dinner with my lass upon my knee, made sure of her with one hand, and ate with the other. Ay, and more than that. She was the worst cook I suppose God made; the things she set her hand to, it would have sickened an honest horse to eat of; yet I made my meal that day on Uma's cookery, and can never call to mind to have been better pleased.

I didn't pretend to myself, and I didn't pretend to her. I saw I was clean gone; and if she was to make a fool of me, she must. And I suppose it was this that set her talking, for now she made sure that we were friends. A lot she told me, sitting in my lap and eating my dish, as I ate hers, from foolery—a lot about herself and her mother and Case, all which would be very tedious and fill sheets if I set it down in Beach de Mar, but which I must give a hint of in plain English—and one thing about myself, which had a very big effect on my concerns, as you are soon to hear.

It seems she was born in one of the Line Islands; had been only two or three years in these parts, where she had come with a white man who was married to her mother and then died; and only the one year in Falesá. Before that, they had been a good deal on the move, trekking about after the white man, who was one of these rolling stones that keep going round after a soft job. They talk about looking for gold at the end of a rainbow; but if a man wants an employment that'll last him till he dies, let him start out on the soft-job hunt. There's meat and drink in it too, and beer and skittles, for you never hear of them starving, and rarely see them sober; and as for steady sport, cockfighting isn't in the same county with it. Anyway, this beachcomber carried the woman and her daughter all over the shop, but mostly to out of the way islands, where there were no police and he thought perhaps the soft job hung out. I've my own view of this old party; but I was just as glad he had kept Uma clear of Apia and Papeete and these flash towns. At last he struck Fale-alii on this island, got some trade—the Lord knows how! muddled it all away in the usual style, and died worth next to nothing, bar a bit of land at Falesá that he had got for a bad debt, which was what put it in the minds of the mother and daughter to come there and live. It seems Case encouraged them all he could, and helped to get their house built. He was very kind those days, and gave Uma trade, and there is no doubt he had his eye on her from the beginning. However, they had scarce settled, when up turned a young man, a native, and wanted to marry her. He was a small chief, and had some fine mats and old songs in his family, and was "very pretty," Uma said; and altogether it was an extraordinary match for a penniless girl and an out-islander.

At the first word of this, I got downright sick with jealousy.

"And you mean to say you would have married him!" I cried.

"*Ioe,*" says she. "I like too much!"

"Well!" I said. "And suppose I had come round after?"

"I like you more better now," said she. "But suppose I marry Ioane, I one good wife. I no common Kanaka. Good girl!" says she.

Well, I had to be pleased with that; but I promise you I didn't care about the business one little bit, and liked the end of that yarn no better than the beginning. For it seems this proposal of marriage was the start of all the trouble. It seems, before that, Uma and her mother had been looked down upon, of course, for kinless folk and out-islanders, but nothing to hurt; and even when Ioane came forward there was less trouble at first than might have been looked for. And then all of a sudden, about six months before my coming, Ioane backed out and left that part of the island, and from that day to this, Uma and her mother had found themselves alone. None called at their house, none spoke to them on the roads. If they went to church, the other women drew their mats away and left them in a clear place by themselves. It was a regular excommunication, like what you read of in the Middle Ages; and the cause or sense of it beyond guessing. It was some *tala pepelo,* Uma said, some lie, some calumny; and all she knew of it was that the girls who had been jealous of her luck with Ioane used to twit her with his desertion, and cry out, when they met her alone in the woods, that she would never be married. "They tell me no man he marry me. He too much 'fraid," she said.

The only soul that came about them after this desertion was Master Case. Even he was chary of showing himself, and turned up mostly by night; and pretty soon he began to table his cards and make up to Uma. I was still sore about Ioane, and when Case turned up in the same line of business, I cut up downright rough.

"Well," I said sneering, "and I suppose you thought Case 'very pretty' and 'liked too much.'"

"Now you talk silly," said she. "White man he come here, I marry him all-e-same Kanaka; very well then, he marry me all-e-same white woman. Suppose he no marry, he go 'way, woman he stop. All-e-same thief; empty hand, Tonga-heart—no can love! Now you come marry me. You big heart—you no 'shamed island-girl. That thing I love you for too much. I proud."

I don't know that ever I felt sicker all the days of my life. I laid down my fork and I put away "the island girl"; I didn't seem somehow to have any use for either; and I went and walked up and down in the house, and Uma followed me with her eyes, for she was troubled, and small wonder! But troubled was no word for it with me. I so wanted, and so feared, to make a clean breast of the sweep that I had been.

And just then there came a sound of singing out of the sea; it sprang up suddenly clear and near, as the boat turned the headland, and Uma, running to the window, cried out it was "Misi" come upon his rounds.

I thought it was a strange thing I should be glad to have a missionary; but if it was strange, it was still true.

"Uma," said I, "you stop here in this room, and don't budge a foot out of it till I come back."

Chapter III

THE MISSIONARY

AS I came out on the verandah, the mission boat was shooting for the mouth of the river. She was a long whale-boat painted white; a bit of an awning astern; a native pastor crouched on the wedge of poop, steering; some four and twenty paddles flashing and dipping, true to the boat-song; and the missionary under the awning, in his white clothes, reading in a book, and set him up! It was pretty to see and hear; there's no smarter sight in the islands than a missionary boat with a good crew and a good pipe to them; and I considered it for half a minute with a bit of envy perhaps, and then strolled down towards the river.

From the opposite side there was another man aiming for the same place, but he ran and got there first. It was Case; doubtless his idea was to keep me apart from the missionary, who might serve me as interpreter; but my mind was upon other things, I was thinking how he had jockeyed us about the marriage, and tried his hand on Uma before; and at the sight of him, rage flew in my nostrils.

"Get out of that, you low, swindling thief!" I cried.

"What's that you say?" says he.

I gave him the word again, and rammed it down with a good oath. "And if ever I catch you within six fathoms of my house," I cried, "I'll clap a bullet in your measly carcase."

"'HAVE YOU HAD ENOUGH?' CRIED I"

"You must do as you like about your house," said he, "where I told you I have no thought of going. But this is a public place."

"It's a place where I have private business," said I. "I have no idea of a hound like you eavesdropping, and I give you notice to clear out."

"I don't take it though," says Case.

"I'll show you, then," said I.

"We'll have to see about that," said he.

He was quick with his hands, but he had neither the height nor the weight, being a flimsy creature alongside a man like me; and besides I was blazing to that height of wrath that I could have bit into a chisel. I gave him first the one and then the other, so that I could hear his head rattle and crack, and he went down straight.

"Have you had enough?" cried I. But he only looked up white and blank, and the blood spread upon his face like wine upon a napkin. "Have you had enough?" I cried again. "Speak up, and don't lie malingering there, or I'll take my feet to you!"

He sat up at that, and held his head—by the look of him you could see it was spinning—and the blood poured on his pyjamas.

"I've had enough for this time," says he, and he got up staggering and went off by the way that he had come.

The boat was close in; I saw the missionary had laid his book to one side, and I smiled to myself. "He'll know I'm a man, anyway," thinks I.

This was the first time, in all my years in the Pacific, I had ever exchanged two words with any missionary; let alone asked one for a favour. I didn't like the lot, no trader does; they look down upon us and make no concealment; and besides they're partly Kanakaised, and suck up with natives instead of with other white men like themselves. I had on a rig of clean striped pyjamas, for of course I had dressed decent to go before the chiefs; but when I saw the missionary step out of his boat in the regular uniform, white duck clothes, pith helmet, white shirt and tie, and yellow boots to his feet, I could have bunged stones at him. As he came nearer, queering me pretty curious (because of the fight I suppose) I saw he looked mortal sick, for the truth was he had a fever on and had just had a chill in the boat.

"Mr Tarleton, I believe?" says I, for I had got his name.

"And you, I suppose, are the new trader?" says he.

"I want to tell you first that I don't hold with missions," I went on, "and that I think you and the likes of you do a sight of harm, filling up the natives with old wives' tales and bumptiousness."

"You are perfectly entitled to your opinions," says he, looking a bit ugly, "but I have no call to hear them."

"It so happens that you've got to hear them," I said. "I'm no missionary nor missionary lover; I'm no Kanaka nor favourer of Kanakas—I'm just a trader, I'm just a common, low, God-damned white man and British subject, the sort you would like to wipe your boots on. I hope that's plain!"

"Yes, my man," said he. "It's more plain than creditable. When you are sober, you'll be sorry for this."

He tried to pass on, but I stopped him with my hand. The Kanakas were beginning to growl. Guess they didn't like my tone, for I spoke to that man as free as I would to you.

"Now you can't say I've deceived you," said I, "and I can go on. I want a service—I want two services in fact; and if you care to give me them, I'll perhaps take more stock in what you call your Christianity."

He was silent for a moment. Then he smiled. "You are rather a strange sort of man," says he.

"'I'M NO MISSIONARY, NOR MISSIONARY LOVER'"

"I'm the sort of a man God made me," says I. "I don't set up to be a gentleman," I said.

"I am not quite so sure," said he. "And what can I do for you, Mr ——?"

"Wiltshire," I says, "though I'm mostly called Welsher; but Wiltshire is the way it's spelt, if the people on the beach could only get their tongues about it. And what do I want? Well, I'll tell you the first thing. I'm what you call a sinner—what I call a sweep—and I want you to help me make it up to a person I've deceived."

THE BEACH OF FALESÁ

He turned and spoke to his crew in the native. "And now I am at your service," said he, "but only for the time my crew are dining. I must be much farther down the coast before night. I was delayed at Papa-mālūlū till this morning, and I have an engagement in Fale-alii tomorrow night."

I led the way to my house in silence and rather pleased with myself for the way I had managed the talk, for I like a man to keep his self-respect.

"I was sorry to see you fighting," says he.

"O, that's part of the yarn I want to tell you," I said. "That's service number two. After you've heard it, you'll let me know whether you're sorry or not."

We walked right in through the store, and I was surprised to find Uma had cleared away the dinner things. This was so unlike her ways, that I saw she had done it out of gratitude, and liked her the better. She and Mr Tarleton called each other by name, and he was very civil to her seemingly. But I thought little of that; they can always find civility for a Kanaka; it's us white men they lord it over. Besides I didn't want much Tarleton just then. I was going to do my pitch.

"Uma," said I, "give us your marriage certificate." She looked put out. "Come," said I. "You can trust me. Hand it up."

She had it about her person as usual; I believe she thought it was a pass to heaven, and if she died without having it handy she would go to hell. I couldn't see where she put it the first time, I couldn't see now where she took it from; it seemed to jump in her hand like that Blavatsky business in the papers. But it's the same way with all island women, and I guess they're taught it when young.

"Now," said I, with the certificate in my hand, "I was married to this girl by Black Jack the negro. The certificate was wrote by Case, and it's a dandy piece of literature, I promise you. Since then I've found that there's a kind of cry in the place against this wife of mine, and so long as I keep her, I cannot trade. Now what would any man do in my place, if he was a man?" I said. "The first thing he would do is this, I guess." And I took and tore up the certificate and bunged the pieces on the floor.

"Aué!" cried Uma, and began to clap her hands, but I caught one of them in mine.

"And the second thing that he would do," said I, "if he was what I would call a man, and you would call a man, Mr Tarleton, is to bring the girl right before you or any other missionary, and to up and say: 'I was wrong married to this wife of mine, but I think a heap of her, and now I want to be married to her right.' Fire away, Mr Tarleton. And I guess you'd better do it in native; it'll please the old lady," I said, giving her the proper name of a man's wife upon the spot.

So we had in two of the crew to witness, and were spliced in our own house; and the parson prayed a good bit, I must say, but not so long as some, and shook hands with the pair of us.

"Mr Wiltshire," he says, when he had made out the lines and packed off the witnesses, "I have to thank you for a very lively pleasure. I have rarely performed the marriage ceremony with more grateful emotions."

That was what you would call talking. He was going on besides with more of it, and I was ready for as much taffy as he had in stock, for I felt good. But Uma had been taken up with something half through the marriage, and cut straight in.

"How your hand he get hurt?" she asked.

"You ask Case's head, old lady," says I.

She jumped with joy, and sang out.

"You haven't made much of a Christian of this one," says I to Mr Tarleton.

"We didn't think her one of our worst," says he, "when she was at Fale-alii; and if Uma bears malice, I shall be tempted to fancy she has good cause."

"Well, there we are at service number two," said I. "I want to tell you our yarn, and see if you can let a little daylight in."

"Is it long?" he asked.

"Yes," I said, "it's a goodish bit of a yarn."

"Well, I'll give you all the time I can spare," says he, looking at his watch. "But I must tell you fairly I haven't eaten since five this morning; and unless you can let me have something, I am not likely to eat again before seven or eight tonight."

"By God, we'll give you dinner!" I cried.

I was a little caught up at my swearing, just when all was going straight; and so was the missionary I suppose, but he made believe to look out of the window and thanked us.

So we ran him up a bit of a meal. I was bound to let the old lady have a hand in it, to show off; so I deputised her to brew the tea. I don't think I ever met such tea as she turned out. But that was not the worst, for she got round with the salt-box, which she considered an extra European touch, and turned my stew into sea-water. Altogether, Mr Tarleton had a devil of a dinner of it; but he had plenty entertainment by the way, for all the while that we were cooking, and afterwards when he was making believe to eat, I kept posting him up on Master Case and the beach of Falesá, and he putting questions that showed he was following close.

"I KEPT POSTING HIM UP ON MASTER CASE AND THE BEACH OF FALESÁ"

"Well," said he at last, "I am afraid you have a dangerous enemy. This man Case is very clever and seems really wicked. I must tell you I have had my eye on him for nearly a year, and have rather had the worst of our encounters. About the time when the last representative of your firm ran so suddenly away, I had a letter from Namu, the native pastor, begging me to come to Falesá at my earliest convenience, as his flock were all 'adopting Catholic practices.' I had great confidence in Namu; I fear it only shows how easily we are deceived. No one could hear him preach and not be persuaded he was a man of extraordinary parts. All our islanders easily acquire a kind of eloquence, and can roll out and illustrate with a great deal of vigour and fancy second-hand sermons; but Namu's sermons are his own, and I cannot deny that I have found them means of grace. Moreover, he has a keen curiosity in secular things, does not fear work, is clever at carpentering, and has made himself so much respected among the neighbouring pastors that we call him, in a jest which is half serious, the Bishop of the East. In short I was proud of the man; all the more puzzled by his letter; and took occasion to come this way. The morning before my arrival, Vigours had been sent on board the *Lion*, and Namu was perfectly at his ease, apparently ashamed of his letter, and quite unwilling to explain it. This, of course, I could not allow; and he ended by confessing that he had been much concerned to find his people using the sign of the cross, but since he had learned the explanation his mind was satisfied. For Vigours had the Evil Eye, a common thing in a country of Europe called Italy, where men were often struck dead by that kind of devil; and it appeared the sign of the cross was a charm against its power.

" 'And I explain it, Misi,' said Namu in this way. 'The country in Europe is a Popey country, and the devil of the Evil Eye may be a Catholic devil, or at least used to Catholic ways. So then I reasoned thus; if this sign of the cross were used in a Popey manner, it would be sinful; but when it is used only to protect men from a devil, which is a thing harmless in itself, the sign too must be harmless. For the sign is neither good nor bad, even as a bottle is neither good nor bad. But if the bottle be full of gin, the gin is bad; and if the sign be made in idolatry, so is the idolatry bad.' And very like a native pastor, he had a text apposite about the casting out of devils.

" 'And who has been telling you about the Evil Eye?' I asked.

"He admitted it was Case. Now I am afraid you will think me very narrow, Mr Wiltshire, but I must tell you I was displeased, and cannot think a trader at all a good man to advise or have an influence upon my pastors. And besides there had been some flying talk in the country of old Adams and his being poisoned, to which I had paid no great heed; but it came back to me at the moment.

" 'And is this Case a man of sanctified life?' I asked.

"He admitted he was not; for though he did not drink, he was profligate with women, and had no religion.

" 'Then,' said I, 'I think the less you have to do with him the better.'

"But it is not easy to have the last word with a man like Namu. He was ready in a moment with an illustration. 'Misi,' said he, 'you have told me there were wise men, not pastors, not even holy, who knew many things useful to be taught, about trees for instance, and beasts, and to print books, and about the stones that are burned to make knives of. Such men teach you in your college, and you learn from them, but take care not to learn to be unholy. Misi, Case is my college.'

"I knew not what to say. Mr Vigours had evidently been driven out of Falesá by the machinations of Case and with something not very unlike the collusion of my pastor. I called to mind it was Namu who had reassured me about Adams and traced the rumour to the ill-will of the priest. And I saw I must inform myself more thoroughly from an impartial source. There is an old rascal of a chief here, Faiaso, whom I daresay you saw today at the council; he has been all his life turbulent and sly, a great fomenter of rebellions, and a thorn in the side of the mission and the island. For all that he is very shrewd, and except in politics or about his own misdemeanours, a teller of the truth. I went to his house, told him what I had heard, and besought him to be frank. I do not think I had ever a more painful interview. Perhaps you will understand me, Mr Wiltshire, if I tell you that I am perfectly serious in these old-wives' tales with which you reproached me, and as anxious to do well for these islands as you can be to please and to protect your pretty wife. And you are to remember that I thought Namu a paragon, and was proud of the man as one of the first ripe fruits of the mission. And now I was informed that he had fallen in a sort of dependence upon Case. The beginning of it was not corrupt; it began doubtless in fear and respect, produced by trickery and pretence; but I was shocked to find that another element had been lately added, that Namu helped himself in the store, and was believed to be deep in Case's debt. Whatever the trader said, that Namu believed with trembling. He was not alone in this; many in the village lived in a similar subjection; but Namu's case was the most influential, it was through Namu Case had wrought most evil; and with a certain following among the chiefs, and the pastor in his pocket, the man was as good as master of the village. You know something of Vigours and Adams; but perhaps you have never heard of old Underhill, Adams's predecessor. He was a quiet, mild old fellow, I remember, and we were told he had died suddenly: white men die very suddenly in Falesá. The truth, as I now heard it, made my blood run cold. It seems he was struck with a general palsy, all of him dead but one eye, which he continually winked. Word was started that the helpless old man was now a devil; and this vile fellow Case worked upon the natives' fears, which he professed to share, and pretended he durst not go into the house alone. At last a grave was dug, and the living body buried at the far end of the village. Namu, my pastor, whom I had helped to educate, offered up prayer at the hateful scene.

"I felt myself in a very difficult position. Perhaps it was my duty to have denounced Namu and had him deposed. Perhaps I think so now, but at the time it seemed less clear. He had a great influence, it might prove greater than mine. The natives are prone to superstition; perhaps by stirring them up, I might but ingrain and spread these dangerous fancies. And Namu besides, apart from this novel and accursed influence, was a good pastor, an able man and spiritually minded. Where should I look for a better? how was I to find as good? At that moment with Namu's failure fresh in my view, the work of my life appeared a mockery; hope was dead in me. I would rather repair such tools as I had, than go abroad in quest of others that must certainly prove worse; and a scandal is, at the best, a thing to be avoided when humanly possible. Right or wrong then, I determined on a quiet course. All that night I denounced and reasoned with the erring pastor; twitted him with his ignorance and want of faith; twitted him with his wretched attitude, making clean the outside of the cup and platter, callously helping at a murder, childishly flying in excitement about a few childish, unnecessary and inconvenient gestures; and long before day, I had him on his knees and bathed in tears of what seemed a genuine repentance. On Sunday I took the pulpit in the morning and preached from First Kings, nineteenth, on the fire, the earthquake and the voice: distinguishing the true

"'Will you know what was in his heart?' cries he"

spiritual power, and referring with such plainness as I dared to recent events in Falesá. The effect produced was great, and it was much increased, when Namu rose in his turn, and confessed that he had been wanting in faith and conduct, and was convinced of sin. So far, then, all was well; but there was one unfortunate circumstance. It was nearing the time of our 'May' in the island, when the native contributions to the mission are received; it fell in my duty to make a notification on the subject, and this gave my enemy his chance, by which he was not slow to profit.

"News of the whole proceedings must have been carried to Case as soon as church was over; and the same afternoon he made an occasion to meet me in the midst of the village. He came up with so much intentness and animosity that I felt it would be damaging to avoid him.

"'So,' says he in native, 'here is the holy man. He has been preaching against me, but that was not in his heart. He has been preaching upon the love of God, but that was not in his heart—it was between his teeth. Will you know what was in his heart?' cries he. 'I will show it you.' And making a snatch at my head, he made believe to pluck out a dollar, and held it in the air.

"There went that rumour through the crowd with which Polynesians receive a prodigy. As for myself, I stood amazed. The thing was a common, conjuring trick, which I have seen performed at home a score of times; but how was I to convince the villagers of that? I wished I had learned leger-demain instead of Hebrew, that I might have paid the fellow out with his own coin. But there I was, I could not stand there silent, and the best that I could find to say was weak.

" 'I will trouble you not to lay hands on me again,' said I.

" 'I have no such thought,' said he, 'nor will I deprive you of your dollar. Here it is,' he said, and flung it at my feet. I am told it lay where it fell three days."

"I must say it was well played," said I.

"O, he is clever," said Mr Tarleton, "and you can now see for yourself how dangerous. He was a party to the horrid death of the paralytic; he is accused of poisoning Adams; he drove Vigours out of the place by lies that might have led to murder; and there is no question but he has now made up his mind to rid himself of you. How he means to try, we have no guess; only be sure it's something new. There is no end to his readiness and invention."

"He gives himself a sight of trouble," says I. "And after all, what for?"

"Why, how many tons of copra may they make in this district?" asked the missionary.

"I daresay as much as sixty tons," says I.

"And what is the profit to the local trader?" he asked.

"You may call it three pounds," said I.

"Then you can reckon for yourself how much he does it for," said Mr Tarleton. "But the more important thing is to defeat him. It is clear he spread some report against Uma, in order to isolate and have his wicked will of her. Failing of that, and seeing a new rival come upon the scene, he used her in a different way. Now the first point to find out is about Namu. Uma, when people began to leave you and your mother alone, what did Namu do?"

"Stop away all-e-same," says Uma.

"I fear the dog has returned to his vomit," said Mr Tarleton. "And now what am I to do for you? I will speak to Namu, I will warn him he is observed; it will be strange if he allow anything to go on amiss, when he is put upon his guard. At the same time, this precaution may fail, and then you must turn elsewhere. You have two people at hand to whom you might apply. There is first of all the priest, who might protect you by the Catholic interest; they are a wretchedly small body, but they count two chiefs. And then there is old Faiaso. Ah! if it had been some years ago, you would have needed no one else; but his influence is much reduced, it has gone into Maea's hands, and Maea, I fear, is one of Case's jackals. In fine, if the worst comes to the worst, you must send up or come yourself to Fale-alii, and though I am not due at this end of the island for a month, I will see what can be done."

So Mr Tarleton said farewell; and half an hour later, the crew were singing and the paddles flashing in the missionary boat.

Chapter IV

DEVIL-WORK

NEAR a month went by without much doing. The same night of our marriage, Galoshes called round, made himself mighty civil, and got into a habit of dropping in about dark and smoking his pipe with the family. He could talk to Uma, of course, and started to teach me native and French at the same time. He was a kind old buffer, though the dirtiest you would wish to see, and he muddled me up with foreign languages worse than the tower of Babel.

That was one employment we had, and it made me feel less lonesome; but there was no profit in the thing; for though the priest came and sat and yarned, none of his folks could be enticed into my store; and if it hadn't been for the other occupation I struck out, there wouldn't have been a pound of copra in the house. This was the idea: Fa'avao (Uma's mother) had a score of bearing trees. Of course, we could get no labour, being all as good as tabooed, and the two women and I turned to and made copra with our own hands. It was copra to make your mouth water, when it was done—I never understood how much the natives cheated me till I had made that four hundred pounds of my own hand—and it weighed so light, I felt inclined to take and water it myself.

When we were at the job, a good many Kanakas used to put in the best of the day looking on, and once that nigger turned up. He stood back with the natives, and laughed, and did the big don and the funny dog, till I began to get riled.

"Here, you, nigger!" says I.

"I don't address myself to you, Sah," says the nigger. "Only speak to gen'le'um."

"I know," says I, "but it happens I was addressing myself to you, Mr Black Jack. And all I want to know is just this: did you see Case's figurehead about a week ago?"

"No, Sah," says he.

"That's all right, then," says I; "for I'll show you the own brother to it, only black, in the inside of about two minutes."

And I began to walk towards him, quite slow and my hands down; only there was trouble in my eye, if anybody took the pains to look.

"You're a low, obstropulous fellow, Sah," says he.

"You bet!" says I.

By that time he thought I was about as near as was convenient, and lit out so it would have done your heart good to see him travel. And that was all I saw of that precious gang, until what I am about to tell you.

It was one of my chief employments these days to go pot-hunting in the woods, which I found (as Case had told me) very rich in game. I have spoken of the cape which shut up the village and my station from the east. A path went about the end of it, and led into the next bay. A strong wind blew here daily, and as the line of the barrier reef stopped at the end of the cape, a heavy surf ran on the shores of the bay. A little cliffy hill cut the valley in two parts, and stood close on the beach; and at high water the sea broke right on the face of it, so that all passage was stopped. Woody mountains hemmed the place all round; the barrier to the east was particularly steep and leafy; the lower parts of it, along the sea, falling in sheer black cliffs streaked with cinnabar; the upper part lumpy with the tops of the great trees. Some of the trees were bright green, and some red, and the sand of the beach as black as your shoes. Many birds hovered round the bay, some of them snow white; and the flying-fox (or vampire) flew there in broad daylight, gnashing its teeth.

For a long while I came as far as this shooting and went no farther. There was no sign of any path beyond; and the cocoa-palms in the front of the foot of the valley were the last this way. For the whole "eye" of the island, as natives call the windward end, lay desert. From Falesá round about to Papa-mālūlū, there was neither house, nor man, nor planted fruit tree; and the reef being mostly absent and the shores bluff, the sea beat direct among crags, and there was scarce a landing place.

I should tell you that after I began to go in the woods, although no one offered to come near my store, I found people willing enough to pass the time of day with me where nobody could see them. And as I had begun to pick up native, and most of them had a word or two of English, I began to hold little odds and ends of conversation, not to much purpose, to be sure, but they took off the worst of the feeling, for it's a miserable thing to be made a leper of.

It chanced one day, towards the end of the month, that I was sitting in this bay in the edge of the bush, looking east, with a Kanaka. I had given him a fill of tobacco, and we were making out to talk as best we could; indeed he had more English than most.

I asked him if there was no road going eastward.

"One time one road," said he. "Now he dead."

"Nobody he go there?" I asked.

"No good," said he. "Too much devil he stop there."

"Oho!" says I, "got-um plenty devil, that bush?"

"Man devil, woman devil; too much devil," said my friend. "Stop there all-e-time. Man he go there, no come back."

I thought, if this fellow was so well posted on devils and spoke of them so free, which is not common, I had better fish for a little information about myself and Uma.

"You think me one devil?" I asked.

"No think devil," said he soothingly. "Think all-e-same fool."

"Uma, she devil?" I asked again.

"No, no; no devil; devil stop bush," said the young man.

I was looking in front of me across the bay, and I saw the hanging front of the woods pushed suddenly open, and Case with a gun in his hand step forth into the sunshine on the black beach. He was got up in light pyjamas, near white, his gun sparkled, he looked mighty conspicuous; and the land crabs scuttled from all round him to their holes.

"Hullo, my friend," says I, "you no talk all-e-same true. Ese he go, he come back."

"Ese no all-e-same; Ese *Tiapolo*," says my friend; and with a good bye, slunk off among the trees.

I watched Case all round the beach, where the tide was low; and let him pass me on the homeward way to Falesá. He was in deep thought; and the birds seemed to know it, trotting quite near him on the sand or wheeling and calling in his ears. Where he passed nearest me, I could see by the working of his lips that he was talking to himself, and what pleased me mightily, he had still my trademark on his brow. I tell you the plain truth, I had a mind to give him a gunful in his ugly mug, but I thought better of it.

All this time, and all the time I was following home, I kept repeating that native word, which I remembered by "Polly, put the kettle on and make us all some tea": tea-a-pollo.

"Uma," says I, when I got back, "what does Tiapolo mean?"

"Devil," says she.

"I thought *aitu* was the word for that?" I said.

"*Aitu* 'nother kind of devil," said she; "stop bush, eat Kanaka. Tiapolo big-chief devil, stop home; all-e-same Christian devil."

"Well then," said I. "I'm no farther forward. How can Case be Tiapolo?"

"No all-e-same," said she. "Ese belong Tiapolo; Tiapolo too much like; Ese all-e-same his son. Suppose Ese he wish something, Tiapolo he make him."

"That's mighty convenient for Ese," says I. "And what kind of things does he make for him?"

Well, out came a rigmarole of all sorts of stories, many of which (like the dollar he took from Mr Tarleton's head) were plain enough to me, but others I could make nothing of; and the thing that most surprised the Kanakas was what surprised me least—namely, that he could go in the desert among all the *aitus*. Some of the boldest, however, had accompanied him, and had heard him speak with the dead and give them orders, and safe in his protection, had returned unscathed. Some said he had a church there where he worshipped Tiapolo, and Tiapolo appeared to him; others swore there was no sorcery at all, that he performed his miracles by the power of prayer, and the church was no church but a prison in which he had confined a dangerous *aitu*. Namu had been in the bush with him once, and returned glorifying God for these wonders. Altogether I began to have a glimmer of the man's position, and the means by which he had acquired it, and though I saw he was a tough nut to crack, I was noways cast down.

"Very well," said I, "I'll have a look at Master Case's place of worship myself, and we'll see about the glorifying."

At this Uma fell in a terrible taking; if I went in the high bush, I should never return; none could go there but by the protection of Tiapolo.

"I'll chance it on God's," said I. "I'm a good sort of a fellow, Uma, as fellows go; and I guess God'll con me through."

She was silent for awhile. "I think," said she, mighty solemn; and then presently: "Victoreea he big chief?"

"You bet," said I.

"He like you too much?" she asked again.

I told her with a grin I believed the old lady was rather partial to me.

"All right," said she. "Victoreea he big chief, like you too much; no can help you here in Falesá; no can do—too far off. Maea he small chief—stop here. Suppose he like you, make you all right. All-e-same God and Tiapolo. God he big chief, got too much work. Tiapolo he small chief, he like too much make-see, work very hard."

"I'll have to hand you over to Mr Tarleton," said I. "Your theology's out of its bearings, Uma."

However we stuck at this business all the evening, and with the stories she told me of the desert and its dangers, she came near frightening herself into a fit. I don't remember half a quarter of them, of course, for I paid little heed; but two come back to me kind of clear.

About six miles up the coast there is a sheltered cove, they call *Fanga-anaana*, "the haven full of caves." I've seen it from the sea myself, as near as I could get my boys to venture in; and it's a little strip of yellow sand. Black cliffs overhang it, full of the black mouths of caves, great trees overhang the cliffs and dangle down lianas, and in one place, about the middle, a big brook pours over in a cascade. Well, there was a boat going by here with six young men of Falesá, "all very pretty," Uma said, which was the loss of them. It blew strong, there was a heavy head sea; and by the time they opened Fanga-anaana, and saw the white cascade and the shady beach, they were all tired and thirsty, and their water had run out. One proposed to land and get a drink; and being reckless fellows, they were all of the same mind except the youngest. Lotu was his name; he was a very good young gentleman and very wise; and he held out they were crazy, telling them the place was given over to spirits and devils and the dead, and there were no living folk nearer than six miles the one way and maybe twelve the other. But they laughed at his words; and being five to one, pulled in, beached the boat, and landed. It was a wonderful pleasant place, Lotu said, and the water excellent. They walked round the beach, but could see nowhere any way to mount the cliffs, which made them easier in their mind; and at last they sat down to make a meal on the food they had brought with them. They were scarce set, when there came out of the mouth of one of the black caves six of the most beautiful ladies ever seen; they had flowers in their hair, and the most beautiful breasts, and necklaces of scarlet seeds; and began to jest with these young gentlemen, and the young gentlemen to jest back with them, all but Lotu. As for Lotu, he saw there could be no living women in such a place, and ran, and flung himself in the bottom of the boat, and covered his face, and prayed. All the time the business lasted, Lotu made one clean break of prayer, and that was all he knew of it, until his friends came back, and made him sit up, and they put to sea again out of the bay, which was now quite desert, and no word of the six ladies. But what frightened Lotu worst, not one of the five remembered anything of what had passed, but they were all like drunken men, and sang and laughed in the boat, and skylarked. The wind freshened and came squally, the sea rose extraordinary high; it was such weather as any man in the islands would have turned his back to and fled home to Falesá; but these five were like crazy folk, and cracked on all sail, and drove their boat into the seas. Lotu went to the bailing; none of the others thought to help him, but sang and skylarked and carried on, and spoke singular things beyond a man's comprehension, and laughed out loud when they said them. So the rest of that day, Lotu bailed for his life in the bottom of the boat, and was all drenched with sweat and cold sea water; and none heeded him. Against all expectation, they came safe in a dreadful tempest to Papa-mālūlū, where the palms were singing out and the cocoa-nuts flying like cannon balls about the village green; and the same night the five young gentlemen sickened and spoke never a reasonable word until they died.

"And do you mean to tell me you can swallow a yarn like that?" I asked.

She told me the thing was well known, and with handsome young men alone, it was even common. But this was the only case where five had been slain the same day and in a company by the love of the women-devils; and it had made a great stir in the island, and she would be crazy if she doubted.

"Well anyway," says I, "you needn't be frightened about me. I've got no use for the women-devils; you're all the women I want, and all the devil too, old lady."

To that she answered there were other sorts, and she had seen one with her own eyes. She had gone one day alone to the next bay, and perhaps got too near the margin of the bad place. The boughs of the high bush over-shadowed her from the cant of the hill, but she herself was outside in a flat place, very stony and growing full of young mummy-apples, four and five feet high. It was a dark day in the rainy season, and now there came squalls that tore off the leaves and sent them flying, and now it was all still as in a house. It was in one of these still times that a whole gang of birds and flying-foxes came pegging out of the bush like creatures frightened. Presently after she heard a rustle nearer hand, and saw coming out of the margin of the trees among the mummy-apples, the appearance of a lean, grey, old boar. It seemed to think as it came, like a person; and all of a sudden, as she looked at it coming, she was aware it was no boar but a thing that was a man with a man's thoughts. At that she ran, and the pig after her, and as the pig ran it hollered aloud, so that the place rang with it.

"I wish I had been there with my gun," said I. "I guess the pig would have hollered so as to surprise himself."

But she told me a gun was of no use with the like of these, which were the spirits of the dead.

Well, this kind of talk put in the evening, which was the best of it; but of course it didn't change my notion, and the next day, with my gun and a good knife, I set off upon a voyage of discovery. I made as near as I could for the place where I had seen Case come out; for if it was true he had some kind of establishment in the bush, I reckoned I should find a path. The beginning of the desert was marked off by a wall—to call it so, for it was more of a long mound of stones. They say it reaches right across the island, but how they know it is another question, for I doubt if anyone has made the journey in a hundred years; the natives sticking chiefly to the sea and their little colonies along the coast, and that part being mortal high and steep and full of cliffs. Up to the west side of the wall, the ground has been cleared, and there are cocoa-palms, and mummy-apples, and guavas, and lots of sensitive. Just across, the bush begins outright; high bush at that, trees going up like the masts of ships, and ropes of liana hanging down like a ship's rigging, and nasty orchids growing in the forks like funguses. The ground where there was no underwood looked to be a heap of boulders. I saw many green pigeons which I might have shot, only I was there with a different idea. A number of butterflies flopped up and down along the ground like dead leaves; sometimes I would hear a bird calling, sometimes the wind overhead, and always the sea along the coast.

But the queerness of the place it's more difficult to tell of, unless to one who has been alone in the high bush himself. The brightest kind of a day it is always dim down there. A man can see to the end of nothing; whichever way he looks, the wood shuts up, one bough folding with another, like the fingers of your hand; and whenever he listens, he hears always something new—men talking, children laughing, the strokes of an axe a far way ahead of him, and sometimes a sort of quick, stealthy scurry near at hand that makes him jump and look to his weapons. It's all very well for him to tell himself that he's alone, bar trees and birds; he can't make out to believe it: whichever way he turns, the whole place seems to be alive and looking on. Don't think it was Uma's yarns that put me out; I don't value native talk a fourpenny piece; it's a thing that's natural in the bush, and that's the end of it.

As I got near the top of the hill, for the ground of the wood goes up in this place steep as a ladder, the wind began to sound straight on, and the leaves to toss and switch open and let in the sun. This suited me better; it was the same noise all the time and nothing to startle. Well, I had got to a place where there was an underwood of what they call wild cocoanut—mighty pretty with its scarlet fruits—when there came a sound of singing in the wind that I thought I had never heard the like of. It was all very fine to tell myself it was the branches; I knew better. It was all very fine to tell myself it was a bird; I knew never a bird that sang like that. It rose, and swelled, and died away, and swelled again; and now I thought it was like some one weeping, only prettier; and now I thought it was like harps; and there was one thing I made sure of, it was a sight too sweet to be wholesome in a place like that. You may laugh if you like; but I declare I called to mind the six young ladies that came, with their scarlet necklaces, out of the cave

THE BEACH OF FALESÁ

at Fanga-anaana, and wondered if they sang like that. We laugh at the natives and their superstitions; but see how many traders take them up, splendidly educated white men, that have been bookkeepers (some of them) and clerks in the old country! It's my belief a superstition grows up in a place like the different kinds of weeds; and as I stood there, and listened to that wailing, I twittered in my shoes.

You may call me a coward to be frightened; I thought myself brave enough to go on ahead. But I went mighty carefully, with my gun cocked, spying all about me like a hunter, fully expecting to see a handsome young woman sitting somewhere in the bush, and fully determined (if I did) to try her with a charge of duckshot. And sure enough I had not gone far, when I met with a queer thing. The wind came on the top of the wood in a strong puff, the leaves in front of me burst open, and I saw for a second something hanging in a tree. It was gone in a wink, the puff blowing by and the leaves closing. I tell you the truth; I had made up my mind to see an *aitu*; and if the thing had looked like a pig or a woman, it wouldn't have given me the same turn. The trouble was that it seemed kind of square; and the idea of a square thing that was alive and sang, knocked me sick and silly. I must have stood quite a while; and I made pretty certain it was right out of the same tree that the singing came. Then I began to come to myself a bit.

"Well," says I, "if this is really so, if this is a place where there are square things that sing, I'm gone up anyway. Let's have my fun for my money."

But I thought I might as well take the off-chance of a prayer being any good; so I plumped on my knees and prayed out loud; and all the time I was praying, the strange sounds came out of the tree, and went up and down, and changed, for all the world like music; only you could see it wasn't human—there was nothing there that you could whistle.

As soon as I had made an end in proper style, I laid down my gun, stuck my knife between my teeth, walked right up to that tree, and began to climb. I tell you my heart was like ice. But presently, as I went up, I caught another glimpse of the thing, and that relieved me, for I thought it seemed like a box; and when I had got right up to it, I near fell out of the tree with laughing. A box it was, sure enough, and a candle box at that, with the brand upon the side of it; and it had banjo strings stretched so as to sound when the wind blew. I believe they call the thing a Tyrolean harp, whatever that may mean.

"Well, Mr Case," said I, "you've frightened me once. But I defy you to frighten me again," I says, and slipped down the tree, and set out again to find my enemy's head office, which I guessed would not be far away.

The undergrowth was thick in this part. I couldn't see before my nose, and must burst my way through by main force and ply the knife as I went, slicing the cords of the lianas and slashing down whole trees at a blow. I call them trees for the bigness, but in truth they were just big weeds and sappy to cut through like a carrot. From all this crowd and kind of vegetation, I was just thinking to myself the place might have once been cleared, when I came on my nose over a pile of stones, and saw in a moment it was some kind of a work of man. The Lord knows when it was made or when deserted, for this part of the island has lain undisturbed since long before the whites came. A few steps beyond, I hit into the path I had been always looking for. It was narrow but well beaten, and I saw that Case had plenty of disciples. It seems indeed it was a piece of fashionable boldness to venture up here with the trader; and a young man scarce reckoned himself grown, till he had got his breech tattooed for one thing, and seen Case's devils for another. This is mighty like Kanakas; but if you look at it another way, it's mighty like white folks too.

A bit along the path, I was brought to a clean stand and had to rub my eyes. There was a wall in front of me, the path passing it by a gap; it was tumbledown and plainly very old, but built of big stones very well laid; and there is no native alive today upon that island that could dream of such a piece of building. Along all the top of it was a line of queer figures, idols, or scare-crows, or what not. They had carved and painted faces, ugly to view; their eyes and teeth were of shell; their hair and their bright clothes blew in the wind, and some of them worked with the tugging. There are islands up west, where they make these kinds of figures till today; but if ever they were made in this island, the practice and the very recollection of it are now long forgotten. And the singular thing was that all these bogies were as fresh as toys out of a shop.

Then it came in my mind what Case had let out to me the first day, that he was a good forger of island curiosities: a thing by which so many traders turn an honest penny. And with that I saw the whole business, and how this display served the man a double purpose: first of all to season his curiosities, and then to frighten those that came to visit him.

But I should tell you (what made the thing more curious) that all the

"Looking around the corner I saw a shining face"

time the Tyrolean harps were harping round me in the trees, and even while
I looked, a green and yellow bird (that I suppose was building) began to tear
the hair off the head of one of the figures.

A little farther on, I found the last curiosity of the museum. The first I
saw of it was a longish mound of earth with a twist to it. Digging off the
earth with my hands, I found underneath tarpaulin stretched on boards, so
that this was plainly the roof of a cellar. It stood right on the top of the hill,
and the entrance was on the far side, between two rocks, like the entrance to
a cave. I went in as far as the bend, and looking round the corner, saw a
shining face. It was big and ugly like a pantomime mask, and the brightness
of it waxed and dwindled, and at times it smoked.

"Oho," says I, "luminous paint!"

And I must say I rather admired the man's ingenuity. With a box of tools and a few mighty simple contrivances, he had made out to have a devil of a temple. Any poor Kanaka brought up here in the dark, with the harps whining all round him, and shown that smoking face in the bottom of a hole, would make no kind of doubt but he had seen and heard enough devils for a lifetime. It's easy to find out what Kanakas think. Just go back to yourself anyway round from ten to fifteen years old, and there's an average Kanaka. There are some pious, just as there are pious boys; and the most of them, like the boys again, are middling honest and yet think it rather larks to steal, and are easy scared and rather like to be so. I remembered a boy I was at school with at home, who played the Case business. He didn't know anything, that boy; he couldn't do anything; he had no luminous paint and no Tyrolean harps; he just boldly said he was a sorcerer, and frightened us out of our boots, and we loved it. And then it came in my mind how the master had once flogged that boy, and the surprise we were all in to see the sorcerer catch it and bum like anybody else. Thinks I to myself. "I must find some way of fixing it so for Master Case." And the next moment I had my idea.

I went back by the path which, when once you had found it, was quite plain and easy walking; and when I stepped out on the black sands, who should I see but Master Case himself? I cocked my gun and held it handy, and we marched up and passed without a word, each keeping the tail of his eye on the other; and no sooner had we passed, than we each wheeled round like fellows drilling and stood face to face. We had each taken the same notion in his head, you see, that the other fellow might give him the load of a gun in the stern.

"You've shot nothing," says Case.

"I'm not on the shoot today," says I.

"Well, the devil go with you for me," says he.

"The same to you," says I.

But we stuck just the way we were; no fear of either of us moving.

Case laughed. "We can't stop here all day, though," said he.

"Don't let me detain you," says I.

He laughed again. "Look here, Wiltshire, do you think me a fool?" he asked.

"More of a knave if you want to know," says I.

"Well, do you think it would better me to shoot you here on this open

"We stuck just the way we were"

beach?" said he. "Because I don't. Folks come fishing every day. There may be a score of them up the valley now, making copra; there may be half a dozen on the hill behind you after pigeons; they might be watching us this minute, and I shouldn't wonder. I give you my word I don't want to shoot you. Why should I? You don't hinder me any. You haven't got one pound of copra but what you made with your own hands, like a negro slave. You're vegetating, that's what I call it; and I don't care where you vegetate, nor yet how long. Give me your word you don't mean to shoot me, and I'll give you a lead and walk away."

"Well," said I, "you're frank and pleasant, ain't you? And I'll be the same. I don't mean to shoot you today. Why should I? This business is beginning; it ain't done yet, Mr Case. I've given you one turn already; I can see the marks of my knuckles on your head to this blooming hour, and I've more cooking for you. I'm not a paralee like Underhill. My name ain't Adams and it ain't Vigours; and I mean to show you that you've met your match."

"This is a silly way to talk," said he. "This is not the talk to make me move on with."

"All right," said I. "Stay where you are. I ain't in any hurry, and you know it. I can put in the day on this beach, and never mind. I ain't got any copra to bother with. I ain't got any luminous paint to see to."

I was sorry I said that last, but it whipped out before I knew. I could see it took the wind out of his sails, and he stood and stared at me with his brow drawn up. Then I suppose he made up his mind he must get to the bottom of this.

"I take you at your word," says he, and turned his back, and walked right into the devil's bush.

I let him go of course, for I had passed my word. But I watched him as long as he was in sight, and after he was gone lit out for cover as lively as you would want to see, and went the rest of the way home under the bush. For I didn't trust him sixpenceworth. One thing I saw, I had been ass enough to give him warning, and that which I meant to do, I must do at once.

You would think I had had about enough excitement for one morning, but there was another turn waiting me. As soon as I got far enough round the cape to see my house, I made out there were strangers there; a little farther, and no doubt about it. There were a couple of armed sentries squatting at my door. I could only suppose the trouble about Uma must have come to a head, and the station been seized. For aught I could think Uma was taken up already, and these armed men were waiting to do the like by me.

However, as I came nearer, which I did at top speed, I saw there was a third native sitting on the verandah like a guest, and Uma was talking with him like a hostess. Nearer still I made out it was the big young chief Maea, and that he was smiling away and smoking; and what was he smoking?— None of your European cigarettes fit for a cat, not even the genuine, big, knock-me-down native article, that a fellow can really put in the time with, if his pipe is broke—but a cigar, and one of my Mexicans at that, that I could swear to. At sight of this, my heart started beating; and I took a wild hope in my head that the trouble was over, and Maea had come round.

Uma pointed me out to him, as I came up, and he met me at the head of my own stairs like a thorough gentleman.

"Vilivili," said he, which was the best they could make of my name, "I pleased."

There is no doubt when an island chief wants to be civil he can do it. I saw the way things were from the word go. There was no call for Uma to say to me: "He no 'fraid Ese now, come bring copra." I tell you I shook hands with that Kanaka like as if he was the best white man in Europe.

The fact was Case and he had got after the same girl, or Maea suspected it and concluded to make hay of the trader on the chance. He had dressed himself up, got a couple of his retainers cleaned and armed to kind of make the thing more public, and just waiting till Case was clear of the village, came round to put the whole of his business my way. He was rich as well as powerful. I suppose that man was worth fifty thousand nuts per annum. I gave him the price of the beach and a quarter cent better, and as for credit, I would have advanced him the inside of the store and the fittings besides, I was so pleased to see him. I must say he bought like a gentleman: rice and tins and biscuit enough for a week's feast, and stuffs by the bolt. He was agreeable besides; he had plenty fun to him; and we cracked jests together, mostly through Uma for interpreter, because he had mighty little English, and my native was still off colour. One thing I made out: he could never really have thought much harm of Uma; he could never have been really frightened, and must just have made believe from dodginess and because he thought Case had a strong pull in the village and could help him on.

This set me thinking that both he and I were in a tightish place. What he had done was to fly in the face of the whole village, and the thing might cost him his authority. More than that, after my talk with Case on the beach, I thought it might very well cost me my life. Case had as good as said he would pot me if ever I got copra; he would come home to find the best business in the village had changed hands; and the best thing I thought I could do was to get in first with the potting.

"See here, Uma," says I, "tell him I'm sorry I made him wait, but I was looking at Case's Tiapolo store in the bush."

"He want savvy if you no 'fraid?" translated Uma.

I laughed out. "Not much!" says I. "Tell him the place is a blooming toyshop! Tell him in England we give these things to the kids to play with."

"He want savvy if you hear devil sing?" she asked next.

"Look here," I said, "I can't do it now because I've got no banjo strings in stock; but the next time the ship comes round, I'll have one of these same contraptions right here in my verandah, and he can see for himself how much devil there is to it. Tell him, as soon as I can get the strings, I'll make one for his picaninnies. The name of the concern is a Tyrolean harp; and you can tell him the name means in English, that nobody but damfools give a cent for it."

This time he was so pleased he had to try his English again. "You talk true?" says he.

"Rather!"said I. "Talk all-e-same Bible. Bring out a Bible here, Uma, if you've got such a thing, and I'll kiss it. Or I'll tell you what's better still," says I, taking a header. "Ask him if he's afraid to go up there himself by day."

It appeared he wasn't; he could venture as far as that by day and in company.

"That's the ticket, then!" said I. "Tell him the man's a fraud and the place foolishness, and if he'll go up there tomorrow, he'll see all that's left of it. But tell him this, Uma, and mind he understands it. If he gets talking, it's bound to come to Case,and I'm a dead man! I'm playing his game, tell him, and if he says one word, my blood will be at his door and be the damnation of him here and after."

She told him, and he shook hands with me up to the hilt, and says he: "No talk. Go up tomollow. You my friend?"

"No, sir!" says I. "No such foolishness. I've come here to trade, tell him, and not to make friends. But as to Case, I'll send that man to glory."

So off Maea went, pretty well pleased, as I could see.

Chapter V

NIGHT IN THE BUSH

WELL, I was committed now. Tiapolo had to be smashed up before next day, and my hands were pretty full, not only with preparations, but with argument. My house was like a mechanics' debating society; Uma was so made up that I shouldn't go into the bush by night, or that if I did I was never to come back again. You know her style of arguing, you've had a specimen about Queen Victoria and the devil; and I leave you to fancy if I was tired of it before dark.

At last, I had a good idea. What was the use of casting my pearls before her? I thought: some of her own chopped hay would be likelier to do the business.

THE BEACH OF FALESÁ

"I'll tell you what, then," said I. "You fish out your Bible, and I'll take that up along with me. That'll make me right."

She swore a Bible was no use.

"That's just your blamed Kanaka ignorance," said I. "Bring the Bible out."

She brought it, and I turned to the title page where I thought there would likely be some English, and so there was. "There!" said I. "Look at that! *London: printed for the British and Foreign Bible Society, Blackfriars*'; and the date, which I can't read, owing to its being in these X's. There's no devil in hell can look near the Bible Society, Blackfriars. Why, you silly!" I said, "how do you suppose we get along with our own *aitus* at home? All Bible Society!"

"I think you no got any," said she. "White man he tell me you no got."

"Sounds likely, don't it?" I asked. "Why would these islands all be chock full of them, and none in Europe?"

"Well, you no got breadfruit," said she.

I could have tore my hair. "Now, look here, old lady," said I, "you dry up, for I'm tired of you. I'll take the Bible, which'll put me as straight as the mail; and that's the last word I've got to say."

The night fell extraordinary dark, clouds coming up with sundown and overspreading all; not a star showed; there was only an end of a moon, and that not due before the small hours. Round the village, what with the lights and the fires in the open houses and the torches of many fishers moving on the reef, it kept as gay as an illumination; but the sea and the mountains and woods were all clean gone. I suppose it might be eight o'clock when I took the road, loaden like a donkey. First there was that Bible, a book as big as your head, which I had let myself in for by my own tomfoolery. Then there was my gun and knife and lantern and patent matches, all necessary. And then there was the real plant of the affair in hand, a mortal weight of gunpowder, a pair of dynamite fishing-bombs, and two or three pieces of slow match that I had hauled out of the tin cases and spliced together the best way I could; for the match was only trade stuff, and a man would be crazy that trusted it. Altogether, you see, I had the materials of a pretty good blow-up! Expense was nothing to me; I wanted that thing done right.

As long as I was in the open, and had the lamp in my house to steer by, I did well. But when I got to the path, it fell so dark I could make no headway, walking into trees and swearing there, like a man looking for the matches in his bedroom. I knew it was risky to light up; for my lantern would be visible all the way to the point of the cape; and as no one went there after dark, it would be talked about and come to Case's ears. But what was I to do? I had either to give the business over and lose caste with Maea, or light up, take my chance, and get through the thing the smartest I was able.

As long as I was on the path, I walked hard; but when I came to the black beach, I had to run. For the tide was now nearly flowed; and to get through with my powder dry between the surf and the steep hill, took all the quickness I possessed. As it was, even, the wash caught me to the knees and I came near falling on a stone. All this time, the hurry I was in, and the free air and smell of the sea, kept my spirits lively; but when I was once in the bush and began to climb the path, I took it easier. The fearsomeness of the wood had been a good bit rubbed off for me by Master Case's banjo strings and graven images; yet I thought it was a dreary walk, and guessed, when the disciples went up there, they must be badly scared. The light of the lantern, striking among all these trunks and forked branches and twisted rope's-ends of lianas, made the whole place, or all that you could see of it, a kind of a puzzle of turning shadows. They came to meet you, solid and quick like giants, and then span off and vanished; they hove up over your head like clubs, and flew away into the night like birds. The floor of the bush glimmered with dead wood, the way the matchbox used to shine after you had struck a lucifer. Big cold drops fell on me from the branches overhead like sweat. There was no wind to mention, only a little icy breath of a land breeze that stirred nothing; and the harps were silent.

The first landfall I made was when I got through the bush of wild cocoanuts, and came in view of the bogies on the wall. Mighty queer they looked by the shining of the lantern, with their painted faces and shell eyes, and their clothes and their hair hanging. One after another I pulled them all up and piled them in a bundle on the cellar roof, so as they might go to glory with the rest. Then I chose a place behind one of the big stones at the entrance, buried my powder and the two shells, and arranged my match along the passage. And then I had a look at the smoking head, just for good-bye. It was doing fine.

"Cheer up," says I. "You're booked."

It was my first idea to light up and be getting homeward; for the darkness, and the glimmer of the dead wood, and the shadows of the lantern made me lonely. But I knew where one of the harps hung; it seemed a pity it shouldn't go with the rest; and at the same time I couldn't help letting on to myself that I was mortal tired of my employment, and would like best to be at home and have the door shut. I stepped out of the cellar, and argued it fore and back. There was a sound of the sea far down below me on the coast; nearer hand, not a leaf stirred; I might have been the only living creature this side Cape Horn. Well, as I stood there thinking, it seemed the bush woke and became full of little noises. Little noises they were, and nothing to hurt—a bit of a crackle, a bit of a brush—but the breath jumped right out of me and my throat went as dry as a biscuit. It wasn't Case I was afraid of, which would have been common sense; I never thought of Case; what took me, as sharp as the cholic, was the old wives' tales, the devil-women and the man-pigs. It was the toss of a penny whether I should run; but I got a purchase on myself, and stepped out, and held up the lantern (like a fool) and looked all round.

In the direction of the village and the path, there was nothing to be seen; but when I turned inland it's a wonder to me I didn't drop. There—coming right up out of the desert and the bad bush—there, sure enough, was a devil-woman, just the way I had figured she would look. I saw the light shine on her bare arms and her bright eyes. And there went out of me a yell so big that I thought it was my death.

"Ah! No sing out!" says the devil-woman, in a kind of a high whisper. "Why you talk big voice? Put out light! Ese he come."

"My God Almighty, Uma, is that you?" says I.

"*Ioe,*" says she. "I come quick. Ese here soon."

"You come alone?" I asked. "You no 'fraid?"

"Ah, too much 'fraid! " she whispered, clutching me. "I think die."

"Well," says I, with a kind of a weak grin, "I'm not the one to laugh at you, Mrs Wiltshire, for I'm about the worst scared man in the South Pacific myself."

She told me in two words what brought her. I was scarce gone, it seems, when Faavao came in, and the old woman had met Black Jack running as hard as he was fit from our house to Case's. Uma neither spoke nor stopped, but lit right out to come and warn me. She was so close at my heels that the lantern was her guide across the beach, and afterwards, by the glimmer of it in the trees, she got her line up hill. It was only when I had got to the top or was in the cellar, that she wandered—Lord knows where!—and lost a sight of precious time, afraid to call out lest Case was at the heels of her, and falling in the bush so that she was all knocked and bruised. That must have been when she got too far to the southward, and how she came to take me in the flank at last, and frighten me beyond what I've got the words to tell of.

Well, anything was better than a devil-woman, but I thought her yarn serious enough. Black Jack had no call to be about my house, unless he was set there to watch; and it looked to me as if my tomfool word about the paint and perhaps some chatter of Maea's had got us all in a clove hitch. One thing was clear: Uma and I were here for the night; we daren't try to go home before day, and even then it would be safer to strike round up the mountain and come in by the back of the village, or we might walk into an ambuscade. It was plain, too, that the mine should be sprung immediately, or Case might be in time to stop it.

I marched into the tunnel, Uma keeping tight hold of me, opened my lantern and lit the match. The first length of it burned like a spill of paper, and I stood stupid, watching it burn, and thinking we were going aloft with Tiapolo, which was none of my views. The second took to a better rate, though faster than I cared about; and at that I got my wits again, hauled Uma clear of the passage, blew out and dropped the lantern, and the pair of us groped our way into the bush until I thought it might be safe, and lay down together by a tree.

"Old lady," I said, "I won't forget this night. You're a trump, and that's what's wrong with you."

She humped herself close up to me. She had run out the way she was with nothing on but her kilt; and she was all wet with the dews and the sea on the black beach, and shook straight on with cold and the terror of the dark and the devils.

"Too much 'fraid," was all she said.

The far side of Case's hill goes down near as steep as a precipice into the next valley. We were on the very edge of it, and I could see the dead wood shine and hear the sea sound far below. I didn't care about the position, which left me no retreat, but I was afraid to change. Then I saw I had made a worse mistake about the lantern, which I should have left lighted, so that I could have had a crack at Case when he stepped into the shine of it. And even if I hadn't had the wit to do that, it seemed a senseless thing to leave the good lantern to blow up with the graven images. The thing belonged to me, after all, and was worth money, and might come in handy. If I could have trusted the match, I might have run in still and rescued it. But who was going to trust the match? You know what trade is; the stuff was good enough for Kanakas to go fishing with, where they've got to look lively anyway, and the most they risk is only to have their hand blown off. But for any one that wanted to fool around a blow-up like mine, that match was rubbish.

Altogether the best I could do was to lie still, see my shot gun handy, and wait for the explosion. But it was a solemn kind of a business. The blackness of the night was like solid; the only thing you could see was the nasty bogy glimmer of the dead wood, and that showed you nothing but itself; and as for sounds, I stretched my ears till I thought I could have heard the match burn in the tunnel, and that bush was as silent as a coffin. Now and then there was a bit of a crack, but whether it was near or far, whether it was Case stubbing his toes within a few yards of me or a tree breaking miles away, I knew no more than the babe unborn.

And then all of a sudden Vesuvius went off. It was a long time coming; but when it came (though I say it that shouldn't) no man could ask to see a better. At first it was just a son of a gun of a row, and a spout of fire, and the wood lighted up so that you could see to read. And then the trouble began. Uma and I were half buried under a waggonful of earth, and glad it was no worse; for one of the rocks at the entrance of the tunnel was fired clean into the air, fell within a couple of fathom of where we lay, and bounded over the edge of the hill, and went pounding down into the next valley.

I saw I had rather under-calculated our distance, or overdone the dynamite and powder, which you please.

And presently I saw I had made another slip. The noise of the thing began to die off, shaking the island; the dazzle was over; and yet the night didn't come back the way that I expected. For the whole wood was scattered with red coals and brands from the explosion; they were all round me on the flat, some had fallen below in the valley, and some stuck and flared in the treetops. I had no fear of fire, for these forests are too wet to kindle. But the trouble was that the place was all lit up, not very bright but good enough to get a shot by; and the way the coals were scattered, it was just as likely Case might have the advantage as myself. I looked all round for his white face, you may be sure; but there was not a sign of him. As for Uma, the life seemed to have been knocked right out of her by the bang and blaze of it.

There was one bad point in my game. One of the blessed graven images had come down all afire, hair and clothes and body, not four yards away from me. I cast a mighty noticing glance all round; there was still no Case, and I made up my mind I must get rid of that burning stick before he came, or I should be shot there like a dog.

It was my first idea to have crawled, and then I thought speed was the main thing, and stood half up to make a rush. The same moment from somewhere between me and the sea there came a flash and a report, and a rifle bullet screeched in my ear. I swung straight round, and up with my gun. But the brute had a Winchester, and before I could as much as see him, his second shot knocked me over like a ninepin. I seemed to fly in the air, then came down by the run and lay half a minute silly; and then I found my hands empty and my gun had flown over my head as I fell. It makes a man mighty wide awake to be in the kind of box that I was in. I scarce knew where I was hurt, or whether I was hurt or not, but turned right over on my face to crawl after my weapon. Unless you have tried to get about with a smashed leg, you don't know what pain is, and I let a howl out like a bullock's.

This was the unluckiest noise that ever I made in my life. Up to then, Uma had stuck to her tree like a sensible woman, knowing she would be only in the way. But as soon as she heard me sing out, she ran forward—the Winchester cracked again—and down she went.

I had sat up, leg and all, to stop her; but when I saw her tumble, I clapped down again where I was, lay still, and felt the handle of my knife. I had been scurried and put out before. No more of that for me. He had knocked over my girl, I had got to fix him for it; and I lay there and gritted my teeth, and footed up the chances. My leg was broke, my gun was gone, Case had still ten shots in his Winchester. It looked a kind of hopeless business. But I never despaired nor thought upon despairing: that man had got to go.

For a goodish bit not one of us let on. Then I heard Case begin to move nearer in the bush, but mighty careful. The image had burned out; there

"THE WINCHESTER CRACKED AGAIN, AND DOWN SHE WENT"

were only a few coals left here and there; and the wood was main dark, but had a kind of a low glow in it like a fire on its last legs. It was by this that I made out Case's head looking at me over a big tuft of ferns; and at the same time the brute saw me and shouldered his Winchester. I lay quite still and as good as looked into the barrel; it was my last chance, but I thought my heart would have come right out of its bearings. Then he fired. Lucky for me it was no shot-gun, for the bullet struck within an inch of me and knocked the dirt in my eyes.

Just you try and see if you can lie quiet, and let a man take a sitting shot at you, and miss you by a hair! But I did, and lucky too. Awhile Case stood with the Winchester at the port-arms; then he gave a little laugh to himself, and stepped round the ferns.

"Laugh!" thought I. "If you had the wit of a louse, you would be praying!"

I was all as taut as a ship's hawser or the spring of a watch; and as soon as he came within reach of me, I had him by the ankle, plucked the feet right out from under him, laid him out, and was upon the top of him, broken leg and all, before he breathed. His Winchester had gone the same road as my shot-gun; it was nothing to me—I defied him now. I'm a pretty strong man anyway, but I never knew what strength was till I got hold of Case. He was knocked out of time by the rattle he came down with, and threw up his hands together, more like a frightened woman, so that I caught both of them with my left. This wakened him up, and he fixed his teeth in my forearm like a weasel. Much I cared! My leg gave me all the pain I had any use for, and I drew my knife, and got it in the place.

"Now," said I, "I've got you; and you're gone up, and a good job too! Do you feel the point of that? That's for Underhill. And there's for Adams. And now here's for Uma, and that's going to knock your blooming soul right out of you!"

With that, I gave him the cold steel for all I was worth. His body kicked under me like a spring sofa; he gave a dreadful kind of a long moan, and lay still.

"I wonder if you're dead? I hope so!" I thought, for my head was swimming. But I wasn't going to take chances; I had his own example too close before me for that; and I tried to draw the knife out to give it him again. The blood came over my hands, I remember, hot as tea; and with that I fainted clean away and fell with my head on the man's mouth.

When I came to myself, it was pitch dark; the cinders had burned out, there was nothing to be seen but the shine of the dead wood; and I couldn't remember where I was, nor why I was in such pain, nor what I was all wetted with. Then it came back; and the first thing I attended to was to give him the knife again a half a dozen times up to the handle. I believe he was dead already, but it did him no harm and did me good.

"I bet you're dead now," I said, and then I called to Uma.

"I HAD HIM BY THE ANKLE"

Nothing answered, and I made a move to go and grope for her, fouled my broken leg, and fainted again.

When I came to myself the second time the clouds had all cleared away except a few that sailed there, white as cotton. The moon was up—a tropic moon. The moon at home turns a wood black; but even this old butt-end of a one showed up that forest as green as by day. The night birds—or rather they're a kind of early morning bird—sang out with their long, falling notes like nightingales. And I could see the dead man that I was still half resting on, looking right up into the sky with his open eyes, no paler than when he was alive; and a little way off, Uma tumbled on her side. I got over to her the best way I was able; and when I got there she was broad awake and crying and sobbing to herself with no more noise than an insect. It appears she was afraid to cry out loud, because of the *aitus*. Altogether she was not much hurt, but scared beyond belief; she had come to her senses a long while ago, cried out to me, heard nothing in reply, made out we were both dead, and had lain there ever since, afraid to budge a finger. The ball had ploughed up her shoulder, and she had lost a main quantity of blood; but I soon had that tied up the way it ought to be with the tail of my shirt and a scarf I had on, got her head on my sound knee and my back against a trunk, and settled down to wait for morning. Uma was for neither use nor ornament, and could only clutch hold of me, and shake, and cry. I don't suppose there was ever anybody worse scared, and to do her justice, she had had a lively night of it. As for me, I was in a good bit of pain and fever, but not so bad when I sat still; and every time I looked over to Case, I could have sung and whistled. Talk about meat and drink! to see that man lying there dead as a herring filled me full.

The night birds stopped after a while; and then the light began to change, the east came orange, the whole wood began to whirr with singing like a musical box, and there was the broad day.

I didn't expect Maea for a long while yet; and indeed I thought there was an off chance he might go back on the whole idea and not come at all. I was the better pleased when, about an hour after daylight, I heard sticks smashing and a lot of Kanakas laughing and singing out to keep their courage up. Uma sat up quite brisk at the first word of it; and presently we saw a party come stringing out of the path, Maea in front, and behind him a white man in a pith helmet. It was Mr Tarleton, who had turned up late last night in

THE BEACH OF FALESÁ

Falesá, having left his boat and walked the last stage with a lantern.

They buried Case upon the field of glory, right in the hole where he had kept the smoking head. I waited till the thing was done; and Mr Tarleton prayed, which I thought tomfoolery, but I'm bound to say he gave a pretty sick view of the dear departed's prospects, and seemed to have his own ideas of hell. I had it out with him afterwards, told him he had scamped his duty, and what he had ought to have done was to up like a man and tell the Kanakas plainly Case was damned, and a good riddance; but I never could get him to see it my way. Then they made me a litter of poles and carried me down to the station. Mr Tarleton set my leg, and made a regular missionary splice of it, so that I limp to this day. That done, he took down my evidence, and Uma's, and Maea's, wrote it all out fair, and had us sign it; and then he got the chiefs and marched over to Papa Randall's to seize Case's papers.

All they found was a bit of a diary, kept for a good many years, and all about the price of copra and chickens being stolen and that; and the books of the business, and the will I told you of in the beginning, by both of which the whole thing (stock, lock, and barrel) appeared to belong to the Sāmoa woman. It was I that bought her out, at a mighty reasonable figure, for she was in a hurry to get home. As for Randall and the black, they had to tramp; got into some kind of a station on the *Papa-mālūlū* side; did very bad business, for the truth is neither of the pair was fit for it; and lived mostly on fish, which was the means of Randall's death. It seems there was a nice shoal in one day, and papa went after them with dynamite; either the match burned too fast or papa was full, or both, but the shell went off (in the usual way) before he threw it; and where was papa's hand? Well, there's nothing to hurt in that; the islands up north are all full of one-handed men, like the parties in the Arabian Nights; but either Randall was too old, or he drank too much, and the short and the long of it was that he died. Pretty soon after, the nigger was turned out of the islands for stealing from white men, and went off to the west, where he found men of his own colour, in case he liked that, and the men of his own colour took and ate him at some kind of a corroborree and I'm sure I hope he was to their fancy!

So there was I left alone in my glory at Falesá; and when the schooner came round I filled her up and gave her a deck cargo half as high as the house. I must say Mr Tarleton did the right thing by us; but he took a meanish kind of a revenge.

"Now, Mr Wiltshire," said he, "I've put you all square with everybody here. It wasn't difficult to do, Case being gone; but I have done it, and given my pledge besides that you will deal fairly with the natives. I must ask you to keep my word."

Well, so I did. I used to be bothered about my balances; but I reasoned it out this way. We all have queerish balances, and the natives all know it and water their copra in a proportion so that it's fair all round. But the truth is, it did use to bother me, and though I did well in Falesá, I was half-glad when the firm moved me on to another station, where I was under no kind of a pledge, and could look my balances in the face.

As for the old lady, you know her as well as I do. She's only the one fault: if you don't keep your eye lifting, she would give away the roof off the station. Well, it seems it's natural in Kanakas. She's turned a powerful big woman now, and could throw a London bobby over her shoulder. But that's natural in Kanakas too; and there's no manner of doubt that she's an A 1 wife.

Mr Tarleton's gone home, his trick being over. He was the best missionary I ever struck, and now it seems he's parsonizing down Somerset ways. Well, that's best for him; he'll have no Kanakas there to get luny over.

My public house? Not a bit of it, nor ever likely. I'm stuck here, I fancy. I don't like to leave the kids, you see; and there's no use talking—they're better here than what they would be in a white man's country, though Ben took the eldest up to Auckland, where he's being schooled with the best. But what bothers me is the girls. They're only half-castes of course; I know that as well as you do, and there's nobody thinks less of half-castes than I do; but they're mine, and about all I've got. I can't reconcile my mind to their taking up with Kanakas, and I'd like to know where I'm to find them whites?

24

THE ISLE OF VOICES

[With illustrations from the First Edition.]

'The Isle of Voices' was serialized in February 1893, and published without revision in Island Nights' Entertainments in April 1893. Stevenson called it "the most extravagant" of the three stories, yet insisted that like the others it had "a queer realism… the manners are exact." He sought the same exactness in presenting Polynesian psychology and supernatural belief, drawing on his earlier Pacific voyages (4, 7, 9). The image of the giant wizard wading the ocean off Molokai, for instance, alludes to a legend of that part of the sea recorded in King Kalalaua's Legends and Myths of Hawaii (1888). The magic isle itself is in the Paumotus, drawn especially from Fakarava, where life was lived around the lagoon, leaving the ocean beach to "wizardry and ghosts", and where Stevenson listened to supernatural tales told, among others, by the half-French M. Donat-Rimarau, who is mentioned in the story and In The South Seas (see 7).

Like the ballads 'A Feast of Famine' (26) and 'The Song of Rahero', 'Isle' gives European readers a version of Polynesian lore that has not been adapted or romanticized for their taste. Kalamake is a distinctly Pacific elder and man of magic, not a Western wizard. Cannibalism exists, though feared, and has its own culinary protocol (Keola is pampered like veal for the table; cf 5). Keola commits adultery with a woman he has first by chance seen near-naked. These were not norms in English fiction in 1893, nor in adaptations of indigenous stories (see 26). The opening plunges us straight into Polynesian beliefs and practices, which are shown inwardly, not exotically. It is the whites who are alien.

At a deeper level of interpretation, the story might be read, like 'The Bottle Imp', as an imaginative response to Stevenson's observation in the Marquesas and

Paumotus of a population in decline yet "beleaguered" by ghosts. In both stories domestic happiness is under threat from death (leprosy, cannibals) and from the powers of darkness (the imp, Kalamake). Happiness in both is achieved through love and resourcefulness, mainly by the female characters.

The idea of an isle of voices can also be read as a response to the Babel of foreign noises that the Pacific had become. Stevenson had an exceptionally acute ear for idiom, and a gift for languages. One of the first things he noticed was the strong similarities between Polynesian languages, and he became proficient in several. Into this relatively homophonous, sparsely populated, and uncommercialized region had come, as 'Isle' describes it, "All the tongues of the earth... the French, the Dutch, the Russian, the Tamil, the Chinese..." all babbling and grabbing. Keola manages to settle at home with his wife and bowl of poi despite the dangers of cannibalism, wizardry and vindictive aliens. Yet the image that remains, especially after reading more of Stevenson's Pacific writings, is that beach of plunder and genocide: "That beach was thick as a cried fair... and he saw the shells vanish before him... the beach babbled with voices and the fires sprang up... and the shells vanished... There was the tribe clustered. They were back to back, and bodies lay, and blood flowed among their feet. The hue of fear was on all their faces."

THE ISLE OF VOICES

KEOLA was married with Lehua, daughter of Kalamake, the wise man of Molokai, and he kept his dwelling with the father of his wife. There was no man more cunning than that prophet; he read the stars, he could divine by the bodies of the dead, and by the means of evil creatures: he could go alone into the highest parts of the mountain, into the region of the hobgoblins, and there he would lay snares to entrap the spirits of ancient.

For this reason no man was more consulted in all the Kingdom of Hawaii. Prudent people bought, and sold, and married, and laid out their lives by his counsels; the King had him twice to Kona to seek the treasures of Kamehameha. Neither was any man more feared: of his enemies, some had dwindled in sickness by the virtue of his incantations, and some had been spirited away, the life and the clay both, so that folk looked in vain for so much as a bone of their bodies. It was rumoured that he had the art or the gift of the old heroes. Men had seen him at night upon the mountains, stepping from one cliff to the next; they had seen him walking in the high forest, and his head and shoulders were above the trees.

This Kalamake was a strange man to see. He was come of the best blood in Molokai and Maui, of a pure descent; and yet he was more white to look upon than any foreigner: his hair the colour of dry grass, and his eyes red and very blind, so that "Blind as Kalamake, that can see across tomorrow" was a byword in the islands.

Of all these doings of his father-in-law, Keola knew a little by the common repute, a little more he suspected, and the rest he ignored. But there was one thing troubled him. Kalamake was a man that spared for nothing, whether to eat or to drink, or to wear; and for all he paid in bright new dollars. "Bright as Kalamake's dollars" was another saying in the Eight Isles. Yet he neither sold, nor planted, nor took hire—only now and then from his sorceries—and there was no source conceivable for so much silver coin.

It chanced one day Keola's wife was gone upon a visit to Kaunakakai, on the lee side of the island, and the men were forth at the sea-fishing. But Keola was an idle dog, and he lay in the verandah and watched the surf beat on the shore and the birds fly about the cliff. It was a chief thought with him always—the thought of the bright dollars. When he lay down to bed he would be wondering why they were so many, and when he woke at morn he would be wondering why they were all new; and the thing was never absent from his mind. But this day of all days he made sure in his heart of some discovery. For it seems he had observed the place where Kalamake kept his treasure, which was a lock-fast desk against the parlour wall, under the print of Kamehameha the Fifth, and a photograph of Queen Victoria with her crown; and it seems again that, no later than the night before, he found occasion to look in, and behold! the bag lay there empty. And this was the day of the steamer; he could see her smoke off Kalaupapa; and she must soon arrive with a month's goods, tinned salmon and gin, and all manner of rare luxuries for Kalamake.

"Now if he can pay for his goods today," Keola thought, "I shall know for certain that the man is a warlock, and the dollars come out of the Devil's pocket."

While he was so thinking, there was his father-in-law behind him, looking vexed.

"Is that the steamer?" he asked.

"Yes," said Keola. "She has but to call at Pelekunu, and then she will be here."

"There is no help for it then," returned Kalamake, "and I must take you in my confidence, Keola, for the lack of anyone better. Come here within the house."

So they stepped together into the parlour, which was a very fine room, papered and hung with prints, and furnished with a rocking-chair, and a table and a sofa in the European style. There was a shelf of books besides, and a family Bible in the midst of the table, and the lock-fast writing desk against the wall; so that anyone could see it was the house of a man of substance.

Kalamake made Keola close the shutters of the windows, while he himself locked all the doors and set open the lid of the desk. From this he brought forth a pair of necklaces hung with charms and shells, a bundle of dried herbs, and the dried leaves of trees, and a green branch of palm.

"What I am about," said he, "is a thing beyond wonder. The men of old were wise; they wrought marvels, and this among the rest; but that was at night, in the dark, under the fit stars and in the desert. The same will I do here in my own house and under the plain eye of day."

So saying, he put the Bible under the cushion of the sofa so that it was all covered, brought out from the same place a mat of a wonderfully fine texture, and heaped the herbs and leaves on sand in a tin pan. And then he and Keola put on the necklaces and took their stand upon the opposite corners of the mat.

"The time comes," said the warlock; "be not afraid."

With that he set flame to the herbs, and began to mutter and wave the branch of palm. At first the light was dim because of the closed shutters; but the herbs caught strongly afire, and the flames beat upon Keola, and the room glowed with the burning, and next the smoke rose and made his head swim and his eyes darken, and the sound of Kalamake muttering ran in his ears. And suddenly, to the mat on which they were standing came a snatch or twitch, that seemed to be more swift than lightning. In the same wink the room was gone and the house, the breath all beaten from Keola's body. Volumes of light rolled upon his eyes and head, and he found himself transported to a beach of the sea under a strong sun, with a great surf roaring: he

THE ISLE OF VOICES

"THE HERBS CAUGHT STRONGLY AFIRE,
AND THE FLAMES BEAT UPON KEOLA"

and the warlock standing there on the same mat, speechless, gasping and grasping at one another, and passing their hands before their eyes.

"What was this?" cried Keola, who came to himself the first, because he was the younger. "The pang of it was like death."

"It matters not," panted Kalamake. "It is now done."

"And, in the name of God, where are we?" cried Keola.

"That is not the question," replied the sorcerer. "Being here, we have matter in our hands, and that we must attend to. Go, while I recover my breath, into the borders of the wood, and bring me the leaves of such and such a herb, and such and such a tree, which you will find to grow there plentifully—three handfuls of each. And be speedy. We must be home again before the steamer comes; it would seem strange if we had disappeared." And he sat on the sand and panted.

Keola went up the beach, which was of shining sand and coral, strewn with singular shells; and he thought in his heart—

"How do I not know this beach? I will come here again and gather shells."

In front of him was a line of palms against the sky; not like the palms of the Eight Islands, but tall and fresh and beautiful, and hanging out withered fans like gold among the green, and he thought in his heart—

"It is strange I should not have found this grove. I will come here again, when it is warm, to sleep." And he thought, "How warm it has grown suddenly!" For it was winter in Hawaii, and the day had been chill. And he thought also, "Where are the grey mountains? And where is the high cliff with the hanging forest and the wheeling birds?" And the more he considered, the less he might conceive in what quarter of the islands he was fallen.

In the border of the grove, where it met the beach, the herb was growing, but the tree further back. Now, as Keola went toward the tree, he was aware of a young woman who had nothing on her body but a belt of leaves.

"Well!" thought Keola, "they are not very particular about their dress in this part of the country." And he paused, supposing she would observe him and escape; and seeing that she still looked before her, stood and hummed aloud. Up she leaped at the sound. Her face was ashen; she looked this way and that, and her mouth gaped with the terror of her soul. But it was a strange thing that her eyes did not rest upon Keola.

"Good day," said he. "You need not be so frightened; I will not eat you." And he had scarce opened his mouth before the young woman fled into the bush.

"These are strange manners," thought Keola. And, not thinking what he did, ran after her.

As she ran, the girl kept crying in some speech that was not practised in Hawaii, yet some of the words were the same, and he knew she kept calling and warning others. And presently he saw more people running— men, women and children, one with another, all running, and crying like people at a fire. And with that he began to grow afraid himself, and returned to Kalamake bringing the leaves. Him he told what he had seen.

"You must pay no heed," said Kalamake, "All this is like a dream and shadows. All will disappear and be forgotten."

"It seemed none saw me," said Keola.

"And none did," replied the sorcerer. "We walk here in the broad sun invisible by reason of these charms. Yet they hear us; and therefore it is well to speak softly, as I do."

With that he made a circle round the mat with stones, and in the midst he set the leaves.

"It will be your part," said he, "to keep the leaves alight, and feed the fire slowly. While they blaze (which is but for a little moment) I must do my errand; and before the ashes blacken, the same power that brought us carries us away. Be ready now with the match; and do you call me in good time lest the flames burn out and I be left."

As soon as the leaves caught, the sorcerer leaped like a deer out of the circle, and began to race along the beach like a hound that has been bathing. As he ran, he kept stooping to snatch shells; and it seemed to Keola that they glittered as he took them. The leaves blazed with a clear flame that consumed them swiftly; and, presently Keola had but a handful left, and the sorcerer was far off, running and stopping.

"Back!" cried Keola. "Back! The leaves are near done."

At that Kalamake turned, and if he had run before, now he flew. But fast as he ran, the leaves burned faster. The flame was ready to expire when, with a great leap, he bounded on the mat. The wind of his leaping blew it out; and with that the beach was gone, and the sun and the sea, and they stood once more in the dimness of the shuttered parlour, and were once more

"'BACK!' CRIED KEOLA. 'BACK! THE LEAVES ARE NEAR DONE'"

shaken and blinded; and on the mat betwixt them lay a pile of shining dollars. Keola ran to the shutter, and there was the steamer tossing in the swell close in.

The same night Kalamake took his son-in-law apart, and gave him five dollars in his hand.

"Keola," said he, "if you are a wise man (which I am doubtful of) you will think you slept this afternoon on the verandah, and dreamed as you were sleeping. I am a man of few words, and I have for my helpers people of short memories."

Never a word more said Kalamake, nor referred again to that affair. But it ran all the while in Keola's head—if he were lazy before, he would now do nothing.

"Why should I work," thought he, "when I have a father-in-law who makes dollars of sea-shells?"

Presently his share was spent. He spent it all upon fine clothes. And then he was sorry.

"For," thought he, "I had done better to have bought a concertina, with which I might have entertained myself all day long." And then he began to grow vexed with Kalamake.

THE ISLE OF VOICES

"This man has the soul of a dog," thought he. "He can gather dollars when he pleases on the beach, and he leaves me to pine for a concertina! Let him beware: I am no child, I am as cunning as he, and hold his secret." With that he spoke to his wife Lehua, and complained of her father's manners.

"I would let my father be," said Lehua. "He is a dangerous man to cross."

"I care that for him!" cried Keola; and snapped his fingers. "I have him by the nose. I can make him do what I please." And he told Lehua the story.

But she shook her head.

"You may do what you like," said she; "but as sure as you thwart my father, you will be no more heard of. Think of this person, and that person; think of Hua, who was a noble of the House of Representatives, and went to Honolulu every year; and not a bone or a hair of him was found. Remember Kamau, and how he wasted to a thread, so that his wife lifted him with one hand. Keola, you are a baby in my father's hands; he will take you with his thumb and finger and eat you like a shrimp."

Now Keola was truly afraid of Kalamake, but he was vain too; and these words of his wife's incensed him.

"Very well," said he, "if that is what you think of me, I will show how much you are deceived." And he went straight to where his father-in-law was sitting in the parlour.

"Kalamake," said be, "I want a concertina."

"Do you, indeed?" said Kalamake.

"Yes," said he, "and I may as well tell you plainly, I mean to have it. A man who picks up dollars on the beach can certainly afford a concertina."

"I had no idea you had so much spirit," replied the sorcerer. "I thought you were a timid, useless lad, and I cannot describe how much pleased I am to find I was mistaken. Now I begin to think I may have found an assistant and successor in my difficult business. A concertina? You shall have the best in Honolulu. And tonight, as soon as it is dark, you and I will go and find the money."

"Shall we return to the beach?" asked Keola.

"No, no!" replied Kalamake; "you must begin to learn more of my secrets. Last time I taught you to pick shells; this time, I shall teach you to catch fish. Are you strong enough to launch Pili's boat?"

"I think I am," returned Keola. "But why should we not take your own, which is afloat already?"

"I have a reason which you will understand thoroughly before tomorrow," said Kalamake. "Pili's boat is the better suited for my purpose. So, if you please, let us meet there as soon as it is dark; and in the meanwhile, let us keep our own counsel, for there is no cause to let the family into our business."

Honey is not more sweet than was the voice of Kalamake, and Keola could scarce contain his satisfaction.

"I might have had my concertina weeks ago," thought he, "and there is nothing needed in this world but a little courage."

Presently after he spied Lehua weeping, and was half in a mind to tell her all was well.

"But no," thinks he; "I shall wait till I can show her the concertina; we shall see what the chit will do then. Perhaps she will understand in the future that her husband is a man of some intelligence."

As soon as it was dark father and son-in-law launched Pili's boat and set the sail. There was a great sea, and it blew strong from the leeward; but the boat was swift and light and dry, and skimmed the waves. The wizard had a lantern, which he lit and held with his finger through the ring; and the two sat in the stern and smoked cigars, of which Kalamake had always a provision, and spoke like friends of magic and the great sums of money which they could make by its exercise, and what they should buy first, and what second; and Kalamake talked like a father.

Presently he looked all about, and above him at the stars, and back at the island, which was already three parts sunk under the sea, and he seemed to consider ripely his position.

"Look!" says he, "there is Molokai already far behind us, and Maui like a cloud; and by the bearing of these three stars I know I am come where I desire. This part of the sea is called the Sea of the Dead. It is in this place extraordinarily deep, and the floor is all covered with the bones of men, and in the holes of this part gods and goblins keep their habitation. The flow of the sea is to the north, stronger than a shark can swim, and any man who shall here be thrown out of a ship it bears away like a wild horse into the uttermost ocean. Presently he is spent and goes down, and his bones are scattered with the rest, and the gods devour his spirit."

Fear came on Keola at the words, and he looked, and by the light of the stars and the lantern, the warlock seemed to change.

"What ails you?" cried Keola, quick and sharp.

"It is not I who am ailing," said the wizard; "but there is one here very sick."

With that he changed his grasp upon the lantern, and, behold! as he drew his finger from the ring, the finger stuck and the ring was burst, and his hand was grown to be of the bigness of three.

At that sight Keola screamed and covered his face.

But Kalamake held up the lantern. "Look rather at my face!" said he—and his head was huge as a barrel; and still he grew and grew as a cloud grows on a mountain, and Keola sat before him screaming, and the boat raced on the great seas.

"And now," said the wizard, "what do you think about that concertina? and are you sure you would not rather have a flute? No?" says he; "that is well, for I do not like my family to be changeable of purpose. But I begin to think I had better get out of this paltry boat, for my bulk swells to a very unusual degree, and if we are not the more careful, she will presently be swamped."

With that he threw his legs over the side. Even as he did so, the greatness of the man grew thirty-fold and forty-fold as swift as sight or thinking, so that he stood in the deep seas to the armpits, and his head and shoulders rose like a high isle, and the swell beat and burst upon his bosom, as it beats and breaks against a cliff. The boat ran still to the north, but he reached out his hand, and took the gunwale by the finger and thumb, and broke the side like a biscuit, and Keola was spilled into the sea. And the pieces of the boat the sorcerer crushed in the hollow of his hand and flung miles away into the night.

"Excuse me taking the lantern," said he; "for I have a long wade before me, and the land is far, and the bottom of the sea uneven, and I feel the bones under my toes."

And he turned and went off walking with great strides; and as often as Keola sank in the trough he could see him no longer, but as often as he was heaved upon the crest, there he was striding and dwindling, and he held the lamp high over his head, and the waves broke white about him as he went.

Since first the islands were fished out of the sea, there was never a man so terrified as this Keola. He swam indeed, but he swam as puppies swim when they are cast in to drown, and knew not wherefore. He could but think of the hugeness of the swelling of the warlock, of that face which was great as a mountain, of those shoulders that were broad as an isle, and of the seas that beat on them in vain. He thought, too, of the concertina, and shame took hold upon him; and of the dead men's bones, and fear shook him.

Of a sudden he was aware of something dark against the stars that tossed, and a light below, and a brightness of the cloven sea; and he heard speech of men. He cried out aloud and a voice answered; and in a twinkling the bows of a ship hung above him on a wave like a thing balanced, and swooped down. He caught with his two hands in the chains of her, and the next moment was buried in the rushing seas, and the next hauled on board by seamen.

They gave him gin and biscuit and dry clothes, and asked him how he came where they found him, and whether the light which they had seen was the lighthouse, Lae o Ka Laau. But Keola knew white men are like children and only believe their own stories; so about himself he told them what he pleased, and as, for the light (which was Kalamake's lantern) he vowed he had seen none.

This ship was a schooner bound for Honolulu, and then to trade in the low islands; and by a very good chance for Keola she had lost a man off the bowsprit in a squall. It was no use talking. Keola durst not stay in the Eight Islands. Word goes so quickly, and all men are so fond to talk and carry news, that if he hid in the north end of Kauai or in the south end of Kaü, the wizard would have wind of it before a month, and he must perish. So he did what seemed the most prudent, and shipped sailor in the place of the man who had been drowned.

In some ways the ship was a good place. The food was extraordinarily rich and plenty, with biscuits and salt beef every day, and pea-soup and puddings, made of flour and suet twice a week, so that Keola grew fat. The captain also was a good man, and the crew no worse than other whites. The trouble was the mate, who was the most difficult man to please Keola had ever met with, and beat and cursed him daily, both for what he did and what he did not. The blows that he dealt were very sore, for he was strong; and the words he used were very unpalatable, for Keola was come of a good family and accustomed to respect. And what was the worst of all, whenever Keola found a chance to sleep, there was the mate awake and stirring him up with a rope's end. Keola saw it would never do; and he made up his mind to run away.

They were about a month out from Honolulu when they made the land. It was a fine starry night, the sea was smooth as well as the sky fair; it blew a steady trade; and there was the island on their weather bow, a ribbon of palm trees lying flat along the sea. The captain and the mate looked at it with the night glass, and named the name of it, and talked of it, beside the wheel where Keola was steering. It seemed it was an isle where no traders came. By the captain's way, it was an isle besides where no man dwelt; but the mate thought otherwise.

"I don't give a cent for the directory," said he. "I've been past here one night in the schooner *Eugenie;* it was just such a night as this; they were fishing with torches, and the beach was thick with lights like a town."

"Well, well," says the captain, "it's steep-to, that's the great point; and there ain't any outlying dangers by the chart, so we'll just hug the lee side. Keep her romping full, don't I tell you!" he cried to Keola, who was listening so hard that he forgot to steer.

And the mate cursed him, and swore that Kanaka was for no use in the world, and if he got started after him with a belaying pin, it would be a cold day for Keola.

And so the captain and mate lay down on the house together, and Keola was left to himself.

"This island will do very well for me," he thought; "if no traders deal there, the mate will never come. And as for Kalamake, it is not possible he can ever get as far as this."

With that he kept edging the schooner nearer in. He had to do this quietly, for it was the trouble with these white men, and above all with the mate, that you could never be sure of them; they would all be sleeping sound, or else pretending, and if a sail shook, they would jump to their feet and fall on you with a rope's end. So Keola edged her up little by little, and kept all drawing. And presently the land was close on board, and the sound of the sea on the sides of it grew loud.

With that, the mate sat up suddenly upon the house.

"What are you doing?" he roars. "You'll have the ship ashore!"

And he made one bound for Keola, and Keola made another clean over the rail and plump into the starry sea. When he came up again, the schooner had payed off on her true course, and the mate stood by the wheel himself, and Keola heard him cursing. The sea was smooth under the lee of the island; it was warm besides, and Keola had his sailor's knife, so he had no fear of sharks. A little way before him the trees stopped; there was a break in the line of the land like the mouth of a harbour; and the tide, which was then flowing, took him up and carried him through. One minute he was without, and the next within: had floated there in a wide shallow water, bright with ten thousand stars, and all about him was the ring of the land, with its string of palm trees. And he was amazed, because this was a kind of island he had never heard of.

The time of Keola in that place was in two periods—the period when he was alone, and the period when he was there with the tribe. At first he sought everywhere and found no man; only some houses standing in a hamlet, and the marks of fires. But the ashes of the fires were cold and the rains had washed them away, and the winds had blown, and some of the huts were overthrown. It was here he took his dwelling; and he made a fire drill, and a shell hook, and fished and cooked his fish, and climbed after green cocoanuts, the juice of which he drank, for in all the isle there was no water. The days were long to him, and the nights terrifying. He made a lamp of

"IN A WIDE SHALLOW WATER, BRIGHT WITH TEN THOUSAND STARS,
AND ALL ABOUT HIM WAS THE RING OF THE LAND,
WITH ITS STRING OF PALM TREES"

THE ISLE OF VOICES

cocoa-shell, and drew the oil of the ripe nuts, and made a wick of fibre; and when evening came he closed up his hut, and lit his lamp, and lay and trembled till morning. Many a time he thought in his heart he would have been better in the bottom of the sea, his bones rolling there with the others.

All this while he kept by the inside of the island, for the huts were on the shore of the lagoon, and it was there the palms grew best, and the lagoon itself abounded with good fish. And to the outer side he went once only, and he looked but the once at the beach of the ocean, and came away shaking. For the look of it, with its bright sand, and strewn shells, and strong sun and surf, went sore against his inclination.

"It cannot be," he thought, "and yet it is very like. And how do I know? These white men, although they pretend to know where they are sailing, must take their chance like other people. So that after all we may have sailed in a circle, and I may be quite near to Molokai, and this may be the very beach where my father-in-law gathers his dollars."

So after that he was prudent, and kept to the land side.

It was perhaps a month later, when the people of the place arrived—the fill of six great boats. They were a fine race of men, and spoke a tongue that sounded very different from the tongue of Hawaii, but so many of the words were the same that it was not difficult to understand. The men besides were very courteous, and the women very towardly; and they made Keola welcome, and built him a house, and gave him a wife; and what surprised him the most, he was never sent to work with the young men.

And now Keola had three periods. First he had a period of being very sad, and then he had a period when he was pretty merry. Last of all came the third, when he was the most terrified man in the four oceans.

The cause of the first period was the girl he had to wife. He was in doubt about the island, and he might have been in doubt about the speech, of which he had heard so little when he came there with the wizard on the mat. But about his wife there was no mistake conceivable, for she was the same girl that ran from him crying in the wood. So he had sailed all this way, and might as well have stayed in Molokai; and had left home and wife and all his friends for no other cause but to escape his enemy, and the place he had come to was that wizard's hunting ground, and the shore where he walked invisible. It was at this period when he kept the most close to the lagoon side, and as far as he dared, abode in the cover of his hut.

The cause of the second period was talk he heard from his wife and the chief islanders. Keola himself said little. He was never so sure of his new friends, for he judged they were too civil to be wholesome, and since he had grown better acquainted with his father-in-law the man had grown more cautious. So he told them nothing of himself, but only his name and descent, and that he came from the Eight Islands, and what fine islands they were; and about the king's palace in Honolulu, and how he was a chief friend of the king and the missionaries. But he put many questions and learned much.

The island where he was was called the Isle of Voices; it belonged to the tribe, but they made their home upon another, three hours' sail to the southward. There they lived and had their permanent houses, and it was a rich island, where were eggs and chickens and pigs, and ships came trading with rum and tobacco. It was there the schooner had gone after Keola deserted; there, too, the mate had died, like the fool of a white man as he was. It seems, when the ship came, it was the beginning of the sickly season in that isle, when the fish of the lagoon are poisonous, and all who eat of them swell up and die. The mate was told of it; he saw the boats preparing, because in that season the people leave that island and sail to the Isle of Voices; but he was a fool of a white man, who would believe no stories but his own, and he caught one of these fish, cooked it and ate it, and swelled up and died, which was good news to Keola.

As for the Isle of Voices, it lay solitary the most part of the year; only now and then a boat's crew came for copra, and in the bad season, when the fish at the main isle were poisonous, the tribe dwelt there in a body. It had its name from a marvel, for it seemed the seaside of it was all beset with invisible devils; day and night you heard them talking one with another in strange tongues; day and night little fires blazed up and were extinguished on the beach; and what was the cause of these doings no man might conceive. Keola asked them if it were the same in their own island where they stayed, and they told him no, not there; nor yet in any other of some hundred isles that lay all about them in that sea; but it was a thing peculiar to the Isle of Voices. They told him also that these fires and voices were ever on the seaside and in the seaward fringes of the wood, and a man might dwell by the lagoon two thousand years (if he could live so long) and never be any way troubled; and even on the seaside the devils did no harm if let alone. Only once a chief had cast a spear at one of the voices, and the same night he fell out of a cocoanut palm and was killed.

Keola thought a good bit with himself. He saw he would be all right when the tribe returned to the main island, and right enough where he was, if he kept by the lagoon, yet he had a mind to make things righter if he could. So he told the high chief he had once been in an isle that was pestered the same way, and the folk had found a means to cure that trouble.

"There was a tree growing in the bush there," says he, "and it seems these devils came to get the leaves of it. So the people of the isle cut down the tree wherever it was found, and the devils came no more."

They asked what kind of tree this was, and he showed them the tree of which Kalamake burned the leaves. They found it hard to believe, yet the idea tickled them. Night after night the old men debated it in their councils, but the high chief (though he was a brave man) was afraid of the matter, and reminded them daily of the chief who cast a spear against the voices and was killed, and the thought of that brought all to a stand again.

Though he could not yet bring about the destruction of the trees, Keola was well enough pleased, and began to look about him and take pleasure in his days; and, among other things, he was the kinder to his wife, so that the girl began to love him greatly. One day he came to the hut, and she lay on the ground lamenting.

"Why," said Keola, "what is wrong with you now?"

She declared it was nothing.

The same night she woke him. The lamp burned very low, but he saw by her face she was in sorrow.

"Keola," she said, "put your ear to my mouth that I may whisper, for no one must hear us. Two days before the boats begin to be got ready, go you to the sea-side of the isle and lie in a thicket. We shall choose that place beforehand, you and I; and hide food; and every night I shall come near by there singing. So when a night comes and you do not hear me, you shall know we are clean gone out of the island, and you may come forth again in safety."

The soul of Keola died within him.

"What is this?" he cried. "I cannot live among devils. I will not be left behind upon this isle. I am dying to leave it."

"You will never leave it alive, my poor Keola," said the girl; "for to tell you the truth, my people are eaters of men, but this they keep secret. And the reason they will kill you before we leave is because in our island ships come, and Donat-Rimarau comes and talks for the French, and there is a white trader there in a house with a verandah, and a catechist. Oh, that is a fine place indeed! The trader has barrels filled with flour; and a French warship once came in the lagoon, and gave everybody wine and biscuit. Ah, my poor Keola, I wish I could take you there, for great is my love to you, and it is the finest place in the seas except Papeete."

So now Keola was the most terrified man in the four oceans. He had heard tell of eaters of men in the south islands, and the thing had always been a fear to him; and here it was knocking at his door. He had heard besides, by travellers, of their practices, and how when they are in a mind to eat a man, they cherish and fondle him like a mother with a favourite baby. And he saw this must be his own case; and that was why he had been housed, and fed, and wived, and liberated from all work; and why the old men, and the chiefs discoursed with him like a person of weight. So he lay on his bed and railed upon his destiny; and the flesh curdled on his bones.

The next day the people of the tribe were very civil, as their way was. They were elegant speakers, and they made beautiful poetry, and jested at meals, so that a missionary must have died laughing. It was little enough Keola cared for their fine ways; all he saw was the white teeth shining in their mouths, and his gorge rose at the sight; and when they were done eating, he went and lay in the bush like a dead man.

The next day it was the same, and then his wife followed him.

"Keola," she said, "if you do not eat, I tell you plainly you will be killed and cooked tomorrow. Some of the old chiefs are murmuring already. They think you are fallen sick and must lose flesh."

With that Keola got to his feet, and anger burned in him.

"It is little I care one way or the other," said he. "I am between the devil and the deep sea. Since die I must, let me die the quickest way; and since I must be eaten at the best of it, let me rather be eaten by hobgoblins than by men. Farewell," said he, and he left her standing, and walked to the seaside of that island.

It was all bare in the strong sun; there was no sign of man, only the beach was trodden, and all about him as he went, the voices talked and whispered, and the little fires sprang up and burned down. All tongues of the earth were spoken there; the French, the Dutch, the Russian, the Tamil, the Chinese. Whatever land knew sorcery, there were some of its people whispering in Keola's ear. That beach was thick as a cried fair, yet no man seen; and as he walked he saw the shells vanish before him, and no man to pick them up. I think the devil would have been afraid to be alone in such a company; but Keola was past fear and courted death. When the fires sprang up, he charged for them like a bull. Bodiless voices called to and fro; unseen hands poured sand upon the flames; and they were gone from the beach before he reached them.

"It is plain Kalamake is not here," he thought, "or I must have been killed long since."

With that he sat him down in the margin of the wood, for he was tired, and put his chin upon his hands. The business before his eyes continued: the beach babbled with voices, and the fires sprang up and sank, and the shells vanished and were renewed again even while he looked.

"It was a by-day when I was here before," he thought, "for it was nothing to this."

And his head was dizzy with the thought of these millions and millions of dollars, and all these hundreds and hundreds of persons culling them upon the beach and flying in the air higher and swifter than eagles.

"And to think how they have fooled me with their talk of mints," says he, "and that money was made there, when it is clear that all the new coin in all the world is gathered on these sands! But I will know better the next time!" said he.

And at last, he knew not very well how or when, sleep fell on Keola, and he forgot the island and all his sorrows.

Early the next day, before the sun was yet up, a bustle woke him. He awoke in fear, for he thought the tribe had caught him napping; but it was no such matter. Only, on the beach in front of him, the bodiless voices called and shouted one upon another, and it seemed they all passed and swept beside him up the coast of the island.

"What is afoot now?" thinks Keola. And it was plain to him it was something beyond ordinary, for the fires were not lighted nor the shells taken, but the bodiless voices kept posting up the beach, and hailing and dying away; and others following, and by the sound of them these wizards should be angry.

"It is not me they are angry at," thought Keola, "for they pass me close."

As when hounds go by, or horses in a race, or city folk coursing to a fire, and all men join and follow after, so it was now with Keola; and he knew not what he did, nor why he did it, but there, lo and behold! he was running with the voices.

So he turned one point of the island, and this brought him in view of a second; and there he remembered the wizard trees to have been growing by the score together in a wood. From this point there went up a hubbub of men crying not to be described; and by the sound of them, those that he ran with shaped their course for the same quarter. A little nearer, and there began to mingle with the outcry the crash of many axes. And at this a thought came at last into his mind that the high chief had consented; that the men of the tribe had set-to cutting down these trees; that word had gone about the isle from sorcerer to sorcerer, and these were all now assembling to defend their trees. Desire of strange things swept him on. He posted with the voices, crossed the beach, and came into the borders of the wood, and stood astonished. One tree had fallen, others were part hewed away. There was the tribe clustered. They were back to back, and bodies lay, and blood

"Came into the borders of the wood, and stood astonished"

THE ISLE OF VOICES

flowed among their feet. The hue of fear was on all their faces; their voices went up to heaven shrill as a weasel's cry.

Have you seen a child when he is all alone and has a wooden sword, and fights, leaping and hewing with the empty air? Even so the man-eaters huddled back to back, and heaved up their axes, and laid on, and screamed as they laid on, and behold! no man to contend with them! only here and there Keola saw an axe swinging over against them without hands; and time and again a man of the tribe would fall before it, clove in twain or burst asunder, and his soul sped howling.

For awhile Keola looked upon this prodigy like one that dreams, and then fear took him by the midst as sharp as death, that he should behold such doings. Even in that same flash the high chief of the clan espied him standing, and pointed and called out his name. Thereat the whole tribe saw him also, and their eyes flashed, and their teeth clashed.

"I am too long here," thought Keola, and ran further out of the wood and down the beach, not caring whither.

"Keola!" said a voice close by upon the empty sand.

"Lehua! is that you?" he cried, and gasped, and looked in vain for her; but by the eyesight he was stark alone.

"I saw you pass before," the voice answered; "but you would not hear me. Quick! get the leaves and the herbs, and let us flee."

"You are there with the mat?" he asked.

"Here, at your side," said she. And he felt her arms about him. "Quick! the leaves and the herbs, before my father can get back!"

So Keola ran for his life, and fetched the wizard fuel; and Lehua guided him back, and set his feet upon the mat, and made the fire. All the time of its burning, the sound of the battle towered out of the wood; the wizards and the man-eaters hard at fight; the wizards, the viewless ones, roaring out aloud like bulls upon a mountain, and the men of the tribe replying shrill and savage out of the terror of their souls. And all the time of the burning, Keola stood there and listened, and shook, and watched how the unseen hands of Lehua poured the leaves. She poured them fast, and the flame burned high, and scorched Keola's hands; and she speeded and blew the burning with her breath. The last leaf was eaten, the flame fell, and the shock followed, and there were Keola and Lehua in the room at home.

Now, when Keola could see his wife at last he was mighty pleased, and

"And the missionary was very sharp on him for taking the second wife in the low island"

he was mighty pleased to be home again in Molokai and sit down beside a bowl of poi—for they make no poi on board ships, and there was none in the Isle of Voices—and he was out of the body with pleasure to be clean escaped out of the hands of the eaters of men. But there was another matter not so clear, and Lehua and Keola talked of it all night and were troubled. There was Kalamake left upon the isle. If, by the blessing of God, he could but stick there, all were well; but should he escape and return to Molokai, it would be an ill day for his daughter and her husband. They spoke of his gift of swelling, and whether he could wade that distance in the seas. But Keola knew by this time where that island was—and that is to say, in the Low or Dangerous Archipelago. So they fetched the atlas and looked upon the distance in the map, and by what they could make of it, it seemed a far way for an old gentleman to walk. Still, it would not do to make too sure of a warlock like Kalamake, and they determined at last to take counsel of a white missionary.

So the first one that came by Keola told him everything. And the missionary was very sharp on him for taking the second wife in the low island; but for all the rest, he vowed he could make neither head not tail of it.

"However," says he, "if you think this money of your father's ill gotten, my advice to you would be, give some of it to the lepers and some to the missionary fund. And as for this extraordinary rigmarole, you cannot do better than keep it to yourselves."

But he warned the police at Honolulu that, by all he could make out, Kalamake and Keola had been coining false money, and it would not be amiss to watch them.

Keola and Lehua took his advice, and gave many dollars to the lepers and the fund. And no doubt the advice must have been good, for from that day to this, Kalamake has never more been heard of. But whether he was slain in the battle by the trees, or whether he is still kicking his heels upon the Isle of Voices, who shall say?

25

THE EBB-TIDE

Stevenson habitually referred to The Ebb-Tide *in phrases like "grisly", or "grim and gloomy". It began in 1889 as 'The Pearl Fisher', a much longer novel with Lloyd Osbourne supplying the framework for "a kind of Monte Cristo yarn". By 1893 Stevenson was "grinding singly", constantly reworking the narration, dialogue and musical tone and structure (the eventual sub-title was 'A Trio and a Quartette'). He called the effort "excruciating", and said it had "sown my head with grey hairs." The result, "black, ugly, trampling, violent", is a critique of the colonial enterprise that is the more disturbing because much is left indeterminate. Meaning is to be found in the dark music of the words, not any easy moral spelling out. Never popular and largely neglected, though there are good recent editions,* The Ebb-Tide *(1894) could, in our post-colonial era, be ready to have its day.*

The novel opens with three white dropouts, "on the beach" and hungry, loitering on the influenza-ravaged waterfront of Papeete. Herrick is an ineffectual Oxford man, Davis an American sea captain who claims to pine for his children, and Huish a cockney of feral cunning and resilience. They contrive to steal a schooner, and sail east, planning to sell it and its cargo of champagne in Peru. After an orgy of drunkenness they find they are not alone in criminality, as most of the bottles have been refilled with water. By chance they make landfall on a coral atoll beyond the Paumotus. They are received by a tall, suave Englishman, exquisitely dressed.

This is Attwater, imperious ruler over the island, with its weird museum of shipwreck debris, its horde of pearls, and its virtually enslaved natives. Attwater is a classically educated, religiously zealous, urbanely domineering, dead-shot epicurean autocrat who is as purring and dangerous as the huge cat he often carries on his shoulder. The novel's ending is too strange to reveal, but it is preceded by an outburst of violence as horrific as anything Stevenson wrote elsewhere, and more significant.

As a self-appointed ruler over a colonial outpost, Attwater preceded H.G. Wells's Dr Moreau *(1896), Joseph Conrad's* Lord Jim *(1900), Kurtz in* Heart of Darkness *(1902), and Axel Heyst in* Victory *(1915), and the Pacific übermensch David Grief, and island monarchs Parlay and Raffy in Jack London's* A Son of the Sun *(1912). Attwater is perhaps the most potent of them all as an image of the dangerous self-justifying immorality of Empire. Unlike Kurtz, he is shown in full view, intelligently self-deluding, despotically charming, and triumphantly in his prime. There is more than a little of King Tembinoka (see* **13**) *in Attwater the potentate; they have the same habit of practising marksmanship on their subjects. The figure-head on the beach and some other details are drawn from Penrhyn (Tongarewa), which Stevenson described in an article 'A Pearl Island' after a visit on the* Janet Nicholl.

The extract given here comprises Chapter 7 and the beginning of Chapter 8, from twelve chapters in all. It represents at an intense imaginative level the essential elements of Stevenson's best Pacific writing. It ranges from exquisite beauty to destructive savagery. It shows humans responding to that vast ocean by striving to comprehend the eternal, and by chanting gibberish rhymes of malevolence. It shows Empire at its most potent, and implies its decay.

*It opens, as Pacific experience always does, with an island landfall. Stevenson draws on the expertise he had gained in the precise sound of breakers, the movement of the ocean and the blots of deeper darkness that indicate land, especially from his own arrival in the dangerous atolls of the Paumotus (**6**). More importantly, he now builds as an artist on his long struggles with "my Pacific book"* (In the South Seas) *to find and craft the right language and style to turn these new experiences into narrative English.*

*As they wait for day, and the dawn magically comes, Stevenson provides a description that might have satisfied Fanny's demand for "enchanting material" (**5**), superficially. But not far beneath the sound of the surf and glowing colours of the dawn lurk, in the first three paragraphs alone, images of danger, the weight of eternity, conflagration, torture, frailty and sudden sinking to destruction. Two paragraphs later the imagery is drawn from Hell. Technically the* accounts of the tides, the reef, the fish, and the schooner's movements into the lagoon are impeccable. Yet it all has such a mystical creepiness that Herrick's cultured Western mind is "tortured" to find analogies. He resorts to sunken ships and circular railways.

When they finally see human habitation, things only become more strange – native huts, a belfry, a palm grove, an English flag, a sense of a place in use yet also deserted, and, weirdly presiding, "a woman of exorbitant stature and as white as snow was to be seen beckoning with uplifted arm." This turns out to be the salvaged figure-head. Never has the strange incongruous litter of colonization been more disturbingly evoked. This first sight of the beach from the schooner is the visual equivalent of the linguistic babble of 'The Isle of Voices' (24).

Attwater's arrival aboard introduces other incongruities. He wears a silk scarf, a white drill suit, and carries a Winchester. His urbanity and virility scarcely conceal a "devastating anger". He and Herrick chatter about wine and Oxford and Cambridge colleges, and he scores condescending English class-system points against the cockney Huish ("Mr. Whish"). Yet all this British ritual is played out against a background of slaughter by smallpox, simmering violence, and the threat of "combat" made in rhyming verse.

When Attwater returns to shore, leaving an invitation that is part threat and part insult, the three thieves fall out over a complex of class resentments, personal jealousies, greed and vindictiveness. Huish breaks into his extraordinary incantation of shocking, hateful, meaningless, savage gibberish (all Stevenson's words). The chapter has gone from "the whole east glowed with gold and scarlet" to "Hikey, pikey, crikey, fikey, chillingawallaba dory." That is Stevenson's Pacific.

Chapter 7 ends with Davis barking violently at Huish like a dog. Chapter 8 opens with Herrick going ashore to socialize with Attwater, among images of pestilence, weeds, the crypt, and that strange figure-head, once so potent and mobile, now idle and ironic. She echoes Shelley's Ozymandias. As a ruined Statue of Liberty she has reappeared more than once in the modern cinema. In each case, the implications for the imperial civilization she embodies are the same.

Chapter 7

THE PEARL-FISHER

bout four in the morning, as the captain and Herrick sat together on the rail, there arose from the midst of the night in front of them the voice of breakers. Each sprang to his feet and stared and listened. The sound was continuous, like the passing of a train; no rise or fall could be distinguished; minute by minute the ocean heaved with an equal potency against the invisible isle; and as time passed, and Herrick waited in vain for any vicissitude in the volume of that roaring, a sense of the eternal weighed upon his mind. To the expert eye the isle itself was to be inferred from a certain string of blots along the starry heaven. And the schooner was laid to and anxiously observed till daylight.

There was little or no morning bank. A brightening came in the east; then a wash of some ineffable, faint, nameless hue between crimson and silver; and then coals of fire. These glimmered a while on the sea line, and seemed to brighten and darken and spread out, and still the night and the stars reigned undisturbed; it was as though a spark should catch and glow and creep along the foot of some heavy and almost incombustible wall-hanging, and the room itself be scarce menaced. Yet a little after, and the whole east glowed with gold and scarlet, and the hollow of heaven was filled with the daylight.

The isle – the undiscovered, the scarce believed-in – now lay before them and close aboard; and Herrick thought that never in his dreams had he beheld anything more strange and delicate. The beach was excellently white, the continuous barrier of trees inimitably green; the land perhaps ten feet high, the trees thirty more. Every here and there, as the schooner coasted northward, the wood was intermitted; and he could see clear over the inconsiderable strip of land (as a man looks over a wall) to the lagoon within – and clear over that again to where the far side of the atoll prolonged its pencilling of trees against the morning sky. He tortured himself to find analogies. The isle was like the rim of a great vessel sunken in the waters; it was like the embankment of an annular railway grown upon with wood: so slender it seemed amidst the outrageous breakers, so frail and pretty, he would scarce have wondered to see it sink and disappear without a sound, and the waves close smoothly over its descent.

Meanwhile the captain was in the forecross-trees, glass in hand, his eyes in every quarter, spying for an entrance, spying for signs of tenancy. But the isle continued to unfold itself in joints, and to run out in indeterminate capes, and still there was neither house nor man, nor the smoke of fire. Here a multitude of sea-birds soared and twinkled, and fished in the blue waters;

and there, and for miles together, the fringe of cocoa-palm and pandanus extended desolate, and made desirable green bowers for nobody to visit, and the silence of death was only broken by the throbbing of the sea.

The airs were very light, their speed was small; the heat intense. The decks were scorching underfoot, the sun flamed overhead, brazen, out of a brazen sky; the pitch bubbled in the seams, and the brains in the brain-pan. And all the while the excitement of the three adventurers glowed about their bones like a fever. They whispered, and nodded, and pointed, and put mouth to ear, with a singular instinct of secrecy, approaching that island underhand like eavesdroppers and thieves; and even Davis from the cross-trees gave his orders mostly by gestures. The hands shared in this mute strain, like dogs, without comprehending it; and through the roar of so many miles of breakers, it was a silent ship that approached an empty island.

At last they drew near to the break in that interminable gangway. A spur of coral sand stood forth on the one hand; on the other a high and thick tuft of trees cut off the view; between was the mouth of the huge laver. Twice a day the ocean crowded in that narrow entrance and was heaped between these frail walls; twice a day, with the return of the ebb, the mighty sur-plusage of water must struggle to escape. The hour in which the *Farallone* came there was the hour of flood. The sea turned (as with the instinct of the homing pigeon) for the vast receptacle, swept eddying through the gates, was transmuted, as it did so, into a wonder of watery and silken hues, and brimmed into the inland sea beyond. The schooner looked up close-hauled, and was caught and carried away by the influx like a toy. She skimmed; she flew; a momentary shadow touched her decks from the shore-side trees; the bottom of the channel showed up for a moment and was in a moment gone; the next, she floated on the bosom of the lagoon, and below, in the trans-parent chamber of waters, a myriad of many-coloured fishes were sporting, a myriad pale flowers of coral diversified the floor.

Herrick stood transported. In the gratified lust of his eye, he forgot the past and the present; forgot that he was menaced by a prison on the one hand and starvation on the other; forgot that he was come to that island, desperately foraging, clutching at expedients. A drove of fishes, painted like the rainbow and billed like parrots, hovered up in the shadow of the schoon-er, and passed clear of it, and glinted in the submarine sun. They were beaut-iful, like birds, and their silent passage impressed him like a strain of song.

Meanwhile, to the eye of Davis in the cross-trees, the lagoon continued to expand its empty waters, and the long succession of the shore-side trees to be paid out like fishing line off a reel. And still there was no mark of habitation. The schooner, immediately on entering, had been kept away to the nor'ard where the water seemed to be the most deep; and she was now skimming past the tall grove of trees, which stood on that side of the channel and denied further view. Of the whole of the low shores of the island, only this bight remained to be revealed. And suddenly the curtain was raised; they began to open out a haven, snugly elbowed there, and beheld, with an astonishment beyond words, the roofs of men.

The appearance, thus 'instantaneously disclosed' to those on the deck of the *Farallone*, was not that of a city, rather of a substantial country farm with its attendant hamlet: a long line of sheds and store-houses; apart, upon the one side, a deep-verandah'ed dwelling-house; on the other, perhaps a dozen native huts; a building with a belfry and some rude offer at architectural features that might be thought to mark it out for a chapel; on the beach in front some heavy boats drawn up, and a pile of timber running forth into the burning shallows of the lagoon. From a flagstaff at the pierhead, the red ensign of England was displayed. Behind, about, and over, the same tall grove of palms, which had masked the settlement in the beginning, prolonged its roof of tumultuous green fans, and turned and ruffled overhead, and sang its silver song all day in the wind. The place had the indescribable but unmistakable appearance of being in commission; yet there breathed from it a sense of desertion that was almost poignant, no human figure was to be observed going to and fro about the houses, and there was no sound of human industry or enjoyment. Only, on the top of the beach and hard by the flagstaff, a woman of exorbitant stature and as white as snow was to be seen beckoning with uplifted arm. The second glance identified her as a piece of naval sculpture, the figure-head of a ship that had long hovered and plunged into so many running billows, and was now brought ashore to be the ensign and presiding genius of that empty town.

The *Farallone* made a soldier's breeze of it; the wind, besides, was stronger inside than without under the lee of the land; and the stolen schooner opened out successive objects with the swiftness of a panorama, so that the adventurers stood speechless. The flag spoke for itself; it was no frayed and weathered trophy that had beaten itself to pieces on the post, flying over desolation; and to make assurance stronger, there was to be descried in the deep shade of the verandah, a glitter of crystal and the fluttering of white napery. If the figure-head at the pier end, with its perpetual gesture and its leprous whiteness, reigned alone in that hamlet as it seemed to do, it would not have reigned long. Men's hands had been busy, men's feet stirring there, within the circuit of the clock. The *Farallones* were sure of it; their eyes dug in the deep shadow of the palms for some one hiding; if intensity of looking might have prevailed, they would have pierced the walls of houses; and there came to them, in these pregnant seconds, a sense of being watched and played with, and of a blow impending, that was hardly bearable.

The extreme point of palms they had just passed enclosed a creek, which was thus hidden up to the last moment from the eyes of those on board; and from this, a boat put suddenly and briskly out, and a voice hailed.

"Schooner ahoy!" it cried. "Stand in for the pier! In two cables' lengths you'll have twenty fathoms water and good holding ground."

The boat was manned with a couple of brown oarsmen in scanty kilts of blue. The speaker, who was steering, wore white clothes, the full dress of the tropics; a wide hat shaded his face; but it could be seen that he was of stalwart size, and his voice sounded like a gentleman's. So much could be made out. It was plain, besides, that the *Farallone* had been descried some time before at sea, and the inhabitants were prepared for its reception.

Mechanically the orders were obeyed, and the ship berthed; and the three adventurers gathered aft beside the house and waited, with galloping pulses and a perfect vacancy of mind, the coming of the stranger who might mean so much to them. They had no plan, no story prepared; there was no time to make one; they were caught red-handed and must stand their chance. Yet this anxiety was chequered with hope. The island being undeclared, it was not possible the man could hold any office or be in a position to demand their papers. And beyond that, if there was any truth in Findlay, as it now seemed there should be, he was the representative of the 'private reasons,' he must see their coming with a profound disappointment; and perhaps (hope whispered) he would be willing and able to purchase their silence.

The boat was by that time forging alongside, and they were able at last to see what manner of man they had to do with. He was a huge fellow, six feet four in height, and of a build proportionately strong, but his sinews seemed to be dissolved in a listlessness that was more than languor. It was only the eye that corrected this impression; an eye of an unusual mingled brilliancy and softness, sombre as coal and with lights that outshone the topaz; an eye of unimpaired health and virility; an eye that bid you beware of the man's devastating anger. A complexion, naturally dark, had been tanned in the island to a hue hardly distinguishable from that of a Tahitian; only his manners and movements, and the living force that dwelt in him, like fire in flint, betrayed the European. He was dressed in white drill, exquisitely made; his scarf and tie were of tender-coloured silks; on the thwart beside him there leaned a Winchester rifle.

"Is the doctor on board?" he cried as he came up. "Dr Symonds, I mean? You never heard of him? Nor yet of the *Trinity Hall?* Ah!"

He did not look surprised, seemed rather to affect it in politeness; but his eye rested on each of the three white men in succession with a sudden weight of curiosity that was almost savage. "Ah, *then!*" said he, "there is some small mistake, no doubt, and I must ask you to what I am indebted for this pleasure?"

He was by this time on the deck, but he had the art to be quite unapproachable; the friendliest vulgarian, three parts drunk, would have known better than take liberties; and not one of the adventurers so much as offered to shake hands.

"Well," said Davis, "I suppose you may call it an accident. We had heard of your island, and read that thing in the Directory about the *private reasons*, you see; so when we saw the lagoon reflected in the sky, we put her head for it at once, and so here we are."

"'Ope we don't intrude!" said Huish.

The stranger looked at Huish with an air of faint surprise, and looked pointedly away again. It was hard to be more offensive in dumb show.

"It may suit me, your coming here," he said. "My own schooner is over-due, and I may put something in your way in the meantime. Are you open to a charter?"

"Well, I guess so," said Davis; "it depends."

"My name is Attwater," continued the stranger. "You, I presume, are the captain?"

"Yes, sir. I am the captain of this ship: Captain Brown," was the reply.

"Well, see 'ere!" said Huish, "better begin fair! 'E's skipper on deck right enough, but not below. Below, we're all equal, all got a lay in the adventure; when it comes to business, I'm as good as 'e; and what I say is, let's go into the 'ouse and have a lush, and talk it over among pals. We've some prime fizz," he said, and winked.

The presence of the gentleman lighted up like a candle the vulgarity of the clerk; and Herrick instinctively, as one shields himself from pain, made haste to interrupt.

"My name is Hay," said he, "since introductions are going. We shall be very glad if you will step inside."

Attwater leaned to him swiftly. "University man?" said he.

"Yes, Merton," said Herrick, and the next moment blushed scarlet at his indiscretion.

"I am of the other lot," said Attwater: "Trinity Hall, Cambridge. I called my schooner after the old shop. Well! this is a queer place and company for us to meet in, Mr Hay," he pursued, with easy incivility to the others. "But do you bear out... I beg this gentleman's pardon, I really did not catch his name."

"My name is 'Uish, sir," returned the clerk, and blushed in turn.

"Ah!" said Attwater. And then turning again to Herrick, "Do you bear out Mr Whish's description of your vintage? or was it only the unaffected poetry of his own nature bubbling up?"

Herrick was embarrassed; the silken brutality of their visitor made him blush; that he should be accepted as an equal, and the others thus pointedly ignored, pleased him in spite of himself, and then ran through his veins in a recoil of anger.

"I don't know," he said. "It's only California; it's good enough, I believe."

Attwater seemed to make up his mind. "Well then, I'll tell you what: you three gentlemen come ashore this evening and bring a basket of wine with you; I'll try and find the food," he said. "And by the by, here is a question I should have asked you when I come on board: have you had smallpox?"

"Personally, no," said Herrick. "But the schooner had it."

"Deaths?" from Attwater.

"Two," said Herrick.

"Well, it is a dreadful sickness," said Attwater.

"'Ad you any deaths?" asked Huish, 'ere on the island?"

"Twenty-nine," said Attwater. "Twenty-nine deaths and thirty-one cases, out of thirty-three souls upon the island. – That's a strange way to calculate, Mr Hay, is it not? Souls! I never say it but it startles me."

"Oh, so that's why everything's deserted?" said Huish.

"That is why, Mr Whish," said Attwater; "that is why the house is empty and the graveyard full."

"Twenty-nine out of thirty-three!" exclaimed Herrick, "Why, when it came to burying – or did you bother burying?"

"Scarcely," said Attwater; "or there was one day at least when we gave up. There were five of the dead that morning, and thirteen of the dying, and no one able to go about except the sexton and myself. We held a council of war, took the... empty bottles... into the lagoon, and... buried them." He looked over his shoulder, back at the bright water. "Well, so you'll come to dinner, then? Shall we say half-past six. *So* good of you!"

His voice, in uttering these conventional phrases, fell at once into the false measure of society; and Herrick unconsciously followed the example.

"I am sure we shall be very glad," he said. "At half-past six? Thank you so very much."

"'For my voice has been tuned to the note of the gun
    That startles the deep when the combat's begun,'"

quoted Attwater, with a smile, which instantly gave way to an air of funereal solemnity. "I shall particularly expect Mr Whish," he continued. "Mr Whish, I trust you understand the invitation?"

"I believe you, my boy!" replied the genial Huish.

"That is right then; and quite understood, is it not?" said Attwater. "Mr Whish and Captain Brown at six-thirty without fault – and you, Hay, at four sharp."

And he called his boat.

During all this talk, a load of thought or anxiety had weighed upon the captain. There was no part for which nature had so liberally endowed him as that of the genial ship captain. But today he was silent and abstracted. Those who knew him could see that he hearkened close to every syllable, and seemed to ponder and try it in balances. It would have been hard to say what look there was, cold, attentive, and sinister, as of a man maturing plans, which still brooded over the unconscious guest; it was here, it was there, it was nowhere; it was now so little that Herrick chid himself for an idle fancy; and anon it was so gross and palpable that you could say every hair on the man's head talked mischief.

He woke up now, as with a start. "You were talking of a charter," said he.

"Was I?" said Attwater. "Well, let's talk of it no more at present."

"Your own schooner is overdue, I understand?" continued the captain.

"You understand perfectly, Captain Brown," said Attwater; "thirty-three days overdue at noon today."

"She comes and goes, eh? plies between here and…?" hinted the captain.

"Exactly; every four months; three trips in the year," said Attwater.

"You go in her, ever?" asked Davis.

"No, one stops here," said Attwater, "one has plenty to attend to."

"Stop here, do you?" cried Davis. "Say, how long?"

"How long, O Lord," said Attwater with perfect, stern gravity. "But it does not seem so," he added, with a smile.

"No, I dare say not," said Davis. "No, I suppose not. Not with all your gods about you, and in as snug a berth as this. For it is a pretty snug berth," said he, with a sweeping look.

"The spot, as you are good enough to indicate, is not entirely intolerable," was the reply.

"Shell, I suppose?" said Davis.

"Yes, there was shell," said Attwater.

"This is a considerable big beast of a lagoon, sir," said the captain. "Was there a – was the fishing – would you call the fishing anyways *good?*"

"I don't know that I would call it anyways anything," said Attwater, "if you put it to me direct."

"There were pearls too?" said Davis.

"Pearls, too," said Attwater.

"Well, I give out!" laughed Davis, and his laughter rang cracked like a false piece. "If you're not going to tell, you're not going to tell, and there's an end to it."

"There can be no reason why I should affect the least degree of secrecy about my island," returned Attwater; "that came wholly to an end with your arrival; and I am sure, at any rate, that gentlemen like you and Mr Whish, I should have always been charmed to make perfectly at home. The point on which we are now differing – if you can call it a difference – is one of times and seasons. I have some information which you think I might impart, and I think not. Well, we'll see tonight! By-by, Whish!" He stepped into his boat and shoved off. "All understood, then?" said he. "The captain and Mr Whish at six-thirty, and you, Hay, at four precise. You understand that, Hay? Mind, I take no denial. If you're not there by the time named, there will be no banquet; no song, no supper, Mr Whish!"

White birds whisked in the air above, a shoal of parti-coloured fishes in the scarce denser medium below; between, like Mahomet's coffin, the boat drew away briskly on the surface, and its shadow followed it over the glittering floor of the lagoon. Attwater looked steadily back over his shoulders as he sat; he did not once remove his eyes from the *Farallone* and the group on her quarter-deck beside the house, till his boat ground upon the pier. Thence, with an agile pace, he hurried ashore, and they saw his white clothes shining in the chequered dusk of the grove until the house received him.

The captain, with a gesture and a speaking countenance, called the adventurers into the cabin.

"Well," he said to Herrick, when they were seated, "there's one good job at least. He's taken to you in earnest."

"Why should that be a good job?" said Herrick.

"Oh, you'll see how it pans out presently," returned Davis. "You go ashore and stand in with him, that's all! You'll get lots of pointers; you can find out what he has, and what the charter is, and who's the fourth man — for there's four of them, and we're only three."

"And suppose I do, what next?" cried Herrick. "Answer me that!"

"So I will, Robert Herrick," said the captain. "But first, let's see all clear. I guess you know," he said with an imperious solemnity, "I guess you know the bottom is out of this *Farallone* speculation? I guess you know it's *right* out? and if this old island hadn't been turned up right when it did, I guess you know where you and I and Huish would have been?"

"Yes, I know that," said Herrick. "No matter who's to blame, I know it. And what next?"

"No matter who's to blame, you know it, right enough," said the captain, "and I'm obliged to you for the reminder. Now here's this Attwater: what do you think of him?"

"I do not know," said Herrick. "I am attracted and repelled. He was insufferably rude to you."

"And you, Huish?" said the captain.

Huish sat cleaning a favourite briar root; he scarce looked up from that engrossing task. "Don't ast me what I think of him!" he said. "There's a day comin', I pray Gawd, when I can tell it him myself."

"Huish means the same as what I do," said Davis. "When that man came stepping around, and saying 'Look here, I'm Attwater' – and you knew it was so, by God! – I sized him right straight up. Here's the real article, I said, and I don't like it; here's the real, first-rate, copper-bottomed aristocrat. *'Aw! don't know ye, do I? God damn ye, did God make ye?'* No, that couldn't be nothing but genuine; a man got to be born to that, and notice! smart as champagne and hard as nails; no kind of a fool; no, *sir!* not a pound of him! Well, what's he here upon this beastly island for? I said. *He's* not here collecting eggs. He's a palace at home, and powdered flunkies; and if he don't stay there, you bet he knows the reason why! Follow?"

"O yes, I 'ear you," said Huish.

"He's been doing good business here, then," continued the captain. "For ten years, he's been doing a great business. It's pearl and shell, of course; there couldn't be nothing else in such a place, and no doubt the shell goes off regularly by this *Trinity Hall*, and the money for it straight into the bank, so that's no use to us. But what else is there? Is there nothing else he would be likely to keep here? Is there nothing else he would be bound to keep here? Yes, sir; the pearls! First, because they're too valuable to trust out of his hands. Second, because pearls want a lot of handling and matching; and the man who sells his pearls as they come in, one here, one there, instead of hanging back and holding up – well, that man's a fool, and it's not Attwater."

"Likely," said Huish, "that's w'at it is; not proved, but likely."

"It's proved," said Davis bluntly.

"Suppose it was?" said Herrick. "Suppose that was all so, and he had these pearls – a ten years' collection of them? – Suppose he had? There's my question."

The captain drummed with his thick hands on the board in front of him; he looked steadily in Herrick's face, and Herrick as steadily looked upon the table and the pattering fingers; there was a gentle oscillation of the anchored ship, and a big patch of sunlight travelled to and fro between the one and the other.

"Hear me!" Herrick burst out suddenly.

"No, you better hear me first," said Davis. "Hear me and understand me. *We've* got no use for that fellow, whatever you may have. He's your kind, he's not ours; he's took to you, and he's wiped his boots on me and Huish. Save him if you can!"

"Save him?" repeated Herrick.

"Save him, if you're able!" reiterated Davis, with a blow of his clenched fist. "Go ashore, and talk him smooth; and if you get him and his pearls aboard, I'll spare him. If you don't, there's going to be a funeral. Is that so, Huish? does that suit you?"

"I ain't a forgiving man," said Huish, "but I'm not the sort to spoil business neither. Bring the bloke on board and bring his pearls along with him, and you can have it your own way; maroon him where you like – I'm agreeable."

"Well, and if I can't?" cried Herrick, while the sweat streamed upon his face. "You talk to me as if I was God Almighty, to do this and that! But if I can't?"

"My son," said the captain, "you better do your level best, or you'll see sights!"

"O yes," said Huish. "O crikey, yes!" He looked across at Herrick with a toothless smile that was shocking in its savagery; and his ear caught apparently by the trivial expression he had used, broke into a piece of the chorus of a comic song which he must have heard twenty years before in London: meaningless gibberish that, in that hour and place, seemed hateful as a blasphemy: "Hikey, pikey, crikey, fikey, chillingawallaba dory."

The captain suffered him to finish; his face was unchanged.

"The way things are, there's many a man that wouldn't let you go ashore," he resumed. "But I'm not that kind. I know you'd never go back on me, Herrick! Or if you choose to – go, and do it, and be damned!" he cried, and rose abruptly from the table.

He walked out of the house; and as he reached the door, turned and called Huish, suddenly and violently, like the barking of a dog. Huish followed, and Herrick remained alone in the cabin.

"Now, see here!" whispered Davis. "I know that man. If you open your mouth to him again, you'll ruin all."

Chapter 8

BETTER ACQUAINTANCE

THE boat was gone again, and already half-way to the *Farallone*, before Herrick turned and went unwillingly up the pier. From the crown of the beach, the figure-head confronted him with what seemed irony, her helmeted head tossed back, her formidable arm apparently hurling something, whether shell or missile, in the direction of the anchored schooner. She seemed a defiant deity from the island, coming forth to its threshold with a rush as of one about to fly, and perpetuated in that dashing attitude. Herrick looked up at her, where she towered above him head and shoulders, with singular feelings of curiosity and romance, and suffered his mind to travel to and fro in her life-history. So long she had been the blind conductress of a ship among the waves; so long she had stood here idle in the violent sun, that yet did not avail to blister her; and was even this the end of so many adventures? he wondered, or was more behind? And he could have found in his heart to regret that she was not a goddess, nor yet he a pagan, that he might have bowed down before her in that hour of difficulty.

When he now went forward, it was cool with the shadow of many well-grown palms; draughts of the dying breeze swung them together overhead; and on all sides, with a swiftness beyond dragon-flies or swallows, the spots of sunshine flitted, and hovered, and returned. Underfoot, the sand was fairly solid and quite level, and Herrick's steps fell there noiseless as in new-fallen snow. It bore the marks of having been once weeded like a garden alley at home; but the pestilence had done its work, and the weeds were returning. The buildings of the settlement showed here and there through the stems of the colonnade, fresh painted, trim and dandy, and all silent as the grave. Only, here and there in the crypt, there was a rustle and scurry and some crowing of poultry; and from behind the house with the verandahs, he saw smoke arise and heard the crackling of a fire.

The store-houses were nearest him upon his right. The first was locked; in the second, he could dimly perceive, through a window, a certain accumulation of pearl-shell piled in the far end; the third, which stood gaping open on the afternoon, seized on the mind of Herrick with its multiplicity and disorder of romantic things. Therein were cables, windlasses and blocks of every size and capacity; cabin windows and ladders; rusty tanks, a companion hutch; a binnacle with its brass mountings and its compass idly pointing, in the confusion and dusk of that shed, to a forgotten pole; ropes, anchors, harpoons, a blubber dipper of copper, green with years, a steering wheel, a tool chest with the vessel's name upon the top, the *Asia:* a whole curiosity-shop of sea curios, gross and solid, heavy to lift, ill to break, bound with brass and shod with iron. Two wrecks at the least must have contributed to this random heap of lumber; and as Herrick looked upon it, it seemed to him as if the two ships' companies were there on guard, and he heard the tread of feet and whisperings, and saw with the tail of his eye the commonplace ghosts of sailor men.

This was not merely the work of an aroused imagination, but had something sensible to go upon; sounds of a stealthy approach were no doubt audible; and while he still stood staring at the lumber, the voice of his host sounded suddenly, and with even more than the customary softness of enunciation, from behind.

"Junk," it said, "only old junk! And does Mr Hay find a parable?"

"I find at least a strong impression," replied Herrick, turning quickly, lest he might be able to catch, on the face of the speaker, some commentary on the words.

Attwater stood in the doorway, which he almost wholly filled; his hands stretched above his head and grasping the architrave. He smiled when their eyes met, but the expression was inscrutable.

"Yes, a powerful impression. You are like me; nothing so affecting as ships!" said he. "The ruins of an empire would leave me frigid, when a bit of an old rail that an old shellback leaned on in the middle watch, would bring me up all standing. But come, let's see some more of the island. It's all sand and coral and palm trees; but there's a kind of quaintness in the place."

"I find it heavenly," said Herrick, breathing deep, with head bared in the shadow...

26

BALLADS

One of Stevenson's first Pacific projects, often referred to in his correspon-
dence, was a volume of 'South Seas Ballads'. In the Marquesas, his first port of
call (2-5), he began a narrative ballad, 'The Feast of Famine', as a first response
to the culture. He fully acknowledged that "It rests upon no authority... I have
strung together some of the more striking particularities of the Marquesas."
The other Pacific ballad that he completed, 'The Song of Rahero. A Legend of
Tahiti', is more consciously authentic. It was, Fanny wrote, "first inspired by the
conversation of Princess Moë in Tautira... My husband drew from her all she
could tell him of the story, afterwards corroborated and enriched by the high
chief Tati."

He did not manage to add more, and these two were published in 1890,
along with some Scottish and other verse narratives, as Ballads, *to unfavourable*
reviews. "My Ballads seem to have been dam bad; all the crickets sing so in their
crickety papers", he wrote. They missed a good deal. Feast and Rahero may be
derived too noticeably from Longfellow's Hiawatha *(1855), but they have a*
toughness and realism that are original, and, for that date, are remarkably
free from poeticized language (apart from the odd "lo!" and "yore") and
romanticized attitudes. They justify Stevenson's claim, in another letter about the
book, that "I do know how to tell a yarn, and two of the yarns are great." They
also show an acute interest in what he called "savage psychology", complaining
that the critics had missed it.

An extract from The Feast of Famine *is chosen here for various reasons. It*
is original, not a version of an inherited story, since we now have different views

about the appropriation of indigenous legend, however "corroborated". It shows Stevenson struggling to find ways of expressing the "despondency and dread" he had found in the current Marquesan psyche (see 4). It is direct and unvarnished, sometimes horrifically, in its rendering of Marquesan custom, lore, war, psychology and even sex. These were not palatable in 1890, a censorious time. Having offered human butchery, cannibal feasting, and unmarried lust in the woods, Stevenson should not have been surprised that "They failed to entertain a coy public."

That is also a measure of its quality in the Pacific context. Other versions of Polynesian legends at this time habitually modified and in effect censored them for Victorian tastes. We now know how radically George Grey transformed the most famous, the Māori story of Hinemoa and Tutānekai, which Stevenson probably drew on for a musical love-call in this ballad. In Polynesian Mythology (1854) Grey turned the story into a sort of soft-medieval romance of innocent love, by eliminating the original's sexuality and its themes of genealogy and class division. These are all present and important in Stevenson's ballad.

The extract below is the third of the ballad's four sections. The first describes the famine, and the frenzied ritual running of the priest that precedes the cannibal feasting (see 5). The second is a meeting in the bush between the lovers, the high-caste Taheia and her "kinless" lover Rua. In hiding from the feasting in which he could be a victim (Section 3, below), Rua encounters (in Section 4) an invading enemy force, and sacrifices himself in a vain attempt to warn his own people.

The extract should be read with caution. The throbbing, drumbeat hexameters well match the pulsing terror of the narrative. 'The Feast of Famine' is not for the faint-hearted.

THE FEAST OF FAMINE
MARQUESAN MANNERS

III. THE FEAST

Dawn as yellow as sulphur leaped on the naked peak,
And all the village was stirring, for now was the priest to speak.
Forth on his terrace he came, and sat with the chief in talk;
His lips were blackened with fever, his cheeks were whiter than chalk;

Fever clutched at his hands, fever nodded his head,
But, quiet and steady and cruel, his eyes shone ruby-red.
In the earliest rays of the sun the chief rose up content;
Braves were summoned, and drummers; messengers came and went;
Braves ran to their lodges, weapons were snatched from the wall;
The commons herded together, and fear was over them all.
Festival dresses they wore, but the tongue was dry in their mouth,
And the blinking eyes in their faces skirted from north to south.

Now to the sacred enclosure gathered the greatest and least,
And from under the shade of the banyan arose the voice of the feast,
The frenzied roll of the drum, and a swift, monotonous song.
Higher the sun swam up; the trade-wind level and strong
Awoke in the tops of the palms and rattled the fans aloud,
And over the garlanded heads and shining robes of the crowd
Tossed the spiders of shadow, scattered the jewels of sun.
Forty the tale of the drums, and the forty throbbed like one;
A thousand hearts in the crowd, and the even chorus of song,
Swift as the feet of a runner, trampled a thousand strong.
And the old men leered at the ovens and licked their lips for the food;
And the women stared at the lads, and laughed and looked to the wood.
As when the sweltering baker, at night, when the city is dead,
Alone in the trough of labour treads and fashions the bread;
So in the heat, and the reek, and the touch of woman and man,
The naked spirit of evil kneaded the hearts of the clan.

Now cold was at many a heart, and shaking in many a seat;
For there were the empty baskets, but who was to furnish the meat?
For here was the nation assembled, and there were the ovens anigh,
And out of a thousand singers nine were numbered to die.
Till, of a sudden, a shock, a mace in the air, a yell,
And, struck in the edge of the crowd, the first of the victims fell.
Terror and horrible glee divided the shrinking clan,
Terror of what was to follow, glee for a diet of man.
Frenzy hurried the chaunt, frenzy rattled the drums;
The nobles, high on the terrace, greedily mouthed their thumbs;

And once and again and again, in the ignorant crowd below,
Once and again and again descended the murderous blow.
Now smoked the oven, and now, with the cutting lip of a shell,
A butcher of ninety winters jointed the bodies well.
Unto the carven lodge, silent, in order due,
The grandees of the nation one after one withdrew;
And a line of laden bearers brought to the terrace foot,
On poles across their shoulders, the last reserve of fruit.
The victims bled for the nobles in the old appointed way;
The fruit was spread for the commons, for all should eat, to-day.

And now was the kava brewed, and now the cocoa ran,
Now was the hour of the dance for child and woman and man;
And mirth was in every heart, and a garland on every head,
And all was well with the living and well with the eight who were dead.
Only the chiefs and the priest talked and consulted a while:
"To-morrow," they said, and "To-morrow," and nodded and seemed to
      smile:
"Rua the child of dirt, the creature of common clay,
Rua must die to-morrow, since Rua is gone to-day."

Out of the groves of the valley, where clear the blackbirds sang,
Sheer from the trees of the valley the face of the mountain sprang;
Sheer and bare it rose, unscalable barricade,
Beaten and blown against by the generous draught of the trade.
Dawn on its fluted brow painted rainbow light,
Close on its pinnacled crown trembled the stars at night.
Here and there in a cleft clustered contorted trees,
Or the silver beard of a stream hung and swung in the breeze.
High overhead, with a cry, the torrents leaped for the main,
And silently sprinkled below in thin perennial rain.
Dark in the staring noon, dark was Rua's ravine,
Damp and cold was the air, and the face of the cliffs was green.
Here, in the rocky pit. accursed already of old,
On a stone in the midst of a river, Rua sat and was cold.
"Valley of mid-day shadows, valley of silent falls,"

Rua sang, and his voice went hollow about the walls,
"Valley of shadow and rock, a doleful prison to me,
What is the life you can give to a child of the sun and the sea?"

And Rua arose and came to the open mouth of the glen,
Whence he beheld the woods, and the sea, and houses of men.
Wide blew the riotous trade, and smelt in his nostrils good;
It bowed the boats on the bay, and tore and divided the wood;
It smote and sundered the groves as Moses smote with the rod,
And the streamers of all the trees blew like banners abroad;
And ever and on, in a lull, the trade-wind brought him along
A far-off patter of drums and a far-off whisper of song.

Swift as the swallow's wings, the diligent hands on the drum
Fluttered and hurried and throbbed. "Ah, woe that I hear you come,"
Rua cried in his grief, "a sorrowful sound to me,
Mounting far and faint from the resonant shore of the sea!
Woe in the song! for the grave breathes in the singers' breath,
And I hear in the tramp of the drums the beat of the heart of death.
Home of my youth! no more, through all the length of the years,
No more to the place of the echoes of early laughter and tears,
No more shall Rua return; no more as the evening ends,
To crowded eyes of welcome, to the reaching hands of friends."

All day long from the High-place the drums and the singing came,
And the even fell, and the sun went down, a wheel of flame;
And night came gleaning the shadows and hushing the sounds
    of the wood;
And silence slept on all, where Rua sorrowed and stood.
But still from the shore of the bay the sound of the festival rang,
And still the crowd in the High-place danced and shouted and sang.
Now over all the isle terror was breathed abroad
Of shadowy hands from the trees and shadowy snares in the sod;
And before the nostrils of night, the shuddering hunter of men
Hurried, with beard on shoulder, back to his lighted den.
"Taheia, here to my side!"—"Rua, my Rua, you!"

And cold from the clutch of terror, cold with the damp of the dew,
Taheia, heavy of hair, leaped through the dark to his arms
Taheia leaped to his clasp, and was folded in from alarms.

"Rua, beloved, here, see what your love has brought;
Coming—alas! returning—swift as the shuttle of thought;
Returning, alas! for to-night, with the beaten drum and the voice,
In the shine of many torches must the sleepless clan rejoice;
And Taheia the well-descended, the daughter of chief and priest,
Taheia must sit in her place in the crowded bench of the feast."
So it was spoken; and she, girding her garment high,
Fled and was swallowed of woods, swift as the sight of an eye.

Night over isle and sea rolled her curtain of stars,
Then a trouble awoke in the air, the east was banded with bars;
Dawn as yellow as sulphur leaped on the mountain height;
Dawn, in the deepest glen, fell a wonder of light;
High and clear stood the palms in the eye of the brightening east,
And lo! from the sides of the sea the broken sound of the feast!
As, when in days of summer, through open windows, the fly
Swift as a breeze and loud as a trump goes by,
But when frosts in the field have pinched the wintering mouse,
Blindly noses and buzzes and hums in the firelit house
So the sound of the feast gallantly trampled at night,
So it staggered and drooped, and droned in the morning light.

27

POEMS

Fanny Stevenson wrote, introducing the verse collection Underwoods *in 1887, "Very few of my husband's poems were conceived with any other purpose than the entertainment of the moment." This is true also of many of his poems of the Pacific, though the drafts left at Vailima at his death include some that look like possible dedications intended for a collection: 'The Far-Farers' (2), for instance, which is alongside another similarly addressed "To friends at home", from "blue horizon and green isles."*

His Pacific poems are to be found scattered in different sections of the volumes of poetry in his collected works. They have not previously been gathered or considered together. His adult poems in general are now difficult to find and are rarely read. The selection here is chosen, like the rest of this book, on merit, and for their interest as literary responses to the Pacific, though clearly some are only drafts. They illustrate his versatility of tone and idiom, and perhaps the way he used verse to hone his verbal skills for prose. It is possible to think that his prose note to the poem for Princess Kaiulani (4) is the best writing in this whole section.

The selection opens and closes with poems that show how deep the idea of the "enchanted island" lay in his imagination and self-mythology. (1) may have been written before 1888 but is pertinent to the Pacific years. (2) represents a number of poems of nostalgia and valediction, some, naturally, in Scots dialect. (3) combines the fantasy island theme with a tribute to Princess Moë of Tautira (see 8), and (4), (5) and (6) arise from his experience in Hawaii and the leper colony of Molokai in early 1889 (9, 10). (8) is roguish, satiric, Kiplingesque

(Above) **RLS's last birthday party, Vailima. RLS is half-hidden, fifth from left, to Fanny's left. (The male with moustache to her right is a neighbour.) The mix of Samoans and Europeans is noteworthy.**

mimicry of the philistine avarice of the English common sailor (cf Huish in The Ebb-Tide*), yet also shows how the Pacific can touch even such men with something of the romantic; (9), about Belle Strong, is part of a long set of poems characterizing the family members at Vailima, and like the last birthday poem he wrote for Fanny (10), gives some colourful authentic glimpses of daily life there. (11) would have made a good epitaph, and deserves to be better known in the nation to which it is addressed.*

(1) [Island of the mind]

Far over seas an island is
    Whereon when day is done
A grove of tossing palms
    Are printed on the sun.
And all about the reefy shore
    Blue breakers flash and fall.
There shall I go, methinks,
    Where I am done with all.

Have I no castle then in Spain,
  No island of the mind,
Where I can turn and go again
  When life should prove unkind?
Up, sluggard soul! And far from here
  Our mountain forest seek;
Or nigh enchanted island, steer
  Down the desired creek.

(2) **The Far-Farers**

The broad sun,
  The bright day,
White sails
  On the blue bay: –
The far-farers
  Draw away.

Light the Fires
  And close the door.
To the old homes,
  To the loved shore,
The far-farers
  Return no more.

(3) **To an Island Princess**

Since long ago, a child at home,
I read and longed to rise and roam,
Where'er I went, whate'er I willed,
One promised land my fancy filled.
Hence the long roads my home I made
Tossed much in ships: have often laid

Below the uncurtained sky my head,
Rain-deluged and wind-buffeted:
And many a thousand hills I crossed
And corners turned—Love's labour lost.
Till, Lady, to your isle of sun
I came, not hoping; and, like one
Snatched out of blindness, rubbed my eyes,
And hailed my promised land with cries.

Yes, Lady, here I was at last;
Here found I all I had forecast:
The long roll of the sapphire sea
That keeps the land's virginity;
The stalwart giants of the wood
Laden with toys and flowers and food;
The precious forest pouring out
To compass the whole town about;
The town itself with streets of lawn,
Loved of the moon, blessed by the dawn,
Where the brown children all the day
Keep up a ceaseless noise of play,

Play in the sun, play in the rain,
Nor ever quarrel or complain;—
And late at night, in the woods of fruit,
Hark! do you hear the passing flute?

I threw one look to either hand,
And knew I was in Fairyland.
And yet one point of being so,
I lacked. For, Lady, (as you know)
Whoever by his might of hand
Won entrance into Fairyland,
Found always with admiring eyes
A Fairy princess kind and wise.

It was not long I waited; soon
Upon my threshold, in broad noon,
Fair and helpful, wise and good,
The Fairy Princess Moë stood.

Tautira, Tahiti, Nov. 5, 1888.

(4) **To Princess Kaiulani**

[Written in April to Kaiulani in the April of her age; and at Waikiki, within
easy walk of Kaiulani's banyan! When she comes to my land and her father's, and
the rain beats upon the window (as I fear it will), let her look at this page; it will
be like a weed gathered and pressed at home; and she will remember her own
islands, and the shadow of the mighty tree; and she will hear the peacocks
screaming in the dusk and the wind blowing in the palms; and she will think of
her father sitting there alone.—R.L.S.]

Forth from her land to mine she goes,
The island maid, the island rose,
Light of heart and bright of face:
The daughter of a double race.

Her islands here, in Southern sun,
Shall mourn their Kaiulani gone,
And I, in her dear banyan shade,
Look vainly for my little maid.

But our Scots islands far away
Shall glitter with unwonted day,
And cast for once their tempests by
To smile in Kaiulani's eye.

Honolulu.

(5) **To Mother Maryanne**

To see the infinite pity of this place,
The mangled limb, the devastated face,
The innocent sufferer smiling at the rod—
A fool were tempted to deny his God.
He sees, he shrinks. But if he gaze again,
Lo, beauty springing from the beast of pain!
He marks the sisters on the mournful shores;
And even a fool is silent and adores.

Guest House, Kalawao, Molokai.

(6) **The High Winds of Nuuanu**

Within the famous valley of that name,
Now twice or thrice the high wind blows each year,
Until you hear it pulsing through the gorge
In spiteful gusts: sometimes it comes with bursts
Of rain, in fiercer squalls; and, howling down the glen,
It breaks great tropic fronds like stems of clay.
Lo! Then, the unbending palms and rugged dates,
Loud-whistling, strain in each recurrent blast,
Like things alive!—or fall, with roots uptorn,
The feathered algarrobas, as the gale
Treads out its wasteful pathway to the sea!
Thus twice or thrice Nuuanu's high winds rage,
Threshing the vale till quakes the Island's heart!
Ten other months are filled with nerveless rest,
Mid cooling breezes and down-dropping showers;
At night the dark-blue vault arching the vale,
Studded with stars innumerable and bright!
While fleecy clouds outdrifting to the sea,
Make shadows in the moonlight on the sward.
Here dwell the Islanders in peace, until
The blasts again sweep down from Northern seas.

(7) One poem published in 'Songs of Travel' sympathizes with Fanny's long wait, "'ere you behold again/ Green forest frame the entry of the lane —/ The wild lane with the bramble and the briar" (he seems to be thinking more of English scenes, than Californian ones). Instead, at sea in the Pacific:

[Aboard the *Equator*]

Here from the sea the unfruitful sun shall rise,
Bathe the bare deck and blind the unshielded eyes;
The allotted hours aloft shall wheel in vain
And in the unpregnant ocean plunge again.
Assault of squalls that mock the watchful guard,
And pluck the bursting canvas from the yard,
And senseless clamour of the calm, at night
Must mar your slumbers by the plunging light,
In beetle-haunted, most unwomanly bower
Of the wild-swerving cabin, hour by hour...

(8) **The Fine Pacific Islands**
      (Heard in a public-house in Rotherhithe)

The jolly English Yellowboy
  Is a 'ansome coin when new,
The Yankee Double-eagle
  Is large enough for two.
O, these may do for seaport towns,
  For cities these may do;
But the dibbs that takes the Hislands
  Are the dollars of Peru:
      O, the fine Pacific Hislands,
      O, the dollars of Peru!

It's there we buy the cocoanuts
  Mast 'eaded in the blue;
It's there we trap the lasses
  All waiting for the crew;

It's there we buy the trader's rum
  What bores a seaman through.
In the fine Pacific Hislands
  With the dollars of Peru:
    In the fine Pacific Hislands,
    With the dollars of Peru!

Now, messmates, when my watch is up,
  And I am quite broached to,
I'll give a tip to 'Evving
  Of the 'ansome thing to do:
Let 'em refit this sailor-man
  And launch him off anew
To cruise among the Hislands
  With the dollars of Peru:
    In the fine Pacific Hislands,
    With the dollars of Peru!

Tahiti, August 1888

(9) The Daughter, Teuila, Native Name for Adorner

Her absent, she shall still be found,
A posse of native maids around
Her and her whirling instrument
Collected and on learning bent.
Oft clustered by her tender knees
(Smiling himself) the gazer sees,
Compact as flowers in garden beds,
The smiling faces and shaved heads
Of the brown island babes: with whom
She exults to decorate her room,
To draw them, cheer them when they cry,
And still to pet and prettify.
Or see, as in a looking glass
Her graceful, dimpled person pass,

Nought great therein but eyes and hair,
On her true business here and there;
Her huge, half-naked staff, intent,
See her review and regiment,
An ant with elephants, and how
A smiling mouth, a clouded brow,
Satire and turmoil, quips and tears,
She deals among her grenadiers!
Her pantry and her kitchen squad,
Six-footers all, hang on her nod,
Incline to her their martial chests,
With school-boy laughter hail her jests,
And do her in her kilted dress
Obsequious obeisances.

(10) *To the Stormy Petrel*
     To His Wife, on her Birthday

Ever perilous

And precious, like an ember from the fire
Or gem from a volcano, we today
When the drums of war reverberate in the land
And every face is for the battle blacked –

No less the sky, that over sodden woods
Menaces now in the disconsolate calm
The hurly-burly of the hurricane,
Do now most fitly celebrate your day.

Yet amid turmoil keep for me, my dear,
The kind domestic faggot. Let the hearth
Shine ever as (I praise my honest gods)
In peace and tempest it has ever shone.

March 10, 1894

315

(11) [**Samoa**]

Fair Isle at Sea – thy lovely name
Soft in my ear like music came.
That sea I loved, and once or twice
I touched at isles of Paradise.

28

"HERE HE LIES
WHERE HE LONGED TO BE":
MOUNT VAEA, UPOLU, SAMOA

Robert Louis Stevenson died suddenly of a brain haemorrhage in the great hall at Vailima on 3 December 1894. He had spent the morning on Weir of Hermiston, *a Scottish story about one third complete, that he considered his best work. The last sentence he wrote, referring to a lover's inexplicable quarrelsomeness, was, "It seemed unprovoked, a wilful convulsion of brute nature."*

When nature had convulsed him for the last time, the Union Jack was hauled down from above the house for him to lie on, and he was wrapped in ceremonial mats brought by the many Samoan mourners. A meeting of chiefs allocated the work of cutting a track to the summit of Mount Vaea, digging a grave in the narrow space there, and carrying the coffin up the steep 300 metres (1000 feet) ascent to his chosen place of burial. He had quite often walked there, the only member of the family to do so. Nineteen Europeans and about sixty Samoans completed the strenuous climb, and took part in the Church of England funeral service.

The chiefs declared a tapu against firearms on the mountain, so that the bush is still vibrant with bird song. A tomb of cement blocks on the model of a Samoan chief's burial place was built, and in 1897 completed by two bronze plates, inscribed with "O Le Oli'olisaga o Tusitala" ("the happy resting place of the Writer of Tales") and with two verses in Samoan from Ruth's Old Testament speech to Naomi ("thy people shall be my people..." ch. 1, verses 16-17), a Scottish thistle and Pacific hibiscus, and two stanzas of his poem 'Requiem' (the penultimate line has a small error that has become commonplace, "home from the sea").

(Above) **"A fable as strange and romantic as one of his own... There have been... for men of letters few deaths more romantically right."** The mourners at RLS's burial, Mt Vaea, Samoa.

Alongside now are the ashes of Fanny, who died in California in February 1914, also of cerebral haemorrhage. Upolu was then under German control, but when the First World War began and New Zealand took the island, Vailima became the British Residence, and Fanny's ashes could be brought and carried in procession by the same track to the summit of Mount Vaea.

It was Henry James, in a generous letter of condolence to Fanny, who first perceived that the time, place and suddenness of Stevenson's death had made his life "into a fable as strange and romantic as one of his own" and that "There have been... for men of letters few deaths more romantically right." Many have sought to explain the meanings of the strange fable, and elaborate on its romantic closure.

Other poems might have been chosen for the grave. His quatrain for Samoa (Poem 11 in 27) would have served well:

> *"That sea I loved, and once or twice*
> *I touched at isles of Paradise."*

'Requiem' was the poem he had ready as his epitaph, an understandable precaution for someone who lived so many years under the volcano of death. It was first written during an earlier confrontation, in San Francisco in 1880, when he had seen the Pacific for the first time. "Here he lies where he longed to be" may or may not have meant Scotland. But a text can take new meaning from its location, much as a person can take new life; or add a life, as Stevenson did, without ever ceasing to be Scottish. 'Requiem' is so associated now with that hill-top in Samoa where it is inscribed that it has become, in effect, a Pacific poem. It expresses and enhances the place, as a poem should. You stand and read it, on his grave, on a hill above his home, under the wide sky, and as you think of his life and work, you look down also at the great sea where for six years he sailed and gladly lived.

1850   ROBERT LOUIS STEVENSON   1894

Under the wide and starry sky,
Dig the grave and let me lie.
Glad did I live and gladly die,
    And I laid me down with a will.

This be the verse you grave for me;
Here he lies where he longed to be;
Home is the sailor, home from sea,
    And the hunter home from the hill.

SOURCES, EDITING, AND FURTHER READING

The Stevenson texts in this book have been prepared from various sources, in each case involving comparison of at least two published versions. Editorial emendations have been made to correct errors that have been perpetuated in previous editions, probably as a result of the original typesetter misreading Stevenson's handwriting. For example, in Section 3, "The paepae is... built without cement of black volcanic stone" seems a better reading than "without cement or volcanic stone"; the point in Section 5 is that some nations show a "willingness to eat the dog", whereas "unwillingness" (as in all editions) makes the whole contrast pointless; and also in 5, I amended "lively haunt of its exercise", a perplexing concept, to "lively height...", which makes perfect sense as a contrast to "scanty survivals."

Punctuation has been changed only to standardize single and double quotation marks, and to modify one or two 19th century publishers' conventions that are now obtrusive, such as the habit of following a semi-colon or comma with a long dash. Select paragraphing has been similarly modified. All editing has sought to combine scholarly accuracy with readability.

For available modern editions of the fiction, see Acknowledgements, p.5. The complete texts of *In the South Seas*, *A Footnote to History*, *Vailima Papers*, *Letters*, *Ballads* and *Poems* are all significant reading, but generally must be sought in libraries or second-hand bookshops. The Tusitala Edition is the one most often found, and especially in its small format is pleasant to read and handle.

Western Samoa's rich and independent culture makes any visit there memorable. To visit the Robert Louis Stevenson Museum at Vailima, walk up Mount Vaea and pause awhile at the grave, is one of the world's most rewarding literary pilgrimages. It is where this book began.

– R.R.

(Right) **RLS with his friend Tuimale Aliifono, probably the last photograph of him.**